Management for Professionals

More information about this series at https://link.springer.com/bookseries/10101

Tracy Dathe • René Dathe • Isabel Dathe
Marc Helmold

Corporate Social Responsibility (CSR), Sustainability and Environmental Social Governance (ESG)

Approaches to Ethical Management

Springer

Tracy Dathe
Macromedia University
Berlin, Berlin, Germany

Isabel Dathe
Technical University of Berlin
Berlin, Berlin, Germany

René Dathe
Berlin, Berlin, Germany

Marc Helmold
iubh University
Berlin, Berlin, Germany

ISSN 2192-8096 ISSN 2192-810X (electronic)
Management for Professionals
ISBN 978-3-030-92356-3 ISBN 978-3-030-92357-0 (eBook)
https://doi.org/10.1007/978-3-030-92357-0

This Springer imprint is published by the registered company Springer Nature Switzerland AG
The registered company address is: Gewerbestrasse 11, 6330 Cham, Switzerland

Preface

The book "Corporate Social Responsibility (CSR), Sustainability and Environmental Social Governance (ESG)" combines the theoretical research and the real-world business practice for ethical management. The symbiosis of theory and practice makes this book a worthwhile reading experience both to the teaching professionals and students of higher educational institutions and the business practitioners.

The presentation of theories provides an extensive overview of the fundamental understanding of business ethics, in particular the concepts of Corporate Social Responsibility (CSR), Sustainability and the operationalisation of sustainability management by means of the process of Environmental Social Governance (ESG). The integration of ethical management in the overall business strategy is depicted both in context of the individual business processes and of interactions with the stakeholder groups. The relationship of value creation and the ethical management is discussed in both short-term and long-term perspectives. A plethora of examples facilitate the comprehension of the theories and inspires the application in the business practice.

The book authors are a combined team of experienced academics, business executives and young activist. The endeavour with this book is intended to help the readers to effectively expand the knowledge of ethical management and to provide a guideline to business executives to enhance long-term, sustainable value chains with national or international business partners.

Finally, the authors would like to thank Ms. Jones-Sepulveda and the Springer team for the friendly and competent assistance for the publication of this book.

Berlin, Germany
Summer, 2022

Tracy Dathe
Marc Helmold
René Dathe
Isabel Dathe

Contents

About the Authors

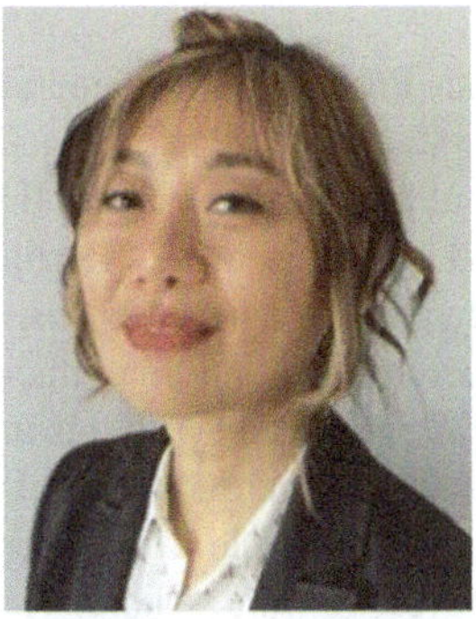

Tracy Dathe is professor for business management at Macromedia University on Campus Berlin, Germany.She is also an experienced finance professional. As CFO of a multinational medium-sized automotive supplier, she was responsible for the overall commercial management at the German headquarters and the overseas subsidiaries in China, France, Italy, Sweden, the Czech Republic, Turkey and the USA. Today, she also supports medium-sized companies as a management consultant.

René Dathe is a business executive in the global research-based pharmaceutical industry with specialization in project management, medical technology and quality management. He leads global development projects and alliances in Asia, Europe and North America with constantly growing fields of responsibility. In terms of CSR, diversity and inclusion in particular, he supports the global talent management of his employer in identifying new talents from China, Japan and other Asian countries who are to develop into future global leaders. Furthermore, he shares his experience and knowledge on business culture in China at various seminars of the global business organization on a regular basis.Dr. René Dathe started his career in the digital research of organic semiconductor materials. He received an MSc degree in Chemistry from the Technical University of Chemnitz, followed by an MBA in Frankfurt am Main. He was awarded a doctorate degree for business administration at the University of Gloucestershire, UK with the specialization in the field of group psychological processes based on SYMLOG and TRIZ (Inventive Problem Solving) theories.

Isabel Dathe decided to study Sustainability Management at the TU Berlin after a 3-year excursion to the Berlin media industry. Already in her early youth, the young academic campaigned for sustainability in the student council. Now she would like to make her well-founded contribution to actionism and represent the interests of the upcoming generation.

Marc Helmold is full-time Professor of General Business Administration, Business Ethics, Performance Management and International Negotiations at the IU Intern. University of applied Sciences at the Berlin campus. Before that, he held various managerial positions and was managing director of leading manufacturers in the automotive and rail industries. With this in mind, he was able to sustainably expand CSR activities. In industry in particular, he was able to transfer sustainability concepts to the entire value chain. He spent several years in Japan and China.

List of Acronyms and Abbreviations

AMWG	Asset Management Working Group
CC	Corporate Citizenship
CRA	Credit Rating Agency
CSR	Corporate Social Responsibility
ERP	Enterprise Resource Planning
ESG	Environmental, Social and Governance
KPI	Key Performance indicators
KQI	Key Quality Indicators
MIS	Management Information System
MNC	Multi-National Corporation
NGO	Non-Governmental Organization
PRI	Principles for Responsible Investment
SRI	Stanford Research Institute
UNEP FI	United Nations Environment Programme Finance Initiative
US SEC	U.S. Securities and Exchange Commission SEC

List of Figures

List of Tables

CSR as Part of the Corporate Strategy 1

The Essence of Strategy is choosing what not to do.

Michael Porter.

1.1 Levels of Strategy

The Three Levels of Strategy, developed by Gerry Johnson and Kevan Scholes along with other major managerial thinkers, are a way of defining the different layers of strategy which, in tandem, orient the direction of the organisation and define its success (Johnson et al., 2017). The Three Levels are:

1. Corporate Supply Chain Strategy Levels
2. Business and tactical Strategy Levels
3. Functional or operational Strategy Levels

When synchronised and coordinated, successful strategies at each of these levels will contribute to successful overall organisational strategy including right measures to prevent and avoid inefficiencies in the supply chain and other functions of an enterprise (Khojasteh, 2018). This is the top layer of strategic planning, and is often associated with the organisation's mission and values, though it is developed in much more significant depth (Helmold, 2020). Enterprises must ensure, that CSR activities are implemented in the strategy of an organisation. Corporate strategy is defined by those at the very top of the organisation – managing directors and executive boards – and is an outline of the overall direction and course of the business. In effect, it defines:

T. Dathe et al., *Corporate Social Responsibility (CSR), Sustainability and Environmental Social Governance (ESG)*, Management for Professionals,
https://doi.org/10.1007/978-3-030-92357-0_1

- General, overall strategy and direction in terms of Markets, Supply and Supply Chains
- What are the CSR activities in each part of the value chain
- How to secure ethical behaviour across the value chain
- Which Markets the Organisation will operate in
- Which Suppliers and Supply Chains to procure from
- How the markets will be entered and the general activities of the organisation
- How to prevent risks in the upstream or downstream supply chains
- How to apply a Supply Chain Risk Management (SCRM)

1.1.1 Corporate Strategy

Corporate strategy is crucial as it will define all other decisions that are made within the organisation along the line. Smaller, newer organisations which are targeting a very specific niche market, or operate with a small set of unique products/services, will find it far easier to develop a corporate strategy as there are fewer variables to consider. However, larger and more developed organisations will find the process much simpler, as they may need to diverge from activities and behaviours which define who they are in order to reach out into new markets and to take new opportunities (Stibbe, 2019).

1.1.2 Business Strategy

Business strategy generally emerges and evolves from the overarching corporate strategy which has been set by those at the helm. They are usually far more specific than corporate strategy and will likely be unique to different departments or subdivisions within the broader organisation. In general, they use corporate strategy as an outline to:

- Define specific tactics and strategies for each market the organisation is involved in
- Define how each business unit will deliver the planned tactics

Due to their nature, they are more common in larger firms that engage in multiple activities, than they are in small businesses. However, they can still be engaged in by smaller organisations who wish to define how they go about each different subsection of their operations, by breaking down the overall scope of the corporate strategy.

1.1.3 Functional Strategy

The functional long-term strategy, also defined as Market-Level Strategy, refers to the day-to-day operation of the company, which will keep it functioning and moving in the correct direction. Whilst many organisations fail because they do not have an overarching corporate strategy, others fail because they have not developed plans for how to engage in everyday activities. Even with an overall direction you wish to head in, without a plan for how to successfully operate, an organisation will be unable to progress. These will be numerous and will define very specific aspects and operations within smaller departments, teams, groups and activities. Overall, they define:

- Day-to-day actions which are required to deliver corporate and business strategies
- Relationships needed between units, departments and teams
- How operational goals will be met, and how they will be monitored

It is at this level, the lowest in strategic development, that leaders should define how different departments and functions will work together to achieve higher goals. There will be managers that will oversee departments (e.g. manufacturing and HR) that do not perform the same functions, but need to be synchronised in order to achieve the goals set out by the corporate and business strategies.

1.1.4 Alignment and Communication of Strategies

Though corporate strategy will get all of the attention, it is success at the bottom of the hierarchy – through day-to-day functions – which will truly define where the organisation as a whole will succeed. You need to build from the ground up, in small steps, in order to keep moving forward. If operations break down, so does the organisation. As mentioned previously, it is crucially important that each level of strategy is synchronised, both from top-to-bottom and horizontally across the organisation. Feedback should down from both corporate strategy to functional strategy, and vice-versa, in order for all three levels to ensure that they are operating in line with one another (Helmold, 2021). Strategies, however, will not work unless there is a proper communication to employees and stakeholders (Wagner, 2019). Companies must ensure the strategies are cascaded throughout the organisation.

Strategy itself will not define organisational success, however, it is a very good place to start. Once sound strategies are in place, an organisation can move forward and begin to execute said strategies. They may need some adjustment along the way – and you should be prepared to do so, in response to feedback from different levels and from the external environment – but they should be initially developed in such a way that they will keep the organisation in line with its long-term objectives.

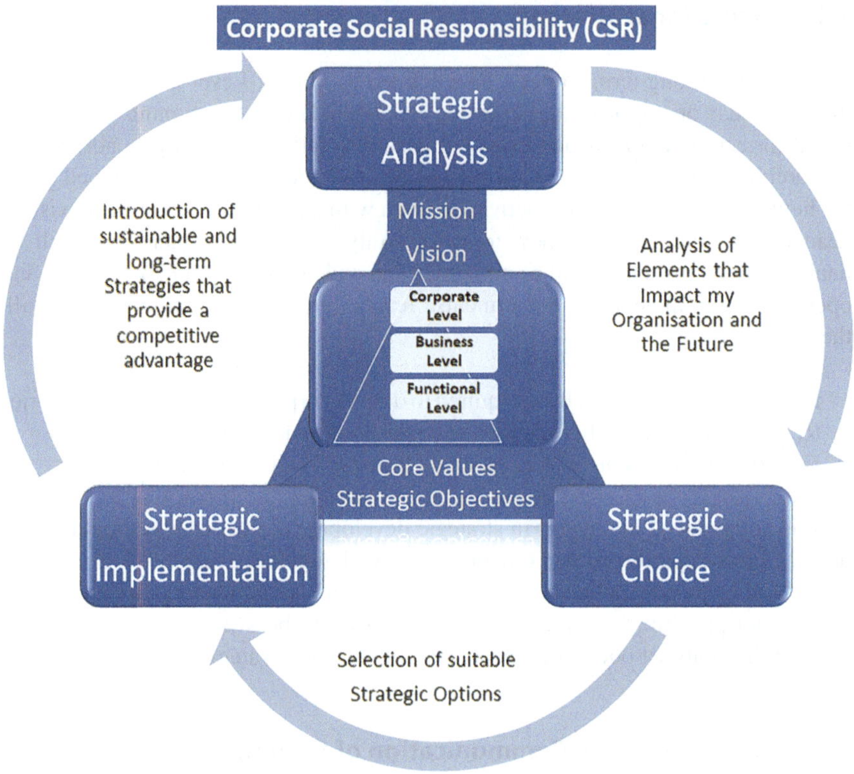

Fig. 1.1 Strategic triangle. (Source: Author's Source, adopted from Johnson et al., 2017)

1.2 Strategic Triangle

The process of strategic management cycle is a process with three elements as outlined in Fig. 1.1 (strategic triangle or strategic cycle) (Johnson et al., 2017). The three steps are (1) the strategic analysis, (2) the strategic choice and (3) the strategic implementation and will be described in the following sections. The triangle is raising the following questions:

1. Where are we in terms of Strategy and Positioning in our Supply Chains?
2. Where do we want to go?
3. How do we achieve this?

1.3 Strategic Analysis

1.3.1 Analysing Important Factors

The strategic analysis of an organisation is about understanding the strategic position of the organisation in terms of Value Chain Management. This stage requires a profound analysis where the organisation stands in terms of Value Chain Management tools and processes (Johnson et al., 2017). The existing competencies and resources of the organisation need to be assessed to determine if there are any opportunities to be gained from these and to determine if they need to be enhanced in order to pursue strategic objectives and goals (Johnson et al., 2017). The major stakeholders which influence the organisation and the opinions or viewpoints must be taken into account as the purpose of all of the strategic analysis is to define the potential future direction of the organisation. The purpose of this phase (strategic analysis) is to create a suitable starting position and to understand the key influences on the present and future state of the organisation and what opportunities are afforded by the environment and the competencies of the organisation Johnson et al., 2017). Assessing the strategic position consists of evaluating the following elements as shown in Table 1.1:

Since strategy is concerned with the position a business takes in relation to its environment, an understanding of the environment's effects on an organisation is of central importance to the strategic analysis. The historical and environmental effects on the business must be considered, as well as the present effects and the expected changes in environmental variables. The analysis of the environment can be done via the macro and micro analysis (PESTEL, Porters 5 Forces). Additionally, strengths, weaknesses, opportunities and threats complete the assessment of the environment (SWOT). This step is a major task because the range of environmental variables is so great. Another area of the strategic analysis is the evaluation of the strategic capability of an organisation and where it is able to achieve a competitive advantage. Considering the resource areas of a business such as its physical plant, its management, its financial structure and its products may identify these strengths and weaknesses (Johnson et al., 2017). The expectations of stakeholders are important because they will affect what will be seen as acceptable in terms of the strategies advanced by management. Stakeholders can be defined as people or groups

Table 1.1 Elements in the strategic analysis

Strategic analysis of elements	Strategic tool
Environment (e.g. markets, regulations, political impacts)	PESTEL Analysis (Macro)
Industry and competition (e.g. rivalry in industry)	Industry Analysis (Micro)
Internal strengths & weaknesses, external threats & opportunities	SWOT Analysis (Internal)
Cultures and beliefs	Cultural Analysis
Strategic capabilities & competencies	Benchmarking Analysis
Expectation of stakeholders	Stakeholder Analysis

Source: Author's Source

inside or outside the organisation, who an interest in the activities of the organisation. A typical list of stakeholders for a large company would include shareholders, banks, employees, managers, customers, suppliers, government and society. Culture affects the interpretation of the environmental and resource influences (Helmold & Terry, 2021).

1.3.2 Analysing the Environment

A PESTEL analysis or PESTLE analysis is a framework or tool used to analyse and monitor the macro-environmental factors that may have a profound impact on an organisation's performance. This tool is especially useful when starting a new business or entering a foreign market. It is often used in collaboration with other analytical business tools such as the SWOT analysis and Porter's Five Forces to give a clear understanding of a situation and related internal and external factors. PESTEL is an acronym that stand for Political, Economic, Social, Technological, Environmental and Legal factors. However, throughout the years people have expanded the framework with factors such as Demographics, Intercultural, Ethical and Ecological resulting in variants such as STEEPLED, DESTEP and SLEPIT. In this article, we will stick simply to PESTEL since it encompasses the most relevant factors in general business. Each element will be elaborated as shown in Fig. 1.2. In the modern shape of the figure, the dimension ethical behaviour or business ethics has been added.

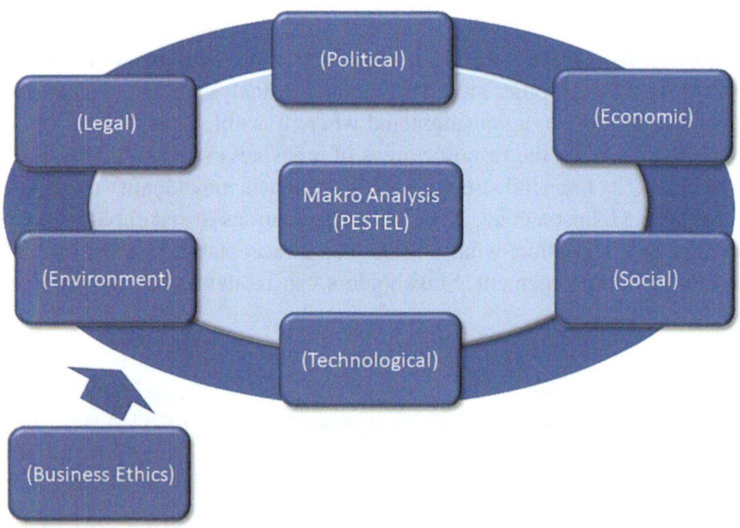

Fig. 1.2 PESTEL analysis. (Source: Author's Source)

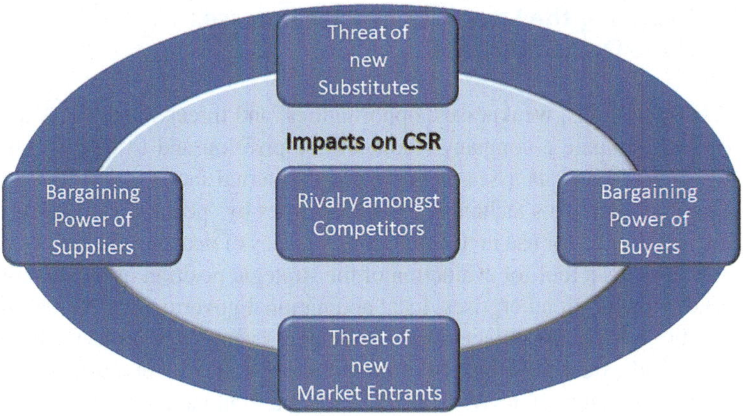

Fig. 1.3 Industry analysis. (Source: Author's source)

1.3.3 Analysing the Industry

Porter is best known for his strategic frameworks and concepts in his paper, which was published in 1980 (Porter, 1980). The five forces model (Industry Analysis) has five elements that can be utilised to assess the attractiveness and competitive situation of the industry as outlined in Fig. 1.3. The five elements are:

1. Rivalry amongst Competitors
2. Bargaining Power of Suppliers
3. Bargaining Power of Buyers
4. Threat of new Market Entrants
5. Threat of new Substitutes

The stronger the threat posed by these five competitive forces, the less attractive the industry under consideration and the more difficult it is to achieve a sustainable competitive advantage. Companies should therefore try to be active in an industry with an attractive industry structure and to build up a defensible position in their industry, i. e. a position in which the five competitive forces are as less threatening as possible. Companies can also influence the five forces with the help of appropriate strategic orientation. This can increase the attractiveness of an industry. If, however, companies influence the distribution of competitive forces to the advantage of their own competitive position without being aware of the long-term effects or consciously accepting them, this can also destroy the structure and profitability of an industry.

1.3.4 Analysing the Strengths and Weaknesses of the Own Enterprise

The SWOT (strengths, weaknesses, opportunities, and threats) analysis is a framework used to evaluate a company's competitive position and to develop strategic planning. SWOT analysis assesses internal and external factors, as well as current and future potential. This technique, which operates by 'peeling back layers of the company is designed for use in the preliminary stages of decision-making processes and can be used as a tool for evaluation of the strategic position of organizations of many kinds (for -profit enterprises, local and national governments, NGOs, etc.). It is intended to specify the objectives of the business venture or project and identify the internal and external factors that are favourable and unfavourable to achieving those objectives. Users of a SWOT analysis often ask and answer questions to generate meaningful information for each category to make the tool useful and identify their competitive advantage (Fig. 1.4).

1.3.5 Analysing the Core Competencies

The core competency concept describes a product, feature, process, skill, brand or activity that a company can perform better than the competition and has thus achieved a competitive advantage. It is determined by the certain characteristics like customer value or benefits, protection against imitation, differentiation, diversification and innovation or unique features as shown in Fig. 1.5. In business, a competitive advantage is the attribute that allows an organization to outperform its competitors.

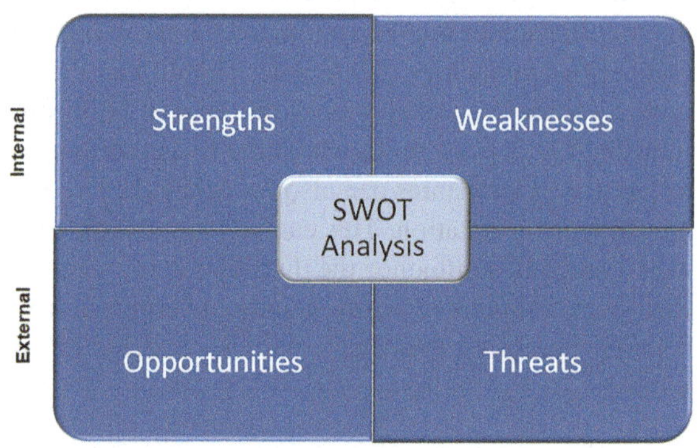

Fig. 1.4 SWOT analysis. (Source: Author's source)

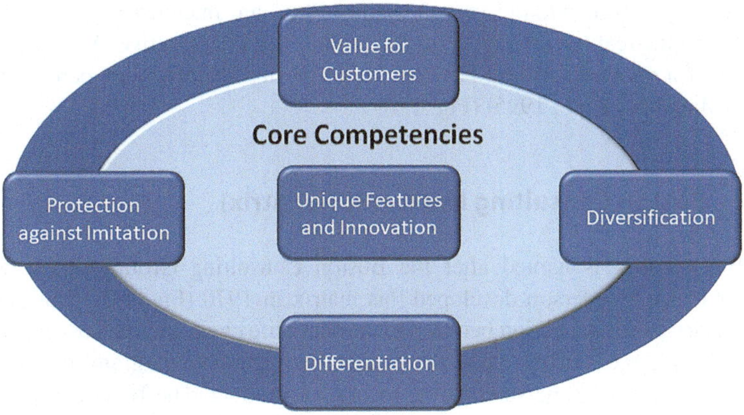

Fig. 1.5 Core competencies. (Source: Author's source)

1.4 Strategic Choice

1.4.1 Generic Strategies

Strategic choice typically follows strategic analysis. Strategic Choice involves a whole process through which a decision is taken to choose a particular option from various alternatives. There can be various methods through which the final choice can be selected upon. Managers and decision makers keep both the external and internal environment in mind before narrowing it down to one. It is based upon the following three elements. First; the generation of strategic options, e. g. growth, acquisition, diversification or concentration. Second; the evaluation of the options to assess their relative merits and feasibility. And third; the selection of the strategy or option that the organisation will pursue. There could be more than one strategy chosen but there is a chance of an inherent danger or disadvantage to any choice made. Although there are techniques for evaluating specific options, the selection is often subjective and likely to be influenced by the values of managers and other groups with an interest in the organisation (Helmold et al., 2020).

The generic strategies differentiation and cost leadership are a good method to define, in which direction a company should go to increase profitability and to acquire a competitive advantage (Porter, 1980, 1985; Helmold & Samara, 2019). Mintzberg provides five definitions of strategy, plan, ploy, pattern, position and perspective (Mintzberg et al., 1995). Firstly, strategy is always a plan. A plan integrates intended actions activities based on previous assessment of the situation. Secondly, as plan, a strategy can be a ploy too, really just a specific manoeuvre intended to outwit an opponent or competitor. If strategies can be intended (whether as general plans or specific ploys), they can also be realised. In other words, defining strategy as plan is not sufficient; we also need a definition that encompasses the resulting behaviour. Thirdly, strategy is a pattern. The definitions of strategy as plan and pattern can be quite independent of one another. Plans may go unrealised, while patterns may appear without preconception. Plans are intended strategy, whereas patterns are the realised strategy. Fourthly, strategy is a perspective. A perspective is not just of a chosen position, but consists of an ingrained way of perceiving the world (Mintzberg et al., 1995) (Fig. 1.6).

1.4.2 Boston Consulting Matrix (BCG-Matrix)

The BCG matrix is named after the Boston Consulting Group (BCG), whose founder Bruce Henderson developed this matrix in 1970 (Fig. 1.7). This concept should clarify the connection between the product life cycle and the cost experience curve. The matrix is often visualized as a scatter or bubble diagram; the area of a circle then represents the sales of the respective product. The BCG matrix is, put simply, a portfolio management framework that helps companies decide how to prioritize their different businesses and supply chains. It is a table, split into four

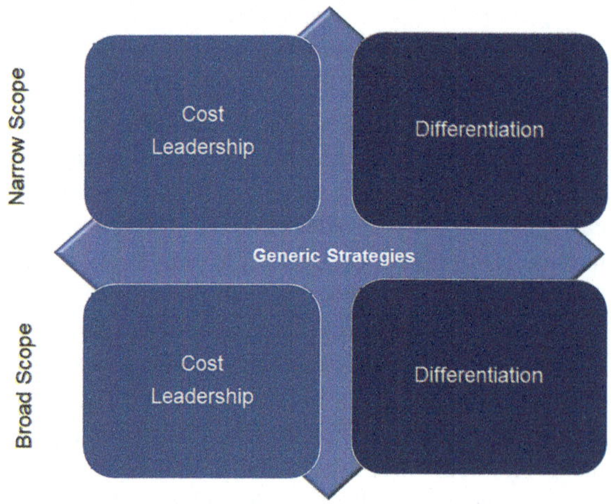

Fig. 1.6 Generic strategies. (Source: Author's own figure, adopted from Porter, 1985))

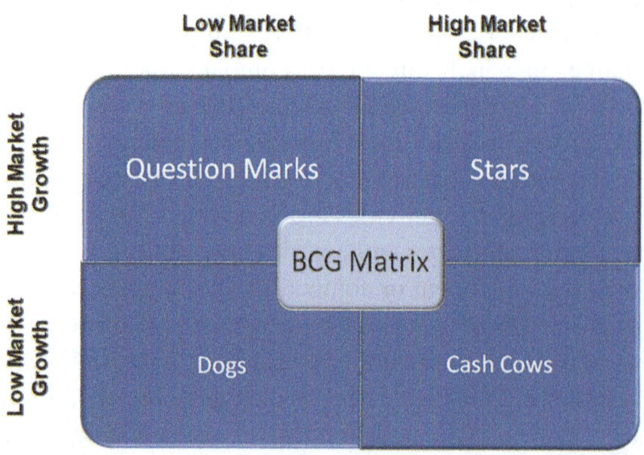

Fig. 1.7 BCG Strategies. (Source: Author's source)

quadrants, each with its own unique symbol that represents a certain degree of profitability: question marks, stars, dogs, and cash cows. By assigning each business to one of these four categories, executives could then decide where to focus their resources and capital to generate the most value, as well as where to cut their losses. The products or business units of a company are assigned to one of the four areas based on their values. Each area embodies a standard strategy. It should give a good recommendation on how to proceed. The life cycle of a typical product runs from the question mark to the star and cash cow to the poor dog. There are also products that do not follow this ideal path. Many product failures and flops do not even reach the star range. An imitating product, on the other hand, may skip the question mark area. The Question Marks, normally young products, are the newcomers among the products. The market has growth potential, but the products only have a small relative market share. Management is faced with the decision of whether to invest or abandon the product. In the case of an investment, the product requires liquid funds, which it cannot generate itself. A typical strategy recommendation is: selection and possibly an offensive penetration strategy to increase market share. The Stars are the company's most promising products. You have a high relative market share in a growth market. They already cover the investment needs resulting from market growth with their own cash flow. The strategy recommendation is: investment and possibly a skimming strategy to increase profit margins without endangering market share. The Cash Cows (milking cows) have a high relative market share in a only slightly growing or static market. They produce stable, high cash flows and can be "milked" without further investment. A fixed price strategy or price competition strategy is appropriate. The Poor Dogs are the discontinued products in the company. They have low market growth, sometimes market contraction, and low relative market share. At the latest as soon as the contribution margin for these products is negative, the portfolio should be adjusted (disinvestment strategy). In addition to assessing the individual products using the standard strategies, the entire portfolio should also be considered. Pay attention to the static financial equalization – the products in the portfolio should support and finance each other. A question mark can only expand if z. B. a cash cow finances this expansion. Future developments can also be seen. The products should be evenly represented in the individual areas – a company without question marks would have little chance in the future market. The matrix reveals two factors that companies should consider when deciding where to invest, company competitiveness, and market attractiveness, with relative market share and growth rate as the underlying drivers of these factors. Each of the four quadrants represents a specific combination of relative market share, and growth:

- Low Growth, High Share. Companies should milk these "cash cows" for cash to reinvest.
- High Growth, High Share. Companies should significantly invest in these "stars" as they have high future potential.
- High Growth, Low Share. Companies should invest in or discard these "question marks," depending on their chances of becoming stars.

- Low Share, Low Growth. Companies should liquidate, divest, or reposition these "dogs."

1.4.3 Ansoff-Matrix

The Product-Market-Matrix (also Ansoff-Matrix, after its inventor Harry Igor Ansoff or Z-Matrix) is a tool for the strategic management of companies. It can be used by a management (= company management) who has decided on a growth strategy as an aid for planning this growth. When it comes to market penetration, the focus is on gaining additional market shares with existing products. The company is trying to sell more of its products to existing, new, and competitive customers. Existing marketing activities usually have to be adapted to achieve this goal. Although the product portfolio does not change, companies often have to experiment with new advertising concepts in order to further promote product adoption in the existing market.

However, this market penetration can only be successfully implemented up to the point at which the market has not yet been fully saturated. The focus of the market development strategy is on creating new sales markets for existing products. By entering new market segments or opening up further geographical regions, a company puts itself in the position of attracting new target groups for its existing products.

A regionally operating bakery can also offer its own products nationwide, for example by setting up digital sales channels, and thus generate growth. Of course, the implementation of this strategy is initially offset by considerable investment costs. The chances of success should therefore first be assessed by means of careful planning and a comprehensive risk analysis. If opening up new markets is not an option, it is often worth taking a look at the product development strategy. The existing range is expanded through product innovations or the creation of product variants in the existing market. The resulting added value should encourage consumers to buy. This strategy is particularly attractive for companies in niche markets in which acquiring new customers and upselling would be almost impossible with a pure market penetration strategy. The reluctance to enter new markets is reinforced by high development costs and the risk of failure of the newly developed product. The most risky quadrant of the Ansoff matrix is that of diversification. This requires the development of a new product while at the same time opening up a new market. The associated investment costs in terms of product development, business analyses, setting up local subsidiaries, etc. can quickly mean the end of a company if the corresponding ROI is not achieved. The diversification strategy can be broken down into horizontal, vertical and lateral diversification, depending on the degree of risk tolerance of a company:

- Vertical Diversification
- Horizontal Diversification

Horizontal Diversification

Horizontal diversification describes the development of a new product that is still factually related to the product range previously offered. The existing value chain can continue to be used with minimal adjustments. With horizontal diversification, a company expands its offerings at the same economic level to reach new customers. An example of this type of diversification is the development of the iPad, which with its introduction gradually expanded Apple's existing smartphone and computer portfolio.

Vertical Diversification

With vertical diversification, a company deepens its commitment to sales-oriented activities (forward integration) and/or the actual manufacturing process of its products (backward integration). Diversification does not take place on the same level of the value chain as with horizontal diversification, but on the upstream or downstream one. With forward integration, a company takes the sales of its products and services into its own hands, for example by opening its own branches or an online shop. Backward integration describes the safeguarding of a company's reference markets, for example by taking over production processes that were previously outsourced to external companies. While horizontal diversification aims to reduce dependency on one product line, vertical diversification focuses on reducing dependence on suppliers and dealers. The acquisition of the necessary skills and know-how for the successful implementation of sales and production processes is in turn associated with high investment costs and thus increased financial risks.

Lateral Diversification

With the lateral diversification strategy, companies expand into completely new markets that have no material connection with the existing business.

The aim and purpose of this alignment is to minimize the dependence on developments in the existing market segment. Google can be mentioned as a good example in this context: In addition to the search engine core business, the company expanded early on into other market segments such as telecommunications (fiber), biotechnology (Calico) or autonomous automotive technology (Waymo). The lateral diversification strategy is used by multinational companies in particular to respond flexibly to changes and trends in the market. The necessary know-how is usually acquired through the acquisition of specialized companies that are already represented in the market of interest. Accordingly, this strategy requires enormous investment costs and harbours not only financial but also immaterial risks, such as a diluted brand image due to product offerings that are too diversified (Fig. 1.8).

1.4.4 Blue and Red Ocean Strategies

Blue Ocean Strategy is a method for developing permanently profitable business models from the field of strategic management: The basic idea is that only through the development of innovative and new markets, which really differentiate and

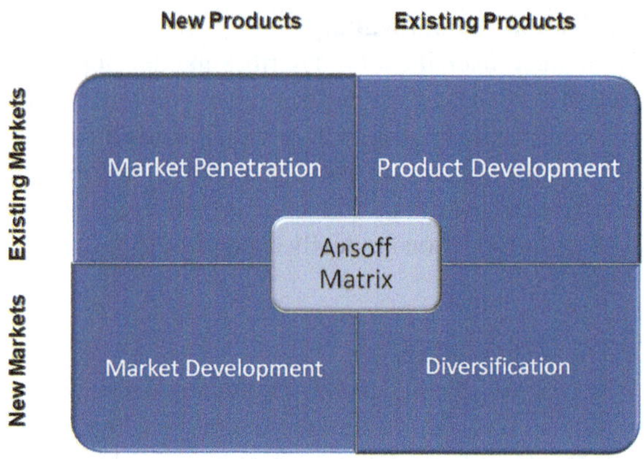

Fig. 1.8 Ansoff Matrix. (Source: Author's source)

relevant benefits for the broad mass of customers or non-customers, "Blue Oceans"offer lasting successes. Among other things, this is to be achieved through competition that has become meaningless, new customer acquisitions and optimized cost structures.

The concept of the Blue Ocean Strategy was developed by W. Chan Kim and Renée Mauborgne at the INSEAD Business School, where it was initially referred to as Value Innovation. Based on empirical studies over a period of 15 years and based on the analysis of more than 100 leading companies, examples of companies were found that opened up new, previously unused sub-markets and thus made the previous competition irrelevant. The term ocean describes a market or branch of industry in connection with the blue ocean strategy. "Blue oceans" are understood as untouched markets or branches of industry with little or no competition. Anyone who plunged into the Blue Ocean would find undiscovered markets or industries. "Red oceans", on the other hand, designate saturated markets, characterized by tough competition, overcrowded with competitors who all offer the same service or the same products. The term "red ocean" is based on the image of bloody fights of predatory fish (the competitors), while the "blue ocean" is free from bloody fights (Table 1.2).

1.5 Strategic Implementation

1.5.1 Assessment of Suitability, Acceptability and Feasibility

Strategic implementation is concerned with the translation of the selected strategy into action (Johnson et al., 2017). The ways in which strategies are implemented are described as the strategic architecture or framework of the organisation (Johnson et al., 2017). Successful implementation of the chosen strategy will be dependent on several factors such as stakeholder's expectations, the employees, the company culture, the will to change and the cooperation within the organisation. These elements and how the management and employees work together to adopt the new plan will

Table 1.2 Red ocean and blue ocean strategies

Red ocean strategy	Blue ocean strategy
Compete in existing Market Spaces	Create uncontested Market Spaces
Defeat the Competition	Make the Competition irrelevant
Apply Differentiation or Cost Leadership	Apply Differentiation and Cost Leadership
Achieve a Competitive Advantage	Achieve Value Innovations
Segment smartly existing Customers	Attract new Customers
Exploit existing Demand	Create and capture new Demands
Achieve a competitive Advantage through CSR	

Source: Author's source, adopted from Kim & Mauborgne (2015)

decide about how successful the strategy implementation is. The available skills and/or the ability to develop new skills when required for the planned change and issues like the structural re-organisation and resulting cultural disturbance would also affect success. Resource availability and planning for the utilisation of such resources need to be addressed as part of the implementation plan. The entire process necessitates the management of strategic change and will concern handling both hard and soft factors of the organisation, i.e. structure and systems and culture and motivation etc. Implementing a strategy has three elements.

- Organisational structure and layout: Where and how should the organisation is split into European, US and Asian divisions? How autonomous should divisions be? What parenting style should be applied?
- Resources: Enabling an organisation's resources should support the chosen strategy: What are the appropriate human and non-human resources? What assets need to be acquired
- Change management: Most strategic planning and implementation will involve change, so managing change, in particular employees' fears and resistance, is crucial

Johnson and Scholes argue that for a strategy to be successful it must satisfy three criteria (Johnson et al., 2017). These criteria can be applied to any strategy decision such as the competitive strategies, growth strategies or development strategies:

1. Suitability- whether the options are adequate responses to the firm's assessment of its strategic position
2. Acceptability- considers whether the options meet and are consistent with the firm's objectives and are acceptable to the stakeholders
3. Feasibility- assesses whether the organisation has the resources it needs to carry out the strategy

1.5.2 Suitability

Suitability is a useful criterion for screening strategies, asking the following questions about strategic options:

- Does the strategy exploit the company strengths, such as providing work for skilled craftsmen or environmental opportunities, e.g. helping to establish the organisation in new growth sectors of the market?
- How far does the strategy overcome the difficulties identified in the analysis? For example, is the strategy likely to improve the organisation's competitive position, solve the company's liquidity problems or decrease dependence on a particular supplier?
- Does the option fit in with the organisation's purposes? For example, would the strategy achieve profit targets or growth expectations, or would it retain control for an owner-manager?

1.5.3 Acceptability

Acceptability is essentially about assessing risk and return and is strongly related to expectations of stakeholders. The issue of "acceptable to whom?" thus requires the analysis to be thought through carefully. Some of the questions that will help identify the likely consequences of any strategy are as follows:

- How will the strategy impact shareholder wealth? Assessing this could involve calculations relating to profitability, e.g. net present value (NPV).
- How will the organisation perform in profitability terms? The parallel in the public sector would be cost/benefit assessment.
- How will the financial risk (e.g. liquidity) change?
- What effect will it have on capital structure (gearing or share ownership)?
- Will the function of any department, group or individual change significantly?
- Will the organisation's relationship with outside stakeholders, e.g. suppliers, government, unions, customers need to change?
- Will the strategy be acceptable in the organisation's environment, e.g. higher levels of noise?

1.5.4 Feasibility

Assesses whether the organisation has the resources it needs to carry out the strategy. Factors that should be considered can be summarised under the M-word model.

- Machinery. What demands will the strategy make on production? Do we have sufficient spare capacity? Do we need new production systems to give lower cost/better quality/more flexibility/etc.?
- Management. Is existing management sufficiently skilled to carry out the strategy?

- Money. How much finance is needed and when? Can we raise this? Is the cash flow feasible?
- Manpower. What demands will the strategy make on human resources? How many employees are needed, what skills will they need and when do we need them? Do we already have the right people or is there a gap? Can the gap be filled by recruitment, retraining, etc.?
- Markets. Is our existing brand name strong enough for the strategy to work? Will new brand names have to be established? What market share is needed for success – how quickly can this be achieved?
- Materials. What demands will the strategy make on our relationships with suppliers? Are changes in quality needed?
- Make-up. Is the existing organisational structure adequate or will it have to be changed?

1.6 Strategic Pyramid

A useful tool for the translation of the corporate strategy and strategic objectives into negotiations is the strategic pyramid. Strategy in this context is the long-term positioning as well as the decision of the enterprise, which business fields and which strategies to choose. Strategy is therefore "the fundamental, long-term direction of three to five years and organization of a company in order to gain competitive advantages in a changing environment through the use of resources and competences and to realize the long-term goals of the stakeholders" (Johnson et al., 2017) (Fig. 1.9).

Fig. 1.9 Strategic pyramid. (Source: Author's own figure)

1.6.1 Mission and Vision

Enterprises must manifest in their strategy to strive for CSR excellence (Helmold & Samara, 2019). The mission is the starting point of the strategic pyramid. The mission statement of an enterprise is the long-term purpose of the company and the strategic direction as defined by Johnson & Scholes (1997). The vision or strategic intent describes more specifically what an organization aims to achieve and the long-term aspirations (Johnson & Scholes, 1997).

Mission Example: Become a CSR Enterprise of excellence on a global basis.
Vision Example: Become the world-leading company in CSR in the industry in the next five years.

1.6.2 Goals and Objectives

The mission and vision are followed by generic goals and specific objectives. Generic Goals are not quantified and more general, but specific objectives are quantified and specific (Helmold & Samara, 2019). The strategists Johnson and Scholes distinguish in longer-term and generic (English: Goals) as well as shorter and quantified objectives (English: Objectives) for the company (Johnson & Scholes, 1997). Quantified goals can include sales, financial, quality, logistics, cost, and alpha goals.

Goal example: Increase and improve quality, reduce cost and provide productivity improvements between 30 and 40 percent within the next three years.
Objectives example: Quantification of the generic aims (goals).

1.6.3 Core Competencies

The next level in the strategic pyramid is the identification of core competencies. Core competences are those competences which allow companies to gain a superior or competitive advantage and that are very difficult for your competitors to emulate (Johnson et al., 2017). These describe the resources, skills, knowledge or any other feature that lead to a competitive advantage. Core competencies must be perceived by customers and clients (Helmold et al., 2020).

Example: Create CSR academy and CSR culture.

1.6.4 Strategies

After defining mission, vision, goals and core competencies, the elements must be translated into strategic objectives and key performance indicators (KPI). The long-term implementation of these elements is defined as the formulation of strategic objectives and important for the negotiations (Helmold & Samara, 2019). In implementing the strategic goals, negotiations will take place with many stakeholders (Helmold et al., 2020). Become a CSR differentiator by answering customer demands: Reduce operating cost by 25 percent in 12 months from now, increase customer satisfaction by 10 percent.

1.6.5 Strategic Architecture

In addition to buildings, machines, plants, offices, resources or employees, the infrastructure in the sense of strategic management also includes knowledge and innovations of the company that ensure long-term success (Helmold & Samara, 2019). This requires facilities, buildings, factories or offices that represent the strategic infrastructure. In addition, however, other success criteria such as resources, knowledge, experts, name recognition, network or innovations are of central importance.

1.6.6 Control and Execution

The final element of the strategic pyramid is the performance control (control and execution) and a target-performance comparison. A suitable tool for this step is the Balance Score Card (BSC) or an action plan. The instrument of the BSC was already developed in 1992 by the professors Norton and Kaplan. The BSC is an instrument in strategic management and includes four categories (Johnson et al., 2017):

1. Customer Satisfaction
2. Financial Category
3. Internal Processes and Improvements
4. Learning Organization

In practice, it seems that companies are adapting or expanding the original four dimensions to their specific needs (Johnson et al., 2017).

Example: Establishing process and key performance indicators (KPI) of monitoring improvements and successful execution of strategy. Creating scorecard and checking running time, sequence, weight and other elements on a daily basis.

1.7 Core Ethical Values

Core ethical values are understood to be the overarching ethical values of an organization that shape its identity and serve as a framework for interacting with customers, colleagues and other stakeholders in a company. Corporate values provide managers and employees with a basis for decision-making, action orientation and behavioural standards. If they are consistently lived in the company, they have a positive influence on the success of an organization.

1.8 Strategies Must Focus on Value-Creation

Porter postulated three generic or broad alternative strategies which may be pursued as a response to the competitive pressures. They are termed generic strategies because they are broadly applicable to any industry or business (Helmold et al., 2020). They are differentiation, cost leadership, and focus. A focus strategy may be further defined as cost focus, differentiation focus, or cost and differentiation focus. A differentiation strategy may be based on actual unique product features or the perception thereof, conveyed through the use of advertising and marketing tactics, in the eyes of the customers. Obviously, the product or service feature must be one the customer needs or desires. Moreover, such enhanced features and designs or advertising and marketing will increase costs, and customers must be price-insensitive – willing to pay for the differentiated product or service. This willingness to pay for the differentiated product of service is what provides the company relief from competitive pressure, cost pressure specifically. Firms pursuing a cost leadership strategy must make lower production and distribution costs their priority (Helmold & Terry, 2021). By keeping their cost lowers than those of their competitors, firms using cost leadership can still price their products up to the level of their competitors and still maintain higher gross profit margins. Alternatively, these firms can price their products lower than those of their competitors in the hope of achieving greater market share and sales volume at the expense of gross profit margins. A focus strategy is based on a particular market, customer, product, or geographic. A Focus strategy is a concentrated, narrowly focused niche strategy. Figure 1.10 shows the example of a Mission Statement of Alstom (formerly Bombardier) Transportation in China International Procurement Office.

1.9 Case Study: Siemens CSR Mission, Vision and Strategy

The company Siemens has outlined the CSR focus in its mission, vision, goals, strategic objectives, core values and cultural specifics in its strategy outline (Siemens, 2019). Innovative technology has been at the heart of Siemens for more than 170 years at Siemens and will continue to be the heart of the future we build. The company strives to develop innovative solutions that provide answers for a better future, answers for more livable and sustainable cities, answers for intelligent energy solutions and answers for the connection of the real and digital world, to reduce energy consumption and to increase competitiveness. Answers to lay the foundations for societies to thrive and people to be empowered. Sustainability is according to the mission and vision of Siemens the core of business activities. It determines formally responsible business practices, risk management approaches and technological contributions to climate protection, resource protection and

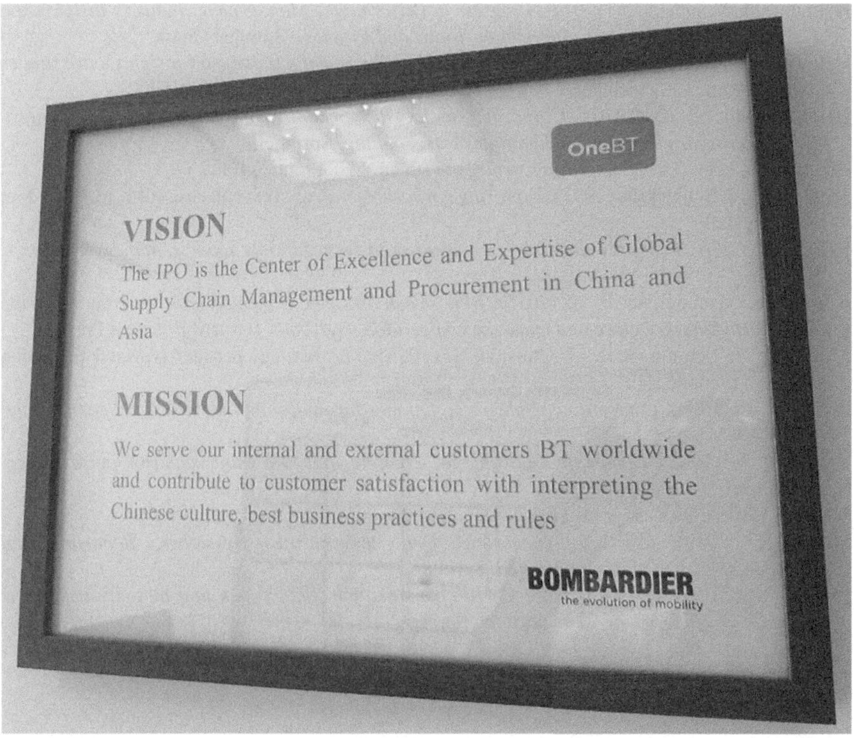

Fig. 1.10 Example of mission statement and vision. (Source: Author's source)

product safety in the interests of future generations. With a strong focus on the fields of industry, infrastructure and transport, we concentrate on creating agile and productive factories, intelligent and efficient buildings and networks or designing a more sustainable transport infrastructure. In this way, Siemens is helping to increase the competitiveness of its customers and at the same time setting the course for a successful energy transition in the key sectors of industry, transport and buildings. Sustainable business practices are based on integrity, fairness, transparency and responsibility. With numerous programs, Siemens promotes the safety, further training and well-being of our employees and are committed to equal rights and the further development of society. Siemens is therefore using the tool DEGREE – A clear framework for sustainability. The DEGREE framework represents a 360-degree approach for all stakeholders – customers, suppliers, investors, employees, the societies the company serves and the planet.

References

Helmold, M. (2020). *Lean Management and Kaizen Fundamentals from Cases and Examples in Operations and Supply Chain Management*. Springer Cham.

Helmold, M. (2021). *Innovatives Lieferantenmanagement. Wertschöpfung in globalen Lieferketten*. Springer.

Helmold, M. & Samara, W. (2019). *Progress in Performance Management. Industry Insights and Case Studies on Principles, Application Tools, and Practice.* Springer Cham.

Helmold, M., & Terry, B. (2021). *Operations and procurement 4.0. Industry insights, case studies and best practices*. Springer.

Helmold, M., et al. (2020). *Corporate Social Responsibility im internationalen Kontext. Wettbewerbsvorteile durch nachhaltige Wertschöpfung*. Springer.

Johnson, G., et al. (2017). *Exploring strategy* (11th ed.). FT Prentice Hall.

Johnson, G., & Scholes, K. (1997). *Exploring corporate strategy*. Text and cases (4th ed.). London: Prentice Hall.

Khojasteh, Y. (2018). *Supply chain risk management. Advanced tools, models, and developments.* Springer.

Kim, C., & Maubourgne, R. A. (2015). *Blue ocean strategy, expanded edition: How to create uncontested market space and make the competition irrelevant.* Harvard Business Press.

Mintzberg, H., Quinn, J. B., & Ghoshal, S. (1995). *The strategy process* (revised European edition). Prentice Hall.

Porter, M. E. (1980). *Competitive strategy: Techniques for analyzing industries and competitors.* Free Press.

Porter, M. E. (1985). *Competitive advantage. Creating and sustaining superior performance.* Free Press.

Siemens. (2019). *Siemens strategy*. www.siemens.de

Stibbe, R. (2019). *CSR-Erfolgssteuerung. Den Reformprozess verstehen, Reporting und Risikomanagement effizient gestalten*. Springer.

Wagner, R. (2019). *Effektive interne CSR-Kommunikation. Sinn stiften und motivieren für eine nachhaltige Unternehmensentwicklung*. Springer.

2 Sustainability Management and Social Responsibility in the Value Chain

It takes 20 years to build a reputation and five minutes to ruin it.

Benjamin Franklin

2.1 CSR as Integral Part in the Value Chain

Corporate social responsibility (CSR) is also known by a number of other names. These include corporate responsibility, corporate accountability, corporate ethics, corporate citizenship or stewardship, business ethics, responsible entrepreneurship, and triple bottom line, to name just a few. As CSR issues become increasingly integrated into modern business practices, there is a trend towards referring to it as "responsible competitiveness" or "corporate sustainability." CSR is understood to be the way firms integrate social, environmental and economic concerns into their values, culture, decision making, strategy and operations in a transparent and accountable manner, and thereby establish better practices within the firm, create wealth and improve society. A key point to note is that CSR is an evolving concept that currently does not have a universally accepted definition. Generally, CSR is understood to be the way firms integrate social, environmental and economic concerns into their values, culture, decision making, strategy and operations in a transparent and accountable manner and thereby establish better practices within the firm, create wealth and improve society. As issues of sustainable development become more important, the question of how the business sector addresses them is also becoming an element of CSR. It is necessary to integrate CSR principles and values across the value chain from the own company towards suppliers and customers (Helmold & Terry, 2021). The World Business Council for Sustainable Development has described CSR as the business contribution to sustainable

T. Dathe et al., *Corporate Social Responsibility (CSR), Sustainability and Environmental Social Governance (ESG)*, Management for Professionals,
https://doi.org/10.1007/978-3-030-92357-0_2

economic development. Building on a base of compliance with legislation and regulations, CSR typically includes "beyond law" commitments and activities pertaining to:

- corporate governance and ethics;
- health and safety;
- environmental stewardship;
- human rights (including core labour rights);
- sustainable development;
- conditions of work (including safety and health, hours of work, wages);
- industrial relations;
- community involvement, development and investment;
- involvement of and respect for diverse cultures and disadvantaged peoples;
- corporate philanthropy and employee volunteering;
- customer satisfaction and adherence to principles of fair competition;
- anti-bribery and anti-corruption measures;
- accountability, transparency and performance reporting; and
- supplier relations, for both domestic and international supply chains.

Value chain concepts focus primarily on improvements of the operational processes and efficiency across the entire value chain (D'heur, 2014). Another goal is to reduce waste and thus to reduce operating costs. In the last years sustainability has become more and more important, so that any organisation must deploy sustainability elements alongside operations management and organisations (Martel & Klibi, 2016). Sustainability or Corporate Social Responsibility (CSR) has the following elements as shown in Fig. 2.1. The figure shows that there is a strong need to align the CSR implementation process with the sustainability strategy in order to avoid the negative impacts that CSR production could have on the environmental and social components of sustainability. Although the concept of corporate social responsibility (CSR) has been advocated for decades and is commonly employed by corporations globally, agreement on how CSR should be defined and implemented remains a contentious debate amongst academia, businesses and society. This gap is problematic for corporations because they are increasingly being required to align

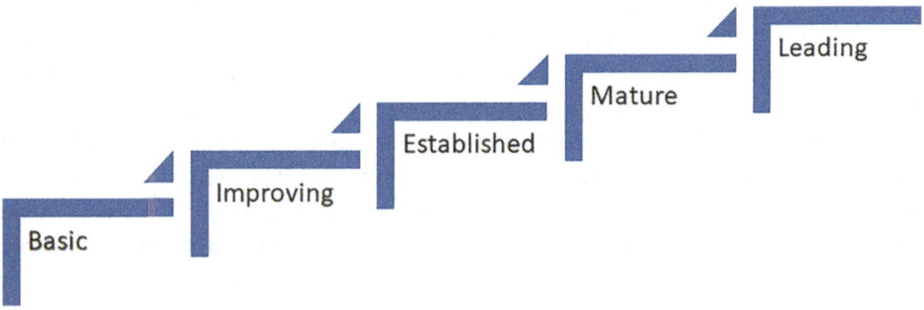

Fig. 2.1 CSR maturity levels (Helmold & Samara, 2019)

with societal norms while generating financial returns. In order to remedy this problem, the following definition is presented: corporate social responsibility is a business system that enables the production and distribution of wealth for the betterment of its stakeholders through the implementation and integration of ethical systems and sustainable management practices. Many of the concepts in the proposed definition are commonplace amongst CSR practitioners and organizations, the validations for the key segments – production and distribution of wealth, stakeholder management, ethical systems, sustainable management practices – coupled with the application of a systems approach and other business practices make the definition unique and conclusive.

2.2 CSR Maturity Levels

Maturity is a measurement of the ability of an organization for continuous improvement in CSR as shown in Fig. 2.1. The higher the maturity, the higher will be the chances that incidents or errors will lead to improvements either in the quality or in the use of the resources of the discipline as implemented by the organization. As part of the maturity levels, it is important to have measurable performance indicators, which will show the level in terms of CSR maturity (Stibbe, 2019).

2.3 Global Compact Principles

Corporate sustainability starts with a company's value system and a principles-based approach to doing business. This means operating in ways that, at a minimum, meet fundamental responsibilities in the areas of human rights, labour, environment and anti-corruption. Responsible businesses enact the same values and principles wherever they have a presence, and know that good practices in one area do not offset harm in another. By incorporating the Ten Principles of the UN Global Compact into strategies, policies and procedures, and establishing a culture of integrity, companies are not only upholding their basic responsibilities to people and planet, but also setting the stage for long-term success. The UN Global Compact is a principle-based framework for businesses, stating ten principles in the areas of human rights, labour, the environment and anti-corruption. Under the Global Compact, companies are brought together with UN agencies, labour groups and civil society. The framework provides a universal language for corporate responsibility and a framework to guide all businesses regardless of size, complexity or location. Joining the UN Global Compact means to take an important, public step to transform our world through principled business. Participation makes a statement about values, and it benefits both society and companies' long-term success (Helmold & Terry, 2016).

Corporate sustainability starts with a company's value system and a principled approach to doing business. This means operating in ways that, at a minimum, meet fundamental responsibilities in the areas of human rights, labour, environment and

Fig. 2.2 Global compact principles. (Source: United Nations)

anti-corruption. Responsible businesses enact the same values and principles wherever they have a presence, and know that good practices in one area do not offset harm in another (Helmold & Samara, 2019). By incorporating the Global Compact principles into strategies, policies and procedures, and establishing a culture of integrity, companies are not only upholding their basic responsibilities to people and planet, but also setting the stage for long-term success. Figure 2.2 Global Compact Principlesshows the Global Compact principles.

2.4 Case Study: Volkswagen's CSR and Green Award

The Volkswagen Wolfsburg plant receives the "CSR & Green Management Award 2019" in the "Automotive OEM" category for its efficient and sustainable production (Fig. 2.3 Volkswagen CSR and Green Award 2019). More than 250 works from more than ten countries and 20 different industries participated in the competition. "We are proud that our persistent work has been successful in saving resources and that we have been awarded the prestigious 'CSR & Green Management Award' for this," said Stefan Loth, Head of Volkswagen's Wolfsburg plant. "At the Wolfsburg location, we prove that efficient vehicle production while at the same time conserving resources is not only possible, but makes sense. Because the production also carries an ecological responsibility. The deliberate use of raw materials and energy

Fig. 2.3 Volkswagen CSR and Green Award 2019. (Source: Volkswagen)

plays a key role in our environmental commitment". In terms of production efficiency, Volkswagen's parent plant focuses on its "PQM" strategy – productivity, quality and crew. Every year more than 400 workshops take place, with which the Wolfsburg workforce improves the processes and thus reduces the production costs per vehicle. The plant consistently uses the Volkswagen Production system that describes the basics, standards and methods by which the manufacturing processes are designed, executed and constantly developed. The Volkswagen parent plant is also on course for sustainability and the implementation of the "Zero Impact Factory" environmental program. An important building block for protecting the environment and promoting biodiversity are, for example, the process water basins located on the plant site. Thanks to the internal operating water cycle, every drop of water passes through the site about four to six times, helping to keep water consumption per vehicle very low. The "CSR & Green Management Award" is awarded annually by the consultants Growth Consulting Europe and Quadriga Consult and the trade publication AUTOMOBIL INDUSTRIE. The award was recently ranked as one of the highest rated sustainability awards in Germany in a study by the University of Hohenheim.

References

D'heur, M. (2014). *CSR und Value Chain Management. Profitables Wachstum durch nachhaltig gemeinsame Wertschöpfung*. Springer.

Helmold, M., & Samara, W. (2019). *Progress in performance management. Industry insights and case studies on principles, application tools, and practice*. Springer Cham.

Helmold, M., & Terry, B. (2016). *Global sourcing and procurement excellence in China. Procurement guide for supply experts*. Springer.

Helmold, M., & Terry, B. (2021). *Operations and procurement 4.0. Industry insights, case studies and best practices*. Springer.

Martel, A., & Klibi, w. (2016). *Designing value-creating supply chain networks*. Springer.

Stibbe, R. (2019). *CSR-Erfolgssteuerung. Den Reformprozess verstehen, Reporting und Risikomanagement effizient gestalten*. Springer.

Volkswagen. (2019). *Volkswagen Werk Wolfsburg erhält den Umweltpreis "CSR and Green Management Award*". Retrieved November 20, 2019, from https://CSR-and-green.de/de/award-gewinner

CSR in Procurement

3

What gets measured gets improved.

Peter Drucker (1909–2005)

3.1 Procurement and Supply Side

The Procurement function and Supply Side is the function, which secures that inputs are available for the transformation process as shown in Fig. 3.1. Transformation is any activity or group of activities that takes one or more inputs, transforms and adds value to them, and provides outputs for customers or clients. Inputs, for which the Procurement is responsible, are mostly products and services coming from suppliers in the upstream side of the value chain. These products or services are directly involved in the transformation into end-products to customers. However, inputs can be also indirect categories or services, which are not directly included in the transformation process (desks, machines, training services etc.).

The term Procurement as key value-adding function replaces old definitions of procurement or purchasing (Helmold & Terry, 2021). This definition is in line with Porter's description of value chains. A value chain is a set of activities that a firm operating in a specific industry performs in order to deliver a valuable product, service for the market. The concept comes from business management and was first described and popularized by Michael E. Porter in his 1985 best-seller, Competitive Advantage: Creating and Sustaining Superior Performance in the upstream Procurement or the supply side. Figure 3.1 displays the operations, the upstream supply side (Procurement) and the downstream supply side (customer or demand side side). In Porter's value chain framework (see Fig. 3.2), Inbound Logistics, Operations, Outbound Logistics, Marketing and Sales, and Service are categorized as primary activities. Secondary activities include Procurement, Human Resource

T. Dathe et al., *Corporate Social Responsibility (CSR), Sustainability and Environmental Social Governance (ESG)*, Management for Professionals,
https://doi.org/10.1007/978-3-030-92357-0_3

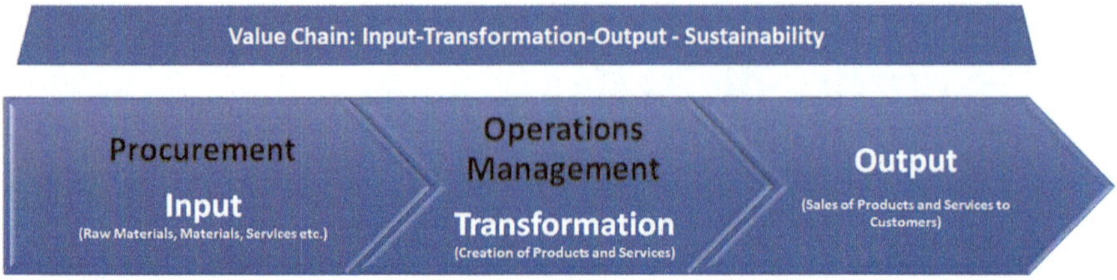

Fig. 3.1 Procurement managing the Input and Supplies. (Source: Author's source, adopted from Helmold & Samara, 2019)

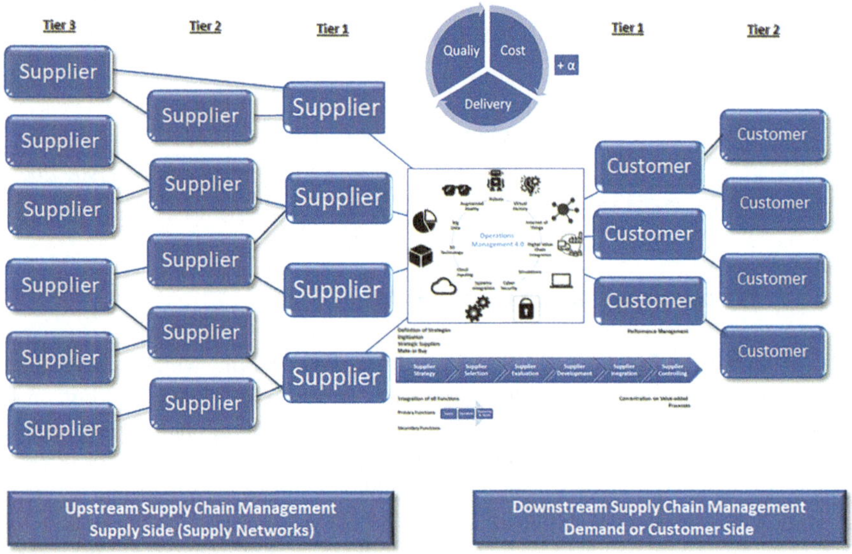

Fig. 3.2 Supply networks within the value chain. (Source: Author's source, adopted from Helmold & Samara, 2019)

management, Technological Development and Infrastructure. As many companies have external value chains (purchase of goods, services) of more than 80%, Procurement has here the most significant role in any enterprise. In many enterprises, functions are still working independently from each other, leading to a large amount of waste and inefficiencies. Many industries are currently faced by fierce competition. This is forcing manufacturing companies to concentrate on core competencies and to transfer the production of components, goods and services to external suppliers (Aberdeen Group, 2005). The number of value-adding activities has decreased constantly and now lies between 10% and 30% in this industry. The company Apple has no production and decided to outsource the manufacturing of iPads or iPhones to the company FoxConn. Such a development has had a great influence on the structure of supply chains and supplier relationships. Supply chains (the terms "supply chains" and "supply networks" are used synonymously in the literature) have become more complex and international, as pointed out by several authors Christopher and Peck see the level of complexity increasing in the upstream supply chain management of manufacturing companies in many industries, a trend which is characterized by the growing transfer of activities to suppliers and supplier networks, high numbers of supply chain layers (tiers), and the ongoing globalization of supply chains. As a consequence, vulnerability and risk exposure have risen significantly. The rapid increase in supplier activities therefore directly affects Procurement, as emphasized by Emmett and Crocker (2009). In recent years, many companies have reduced their value-adding activities and implemented efficiency-oriented cost reductions, e.g. outsourcing, single sourcing, low-cost country sourcing, platform concepts, CSR management, design-to-cost approaches (Aberdeen Group, 2005). Procurement has become more important in core and peripheral business areas and is aimed at building resilient supply chains. Resilience is based on being able to anticipate, manage and prevent supply chain disruptions at an early stage. On the other hand, supply risks have risen due to increased dependency on supplier networks (Fig. 3.3).

In their research "An Empirical Analysis of the Effect of Supply Chain Disruptions on Long-Run Stock Price", found that enterprises without operational slack and redundancies in their supply chains experience negative stock effects. The authors revealed the tremendous impact of supply chain disruptions on stock price performance and shareholder value. Supply disruptions can easily lead to high recovery cost, waste and sharp decreases in sales. External customers become dissatisfied and internal core functions (e.g. assembly) are disturbed. In most cases, supply disruptions have negative impacts on brand image, sales figures and the company's own financial situation as stressed by many authors writing about supply disruptions and resilient supply chains. Recent incidents in the media about disruptions caused by upstream Procurement inefficiencies from China show that the Procurement excellence approach needs to tackle these issues in a proactive and sustainable way.

Fig. 3.3 Porter's value chain. (Source: Authors source, adopted from Helmold et al., 2020)

Procurement risks have mainly been investigated at the direct level of tier-one relationships, but consideration has not been fully extended to sub-suppliers, i.e. tiers one, two, three and beyond. The new concept of Procurement therefore seeks to address these concerns by investigating how disruptions can be anticipated, prevented and managed over the entire value chain including all tiers on the supply and demand side as shown in the figure. Recent supply disruptions show that current Procurement organisations, Procurement tools and concepts are not smart and resilient enough to avoid these supply chain discrepancies. Recent articles for example in the magazine "Automotive News" show that all car producers are facing severe problems due to suppliers' problems. Not only the automotive industry but also many other industries face these issues.

The CSR Procurement concept was developed by Taichi Ohno (1990), who worked for Toyota Motors. It derived from a bundle of instruments which come from sophisticated production methods or supporting functions such as logistics. The ideal interplay and optimal combination of all instruments are essential for success. The vision of CSR production is based on the JUST-IN-TIME (JIT) philosophy and the Toyota Production System (TPS: Japanese = トヨタ生産システム) and focuses on the elimination of waste and the minimization of stock.

3.2 History of Procurement and Procurement 4.0 (Fig. 3.4)

3.3 Procurement Objectives

Supply Side objectives are important. The seven rights (7R), which are the major objectives according to the CSR Procurement philosophy can be defined as:

1. Right Products
2. Right Quality
3. Right Time
4. Right Quantity
5. Right Location
6. Right People
7. Right Cost

The right product refers to the right specification and requirements by the demanding customer. The products must have the required dimensions, layout, material, colour etc. The right quality means the clarification of all requirements in terms of quality and improvement measures to have the optimum quality levels. Quality is normally measured by hard factors such as non-conformities, field rejects or defects at receipt (0 km defects). The right quantity is the placing of a specific order quantity triggered by internal and customer demands. Procurement has to transfer the customer and company demands to the supply networks. The right time

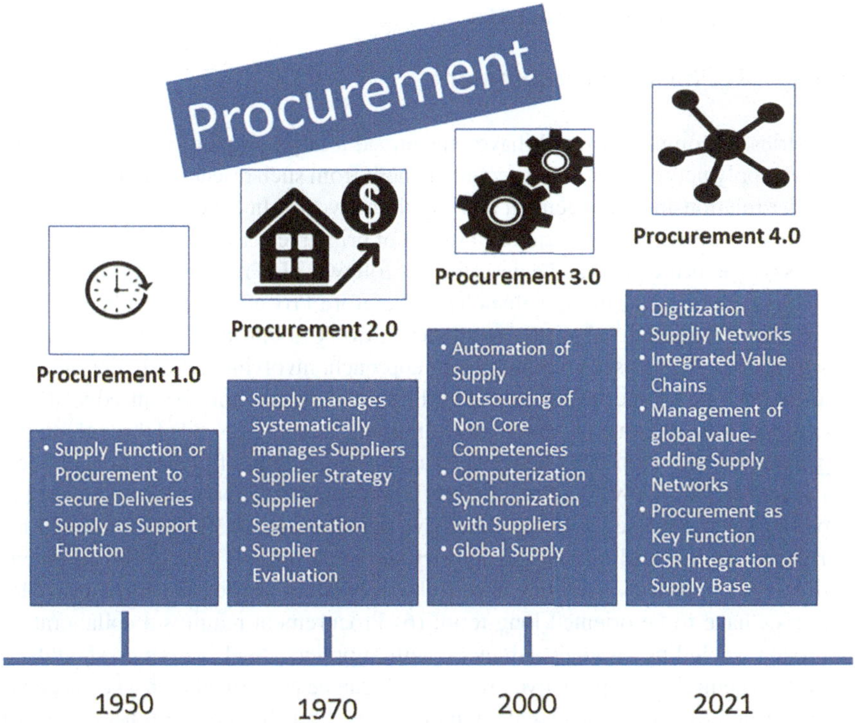

Fig. 3.4 History of Procurement 4.0. (Source: Author's source)

means that products ordered have to be at the buyer's place in time, neither too early nor too late. Procurement has to recognize suppliers' lead times. The lead time for any product starts from the order until the physical receipt of goods at the ordering party. The right location can be defined as the place, where the products are required. Shipment of products from China to Europe take more than eight weeks, so that that the right location is closely linked to the lead time of products. The meaning of right people extends current definition of the five Rights (Emmett & Crocker, 2009) in line with the modern and CSR philosophy of the new paradigm of Procurement. Suppliers in global markets need to have the right sales people, project managers and operators to meet the requested criteria. Project managers must have sufficient language skills and as well operators must be trained to produce good quality parts. People are becoming in a changing and global trade situation more and more important. Any product needs to have the right cost level, otherwise it will not be demanded and bought.

3.4 Procurement Process

3.4.1 Six Phases in Procurement

Industries or companies which have outsourced a large scope of their products to global supply networks would especially benefit from such research in Procurement, supplier relationship management and supply networks. In conclusion, it is evident that proactive Procurement requires a subset of principles (see Fig. 3.5 Procurement Process): The principles can be described as follows: (1) Procurement is a function which is managing the entire value chain; therefore Procurement must be incorporated into the mission, values and strategies of every organization. (2) Procurement best practices are focused on a multilayer approach, involving not only tier one, but also tier two and three levels; proactive Procurement can only be introduced and executed if the corporate objectives are communicated and cascaded throughout the organization; the setup must be centralized as single point of contact to suppliers; (3) advanced and innovative Procurement has standardized tools and processes; (4) Procurement best practice companies have sophisticated B2B platforms/supplier portals in terms of quality, cost and delivery and other suitable KPI; (5) Procurement and mitigation actions activities have to be preventive, proactive and sustainable; activities have to be oriented long-term; (6) Procurement requires a collaborative approach, including strategic alliances with suppliers. Such activities should be organized centrally; (7) proactive Procurement can be performed with a key account manager in terms of being a single point of contact for the supplier (customer); (8) performance indicators have to be mutually agreed upon and may comprise both hard and soft factors. The assessment process should consist of quality, cost, delivery and technological criteria; (9) the learning organization should, among other things, be characterized by the capability and competencies of coaching suppliers;

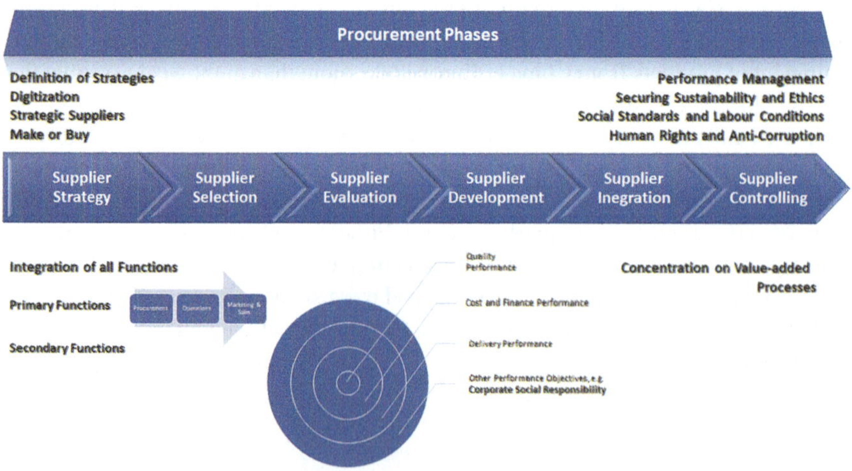

Fig. 3.5 Procurement process. (Source: Author's source)

(10) all the above mentioned principles should be combined with a philosophy of continuous improvement (Japanese: Kaizen) and reflection (Japanese: Hansei) to achieve a best practice model in Procurement. Companies that want to distance themselves from their competitors through best-in-class Procurement must implement the ten principles and adopt a collaborative approach in dealing with their supply base. Appropriate management of one's supply base can lead to competitive advantage. The strategic objective of Procurement is the establishment, design and management of supplier networks and the successful collaboration within these networks as the figure shows. The network consists of internal and external suppliers. The collaboration between supply partners and the management of the interactions are a key responsibility of the Procurement function. A sophisticated information system is a pre-requisite for proper interactions.

3.4.2 Supplier Strategy

By shifting value-adding activities and non-core competencies to supplier networks that are in competition with each other, new performance concepts, strategies and processes arise that have to be mastered. For a long time now, the focus in the future has not only been on increasing company-internal cost advantages, but much more on the exchange of information and the exploitation of global cross-company potential. In general, supplier management aims to provide a uniform method for analysing potential and existing suppliers in order to make strategic decisions based on the results. At the operational level, this means making the performance of suppliers comparable, uncovering optimization potential and reducing procurement costs. The strategic dimension of supplier management, on the other hand, aims primarily to define suitable procurement strategies based on a transparent basis for decision-making in order to reduce supply risks and dependencies and to increase procurement quality. The strategic goals of supplier management deal with the medium to long-term optimization of the company's supplier base. Based on category or material group-specific procurement strategies, it is important to define precise development measures that enable a continuous increase in delivery quality or a reduction in procurement costs. The supply risk can be sustainably reduced, for example, through the collaborative optimization of cross-company processes. The early establishment of possible alternative suppliers and the targeted control of the procurement volume prevent the company from becoming dependent. Figure 3.6 shows the first of the six phases of supplier strategy. In addition, the relationship with strategically important suppliers that are difficult to substitute should be strengthened through cooperative and integrative measures. This ensures the competitiveness of your own company. Due to the long-term orientation, all measures to achieve the strategic goals should be regularly checked as part of a continuous process and adjusted if necessary. Figure 3.7 shows the main elements in the phase of the supplier strategy with segmentation of suppliers, development of a material group strategy, feasibility studies on in-house or third-party production, the evaluation of

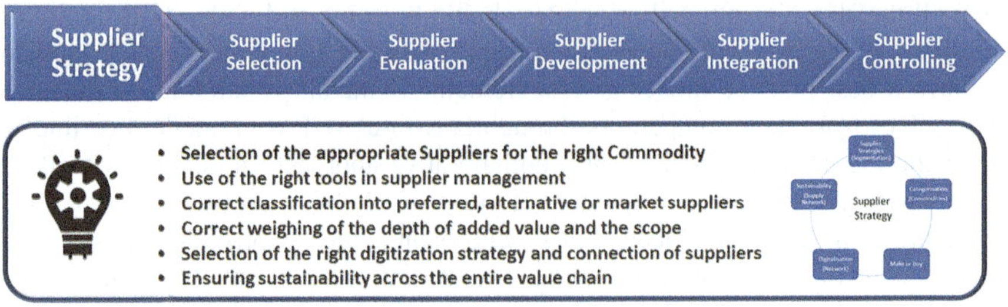

Fig. 3.6 Procurement process. (Source: Author's source)

Fig. 3.7 Elements of the Supplier Strategy Phase. (Source: Author's source)

degrees of digitization in supply chains and the constant review of sustainability requirements of suppliers. The main tasks can be described as follows:

- Choosing the right suppliers for the right material groups
- Use of the right tools in supplier management
- Correct classification into preferred, alternative or market suppliers
- Correct weighing of the depth of added value and the scope
- Selection of the right digitization strategy and connection of suppliers
- Ensuring sustainability across the entire value chain

Supplier Segmentation

Every supplier strategy must be based on core elements such as classification, categorization, digitization, in-house or external production, digitization and sustainability. Figure 3.8 shows these elements. As part of the supplier segmentation, the suppliers are grouped into company-wide classes according to preferred suppliers, alternative, benchmark, market and other suppliers. Preferred suppliers are selected suppliers with excellent performance characteristics in terms of innovation, quality, costs, delivery reliability, sustainability and processes. Preferred suppliers are given preferential treatment and are given specified volumes, order volumes and procurement quotas. Preferred suppliers are usually involved in the development and product creation process of their own company at an early stage. The relationship is based on partnership. Alternative suppliers are suppliers who can be used alongside the preferred suppliers. Alternative suppliers are in the group of bidders, but their performance is not as good as the preferred suppliers in terms of quality, costs, delivery and other characteristics, so they usually only receive smaller volumes and procurement quotas. The alternatives are followed by benchmark suppliers who serve as benchmarks and can be included in the group of bidders. Benchmarking in supplier management is a useful method for the systematic and structured acquisition of information and for the comparison of suppliers based on characteristics such as innovative strength, technological leadership, cost efficiency or quality awareness. Benchmarking is thus a constant creative process to improve the supplier portfolio by determining and comparing the best-known services of existing suppliers and the comparison with new suppliers who show particularly strong performance characteristics (English: benchmark = the best; best practice). By adopting and continuously improving the identified best practice processes, the performance of your own area, competitiveness and ultimately customer satisfaction are improved. Seen in this way, a benchmarking project within the scope of a tender offers the possibility of comparison with the best solutions, reveals deficits and weak points, clarifies the need for action and can be used as an ideal tool for the

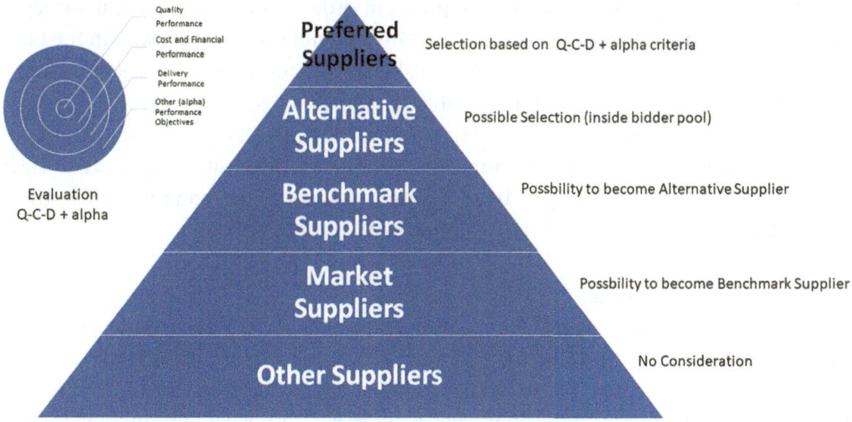

Fig. 3.8 Supplier segmentation and classification. (Source: Author's source)

development of new suppliers and constant competition. Benchmarking is not just a comparison of key figures or operations, but is a comprehensive, holistically applicable process analysis for improving performance that can be used for all performance areas and the entire company. The benchmark suppliers are followed by market suppliers and all other suppliers. Market suppliers can be included in the group of benchmark suppliers if their supplier management has been qualified and evaluated. All other suppliers are not taken into account (Helmold & Terry, 2016).

Commodity Strategies

A material or product group or category (English: commodity or category) combines different individual parts or categories in a material group, which are usually made from the same basic material or raw material or can be divided into the same category. The differentiation of material groups can be freely defined and can be relatively coarse or fine, this depends on the respective purpose. Examples of material groups: iron or ferrous metal, copper, plastic, rubber, leather, wood, etc. Other subdivisions are made e. g. according to electrical, mechanical, aluminium or steel.

The primary goal for bottleneck materials is to secure the supply. To reduce the supply risk, one should look at the global procurement markets. As a rule, the local markets offer only inadequate sources of supply for shortage materials. By expanding the number of suppliers, the dependency on individual suppliers for bottleneck materials is reduced. The focus is not on the cost of the material, but on securing the supply. Since these are mostly low-value individual parts, product development is not very important. A reduction in the supply risk can be achieved by standardizing bottleneck materials. Figure 3.9 Commodity Strategies shows the possible material group strategies. This matrix is subdivided into strategic, lever, bottleneck and non-critical material groups and market segments (suppliers). In the case of strategic material groups and market segments, it is advisable to enter into close ties with suppliers. This can take place through collaboration, joint or competitive development projects, collaborations or even company mergers (e.g. founding a new company or a joint venture). For leverage products, companies should bundle volumes and proactively approach potential suppliers in order to achieve the ideal strategy. Purchasing co-operations can also help to gain advantages in the market. In the case of bottleneck products, the strategy must be based on security of needs, so that long-term contracts prove advantageous. Global tenders or substitution are further strategies for ensuring security of supply. For standardized products, on the other hand, it is advantageous to regularly examine the market and exploit the potential. B2B platforms, C-parts management from a single source or the bundling of requirements after a detailed market study (Helmold & Terry, 2016).

Make or Buy Strategies

A make-or-buy decision addresses the in-house production or external procurement of a product. It's about producing a product (make) or buying it (buy). The operational function of production is always understood to mean in-house production. Goods are manufactured with their own resources, employees, production factors and production processes. In-house production means internalization, i.e. the

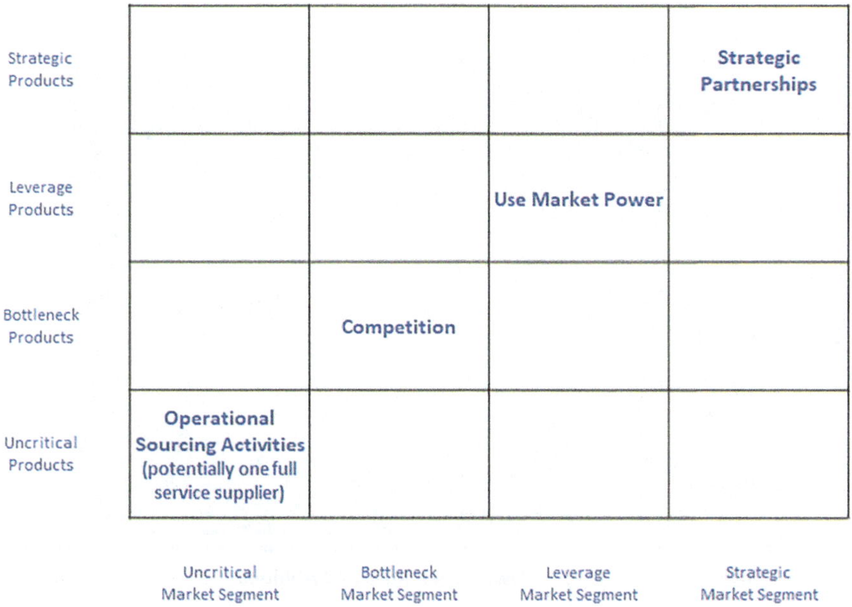

Fig. 3.9 Commodity strategies. (Source: Author's source)

organization of economic activities and the production of a material group in your own company organization. External production, on the other hand, means that material groups and production volumes are outsourced to suppliers. In the case of external production, there are usually only variable costs. In the case of in-house production, the fixed costs are added. The difference between the two variable cost amounts is used to cover the fixed costs more with each piece (fixed cost degression) until they are completely covered. Figure 3.10 shows recommendations for action for companies according to the strategic importance and relevance of the material group on the Y-axis and skills and competencies for developing and manufacturing the material group on the X-axis. Companies must therefore concentrate on their own skills and competencies for the development and production of the material group and prefer a strategy of in-house production (make) in this segment, especially if the strategic importance and relevance of the material group is very high. With the same level of skills and competencies for a product group, but relatively low strategic relevance and value, a hybrid strategy with partial outsourcing can take place. However, companies must ensure that the knowledge for this material group remains in their own company. If your own company does not have competencies in a special material group that is of high strategic importance, we recommend cooperative partnerships with one or a few suppliers (external production or buy). Due to its strategic importance, it is worth pursuing long-term contracts, collaborations or joint project developments with suppliers. With less relevant material groups and no know-how in your own company, the market potential and competition can be fully exploited. The decision to purchase from a third party should therefore be carefully

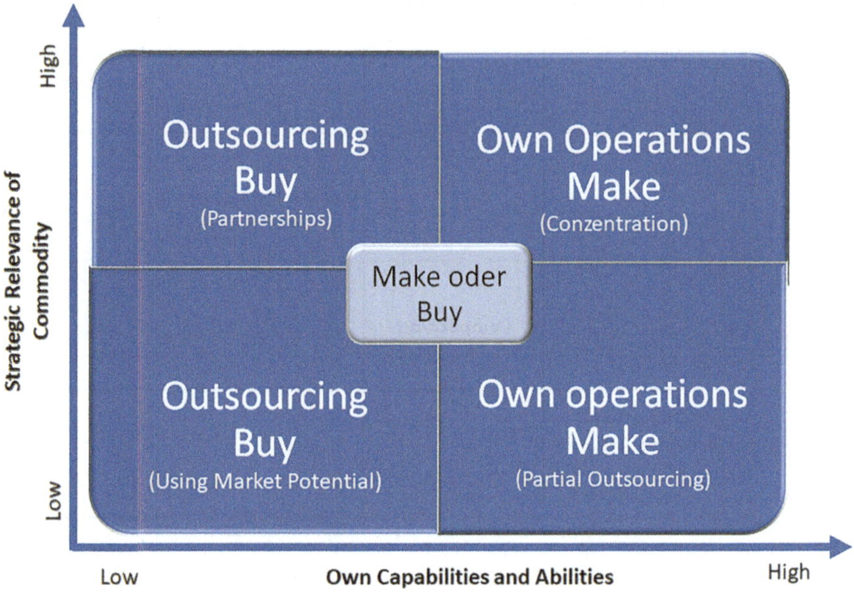

Fig. 3.10 Make or buy strategies. (Source: Author's source)

considered. It is therefore important to think about the basic advantages and disadvantages in advance. Some important ones are noted below.

The Advantages of Outsourcing Are

- Concentration on core competencies and focusing of activities and resources on one's own core business
- Possibility and opportunity to establish a proactive and preventive supplier management
- Reduction of the vertical range of manufacture and transformation towards a CSR production structure
- Long-term optimization of the cost structure by reducing fixed costs and changing from fixed to variable costs
- Improvement of the liquidity situation and, if necessary, improvement of the balance sheet ratios (e.g. by reducing the level of indebtedness if investments for which loans have to be taken out are not made)
- Flexible reaction to changes in demand is possible and part of the entrepreneurial risk is shifted to the supplier
- Possibility of partnerships and the preservation of innovations that are not in one's own area of competence

Disadvantages of Outsourcing Are

- Far-reaching cuts in existing structures in the event of outsourcing and unrest in the workforce
- Loss of know-how and personnel with a possibly significant dependence on one provider
- Long-term loyalty to suppliers limits flexibility to actively react to market changes
- The possibility that trade secrets will not be kept, especially in international business
- Increasing coordination effort, especially in logistics and other departments that are involved in the value creation process

ABC-XYZ Analysis

The ABC-XYZ analysis is a method in supplier management for the classification of material groups according to consumption, value and according to the predictability of the consumption of procurement volumes in a company. The ABC analysis is often combined with the XYZ analysis for the procurement of products, the planning of production quantities and other logistical issues. While the ABC analysis is primarily about the value and importance of customers, products, suppliers or purchased parts, the XYZ analysis analyzes their predictability and the possibility of making forecasts. It is made up of the ABC and the XYZ analysis as shown in Fig. 4.7. The classification looks like this:

ABC article

- A-Article: High value proportion of approx. 70–80%
- B item: Average value share of approx. 15–20%
- C-article: low value share of approx. 5–10%

XYZ item

- X-Articles: Articles with constant demand and high predictive accuracy
- Y article: article with fluctuating demand and medium forecast accuracy
- Z item: Item with irregular demand and poor forecast accuracy

AX and BX articles have a high share of value and can be easily forecast in terms of consumption, as they are subject to uniform consumption. They are therefore relatively easy to control. AZ and BZ articles are to be regarded as problematic. They make up a high proportion of sales, but are difficult to control due to their irregular needs. If too many articles in this category are stored, the storage costs increase. Insufficient storage can lead to bottlenecks in production (Fig. 3.11).

Internationalisation Strategies

Supplier management must ensure resilience in international transactions and business. In 2019, German companies imported preliminary products to the value of 606

		Value and strategic relevance		
		A High value product or material, mostly low-volume articles. Very high strategic importance.	**B** Medium value product or material, mostly low-volume items. Medium strategic importance.	**C** Low value product or material, mostly low-volume articles. Low strategic importance.
Predictability and consumption	**X** Relatively uniform, low consumption fluctuations. High forecast accuracy, very easy to plan.	• High share of value • Planned consumption • Detailed planning • Low or no inventory • Ensure fast availability at the supplier • JIT deliveries	• Average value share • Planned consumption • Detailed planning • Low or no inventory • Ensure fast availability at the supplier • JIT deliveries	• Low value share • Planned consumption • Low capital commitment • Uncritical treatment
	Y Inconsistent, absent or rising trend. Seasonal business with fluctuations. Medium prediction accuracy. Can be planned to a limited extent.	• High share of value • Irregular consumption • Detailed planning • Possibly. Create a safety reserve with the supplier • Ensure fast availability at the supplier	• Average value share • Irregular consumption • Detailed planning • Treatment like AY or BY • Ensure availability at the supplier	• Low value share • Irregular consumption • Consumption cannot be planned • Build up safety reserves as long as there is no bottleneck in the warehouse
	Z Inconsistent and absolutely irregular demand. Very low prediction accuracy. Difficult to plan.	• High share of value • Chaotic and sporadic consumption • Agree on a safety reserve with the supplier • JIT deliveries	• Average value share • Chaotic and sporadic consumption • Agree on a safety reserve with the supplier • Ensure availability at the supplier • Like AZ or CZ	• Low value share • Chaotic and sporadic consumption • Consumption cannot be planned • Build safety reserves

Fig. 3.11 ABC-XYZ analysis. (Source: Author's source)

billion euros, which made up a good 55% of Germany's total goods imports. Two thirds of the imported primary products came from other EU member states, a further 5.3% and 5.0% from the USA and China (Kolev & Obst, 2020). Supplier management must ensure through a clear structure and risk assessment that international supply chains are stable and do not lead to supply bottlenecks. The COVID-19 crisis in particular has shown that strategies for products from the health sector were not sustainable and good, so that supply bottlenecks, e.g. Masks or protective equipment has come (Helmold et al., 2020).

Sustainability and CSR Strategies

The primary task of classic supplier management is to create value-adding supply chains based on suitable criteria and strategies. This happens on the basis of the criteria quality, costs, delivery performance and other significant aspects (QCD plus alpha). In times of political unrest, trade in an international context, climate change, stricter environmental guidelines, rising energy prices and enlightened, environmentally friendly consumers, supplier management has a key role in ensuring sustainable supply chains. Studies show: "Sustainability" as an integral part of the value chain offers companies good opportunities to differentiate themselves from the competition and thus increase sales. Sustainable (Fig. 3.12) includes elements such as working conditions, environmental protection, human rights, anti-corruption, social standards, compliance with human rights and respect for intellectual property.

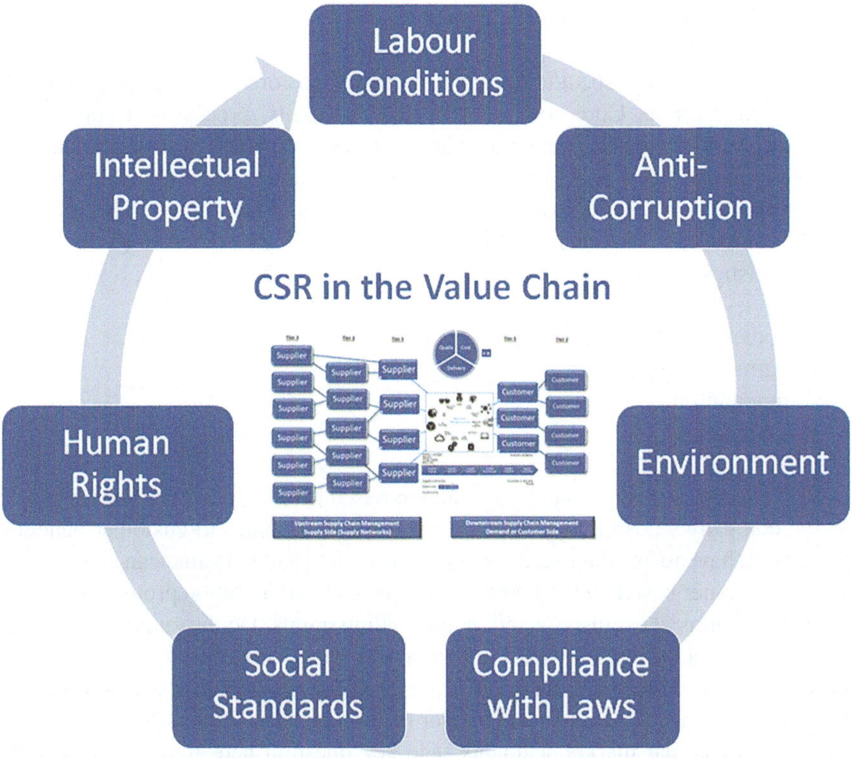

Fig. 3.12 CSR in operation and Procurement 4.0. (Source: Author's source)

Digitization Strategies

The digitization and linking of one's own company with the supply chain will, in the medium term, significantly increase the distance between companies that successfully apply this to their business model and those that miss this opportunity. Digitization also opens up an opportunity for smaller, faster and more flexible companies to skip entire evolutionary stages of organizations, to overtake their competitors and to create their own markets. This also applies to supplier management or, in a broader sense, to the management of the supply chain. In the medium term, digitization will significantly increase the gap between companies that successfully apply it to their business model and those that miss this opportunity. Digitization also opens up an opportunity for smaller, faster and more flexible companies to skip entire evolutionary stages of organizations, to overtake their competitors and to create their own markets. This also applies to supplier management or, in a broader sense, to the management of the supply chain (Immerthal, 2017).

3.4.3 Supplier Selection

Every company has its specific strengths, the so-called core competencies, on which it must concentrate. Core competencies refer to skills, processes, technologies, knowledge advantages or activities that a company can carry out better than the competition and has thus achieved a competitive advantage. Core competencies are the skills of a company to be able to do something better than others. This is a strategic competitive advantage. Core competencies are determined by four characteristics:

- customer benefits
- Imitation protection
- differentiation
- diversification

The concept is a variation of the resource-based approach that has been opposed to the company's positioning in the market. When it comes to customer benefits, companies have to ask themselves whether sustainable added value can be provided for the customer based on their core competencies? The imitation protection, on the other hand, aims at exclusivity and unique selling points. Do the companies master the core competencies exclusively or can they be easily imitated by the competitor? Differentiation reflects the duration of the benefit. Does the core ability lead to a long-term and sustainable advantage over the competition? Diversification focuses on the markets and market segments. The key question here is whether the core capabilities offer potential access to new markets? Peripheral competencies, on the other hand, can be outsourced to suppliers, as these do not represent a competitive advantage. The relocation is called "outsourcing" and includes a corporate strategy that outsources individual product scopes, tasks, sub-areas or even entire business processes to third-party companies. The selection of suppliers when relocating products, processes and services is part of supplier management and the second phase after the supplier strategy, as Fig. 3.13 shows.

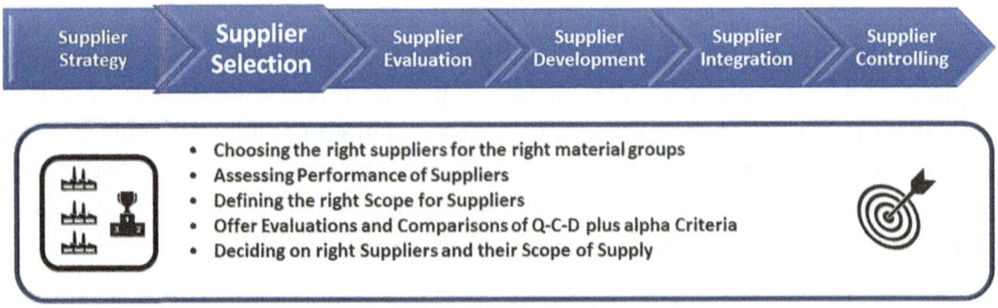

Fig. 3.13 Supplier selection. (Source: Author's source)

	Criteria of Supplier Selection	Supplier 1	Supplier 2	Supplier 3	Supplier 4
1.	Quality - Delivery Quality - Field Quality - Warranty Processing	10	10	5	5
2.	Cost - Material Cost (Recurring) - Non-Recurring Cost - Cost Reduction Ideas	9	5	5	5
3.	Delivery - On-Time-Delivery (OTD) - Flexibility - Supply and Delivery Concepts, e.g. VMI	10	5	5	5
4.	Technology Leadership	5	5	0	5
5.	Relationship Management	10	10	0	5
6.	Innovation Capability	10	5	10	5
7.	Financial Strength	5	5	10	5
8.	Quality Management System, ISO 9001:2015	10	5	10	5
9.	Sustainability (CSR)	10	5	5	5
10.	Other Criteria	10	5	5	5
	Total Result	**89**	**60**	**55**	**50**

Fig. 3.14 Supplier selection matrix. (Source: Author's source)

Supplier Selection Criteria

Before there can be a cooperation and a contractual agreement, a supplier selection must therefore take place on the basis of standardized selection criteria in a supplier selection matrix. Important criteria for the selection of suitable suppliers are shown in Fig. 3.14. One of the central criteria is the quality and nature of the products and services supplied. In addition, there are other important elements that need to be considered. An excellent supplier is not only characterized by high quality, low costs and stable delivery performance, but also in other ways. The following criteria should therefore be considered when selecting a supplier:

- High quality of the goods and low error rate
- A quality management system, e.g. DIN EN ISO 90001: 2015
- Distinct goodwill behavior on the part of the supplier if there are complaints
- Constant readiness for delivery and high adherence to delivery dates
- Strict adherence to promised delivery times or changes
- Good accessibility and fixed contact persons at the supplier
- High flexibility (enables quick reactions, e.g. to customer requests)
- Price guarantees (how long are negotiated prices promised)

- Few or well-founded or only moderate price increases in the past
- Financial stability and good credit ratings
- Offer transparency (no hidden costs, fees or minimum quantities)
- Sustainability and innovation

Supplier Risk Management

Supplier selection includes measures that companies take before a need arises and a supplier is contacted. One of the main goals of supplier selection is to minimize risk. If a company chooses an unsuitable supplier, it is exposed to one or more of the following risks:

- Failure to perform the contract because a supplier is in financial difficulties
- poor performance of the contract
- Supplier supplies poor quality
- Lack of adherence to deadlines
- The price for the services provided is too high

Careful supplier selection is necessary in order to contain these risks. As part of the supplier evaluation, certain criteria are used to assess performance according to a defined system. In view of the trend that the integration of suppliers into company processes is becoming more and more important, the demands on suppliers are increasing. An ideal supplier portfolio is created when certain requirements are taken into account when making the selection.

- Selection of suppliers based on the supplier strategy
- Cross-departmental supplier decisions and coordination processes
- Selection based on objective and uniform evaluation criteria
- Use of qualitative and quantitative criteria
- Transparent, cost- and time-efficient selection process
- Selection of the most innovative and best supplier based on the selection criteria

Quality management systems such as DIN EN ISO 9001:2015 also refer to a selection of suppliers taking into account central elements such as the selection and evaluation of suppliers. The standard indicates that the processes, products and services provided meet the requirements and that the companies must determine and apply criteria for selection and evaluation.

3.4.4 Supplier Evaluation

The third phase in supplier management is the supplier evaluation. The instrument of the supplier evaluation comparable systematic assessment, which is to evaluate the performance of suppliers or service providers on the basis of previously defined characteristics, and is mainly used for continuous and preventive supplier

Fig. 3.15 Supplier evaluation. (Source: Author's source)

monitoring. During observation, the delivery services are regularly monitored in order to identify changes in performance at an early stage. The supplier evaluation helps to an objective and systematic supplier selection, to the development of an optimal supplier portfolio and to a continuous improvement process. The supplier evaluation is carried out with the help of certain evaluation criteria that are important for the evaluation of the supplier. Evaluation criteria are static and dynamic factors. Figure 3.15 shows an example of a supplier evaluation with internal and external company data.

Appropriate Selection of Evaluation Criteria

Depending on the complexity and industry spectrum, the departments of quality, purchasing, production, logistics, sales, data processing, finance or research and development can be included in the process. Supplier management takes on the coordination of this interface between the company and its suppliers. The result of the supplier evaluation is recorded in the form of a holistic degree of fulfilment and can later be used for the strategy derivation and selection. The criteria used to evaluate suppliers should be defined and weighted appropriately for the company. The basis for determining the criteria are the goals that the company pursues in cooperation with the supplier, as well as special requirements for the supplier or for the product or service to be delivered. The assessment criteria are best determined with the help of a requirements analysis. Depending on the exact requirements a company places on the supplier and its product or service, the evaluation criteria can also be different and, above all, their weighting can be different. However, there are some criteria that must be considered in most cases when evaluating a supplier. These include:

- Quality of the product/frequency of errors
- Costs and pricing conditions
- Delivery time, delivery reliability and logistics
- terms of payment
- capacity
- Reliability/risk of delivery failure
- location and transport
- flexibility
- Sustainability

The most important methods for supplier evaluation are point evaluation methods, profile analysis and price structure analysis. A point evaluation method for supplier evaluation is a relatively simple way of evaluating and comparing suppliers based on the allocation of weighted points or grades. A point evaluation procedure based on measurable key figures has the best informative value. As part of a profile analysis for supplier evaluation, supplier performance profiles are juxtaposed and compared. In this way, a profile analysis reveals the advantages and disadvantages of the individual suppliers. The biggest difference between the point evaluation method and the profile analysis is that the individual criteria are not weighted in the profile analysis and are also not combined into a single performance value. The price structure analysis is primarily about the criterion of the costs that a supplier causes. For the price structure analysis, the price criterion is therefore broken down into the supplier's cost and profit components. Material costs, hourly rates, purchase costs, etc. are to be named here as sub-criteria.

Supplier Evaluation as Predictive and Preventive Tool
These categories can be performance of the delivery, price evolution, production capacity, quality of management, technical capabilities, and service. Once there is a mechanism in place to periodically collect performance data from suppliers, the next step is to review the performance data. Ideally, the format that the data is in should lend itself to comparison and analysis. The data should also be in a format that can be quantified and scored. Many companies use a supplier evaluation or scorecard for this. Moreover, data from different types of assessments such as internal surveys, external surveys, and site visits should be incorporated into the analysis. Since most large organizations have many strategic suppliers and lots of data, it is almost impossible to obtain, organize and review data from assessments effectively on a large scale without automation or software. When evaluating supplier performance data, the two things to look for (besides the obvious) are large changes in the performance metrics and overall trends. By identifying trends, a company can make projections about where the performance data will be in the future and can take action accordingly. Downward trends and deterioration in performance can signal a problem. Moreover, an abrupt change in performance metrics might signal an imminent problem. However, there could be another explanation. In this case it makes sense to obtain more data from the supplier and to dig deeper to find the source of the problem. It may be a one-time anomaly or it could be something more. Monitoring supplier performance proactively can ensure that exceptions to policies are tracked and personnel and resources are assigned to address the problem quickly. Alerts and notifications can provide up to the minute information to company personnel letting them know of changes in supplier performance.

Having a system that can take the assessment/scorecard data and can output it in a report or other format is helpful because members of the team can all access and review the information quickly and easily. The performance evaluation of Daimler shown in Fig. 13.5 is an example of a supplier evaluation. For a supplier the performance is very bad, so that immediate actions have to be taken. Once there is sudden drop in supplier performance or a downward trend, it is important to take action quickly. Quick action can reduce the risk of disaster significant loss, and gives the company the ability to take steps to prevent bad outcomes. Some actions that can be instigated include communicating with the supplier, conducting further evaluations, developing an improvement plan, or finding an alternative supplier. The actions taken may depend on many factors. These include the supplier's past performance, level of current performance, strategic importance, possible damages, and overall risk. One of the first things to do is to contact the supplier and find out what went wrong and why. The results of the performance assessment should be provided to the supplier and can create a basis for discussions.

The poor performance could have been the result of something outside of the supplier's control. It could have been a problem with process, personnel, a supplier, or something else. By communicating with the supplier, personnel can determine the cause of the problem and try to work with the supplier to make changes to bring the supplier performance back into compliance with the contract or with company policies. If the vendor does not have a good explanation or understanding of why the problem occurred, this may be a sign of trouble. Once the causes of a problem or set of problems have been identified, the next step is to devise a supplier improvement plan. The plan should be specific to the problem, should involve both company personnel and supplier personnel, and should involve a timeline for addressing the problem or bringing the performance into compliance. This process should also be a collaborative process and should be aimed at improving the overall supply chain. Even if a supplier's performance is acceptable, the company may wish to invest time and resources in developing suppliers and improving suppler performance. If the problem is too severe, cannot be fixed in a timely manner, or poses too great of a risk, the company may wish to stop doing business altogether with the supplier. This means that the company should carefully find an alternative source of supply and, if possible, reduce its reliance on the supplier in question. Emmett and Crocker (2009) and also propose using such criteria for evaluating the performance of suppliers. Interestingly, the interviews revealed that many companies have created sub-criteria of Q-C-D-SF according to their own needs. Regarding the question of how often manufacturing companies in the European transportation industry measure supplier performance, what they do internally with the data and how they communicate the results to suppliers, several different answers were given. In the best case, data was updated on a weekly basis and made available to suppliers through a web-based tool. Concerning the evaluation of supplier performance, all interviewees outlined three to four categories, like traffic lights:

- Category one (green): acceptable with minor deviations and without conditions
- Category two (yellow): acceptable with conditions
- Category three (red): not acceptable

In category one (green), the evaluation is approved and accepted with minor deviations. In category two (yellow) the evaluation is accepted with conditions.

Conditional acceptance means that any subsequent action plan has to be approved by the Procurement department. If a supplier shows severe deficiencies and is categorised three (red), the evaluation is not accepted. This can mean that a new supplier is not allowed to supply parts. In cases where category three is measured during serial production, specific Procurement actions (e. g. management escalation, supplier audits, dual-sourcing) might be the consequence. Some of the challenges associated with supplier evaluation may be mitigated by the use of appropriate tools. For simple projects a spreadsheet can be used. But as evaluations become more complex or more frequent data management and data integrity issues become significant. Web Electronic RFP/Tendering systems are often used for initial selection projects. Some products provide functionality for combining both initial selection and ongoing evaluation and benchmarking. Without few exceptions, there is no evaluation model which considers the maturity and level of relationship with suppliers. The doctoral thesis "Establishing a best practice model of supplier relationship management (SRM) for multinational manufacturing companies in the European transportation industry" makes suggestions for this aspect. There is also an M.B.A. thesis available, which includes the assessment of the Guanxi for Procurement in China (Lee, 2015). Wider, within established Procurement evaluation methodologies, the Carter 10 C's model is an internationally recognised approach (Emmett & Crocker, 2009). This model looks at aspects which should be evaluated before contracting and as part of the ongoing supplier performance appraisal. The ten categories can be summarized as the following:

1. Capacity (Does the organization have the capacity and capability to deliver the order)
2. Competency (Is the organization, its people or its process competent)
3. Consistency (Does the organization produce a consistent output)
4. Control of process (Can the organization control its process and offer flexibility)
5. Commitment to Quality (Does the organization effectively monitor and manage quality)
6. Cash (Has the organization got a strong enough financial base)
7. Cost (Is the product or service offered at a competitive price)
8. Culture (Are the supplier and buyer cultures compatible)
9. CCSR (is the organization ethical, funded legitimately, doesn't engage Child labor
10. Communication efficiency (Does the organisation have support technology of information integration) to support collaboration and co-ordination in the supply chain.

Supplier Evaluation as Management Tool

As an essential component of supplier management, the supplier evaluation contributes to the control of supplier relationships, the development and maintenance of suppliers and to improved quality and logistics performance. In order to achieve these goals in the best possible way and to get a global picture of the supplier's

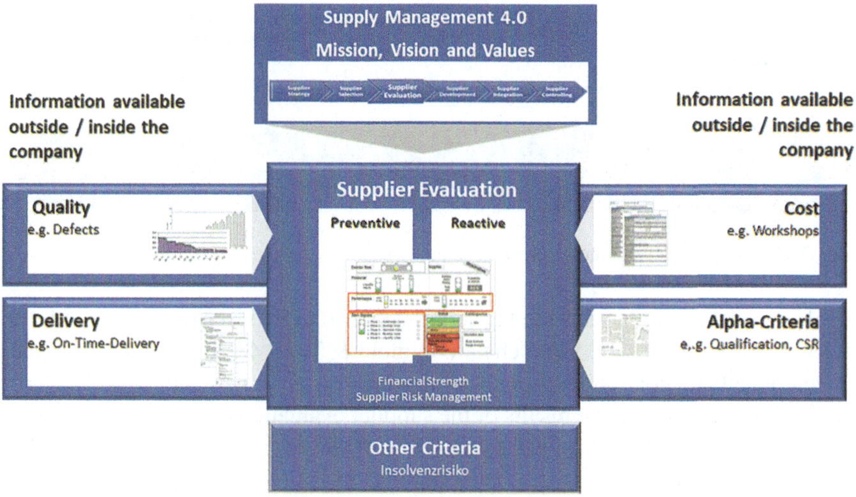

Fig. 3.16 Supplier evaluation tool. (Source: Author's source)

Fig. 3.17 Supplier development phases. (Source: Author's source)

performance, an assessment is necessary, which not only focuses on so-called "hard facts" such as adherence to deadlines and quantities, but also on "soft facts" such as Example communication skills fall back. Furthermore, the supplier evaluation is carried out globally according to the same standards and criteria, thus allowing a location-based evaluation and comparability of supplier performance. By expanding the evaluation criteria, we want to optimize future cooperation with our suppliers at all essential interfaces and reward constructive cooperation. The supplier evaluation is often carried out digitally using real-time data, but it can also be carried out monthly, quarterly or semi-annually (Fig. 3.16).

3.4.5 Supplier Development

Supplier Development is the fourth phase in the Procurement process as shown in Fig. 3.17. The term supplier development describes the activities and improvements

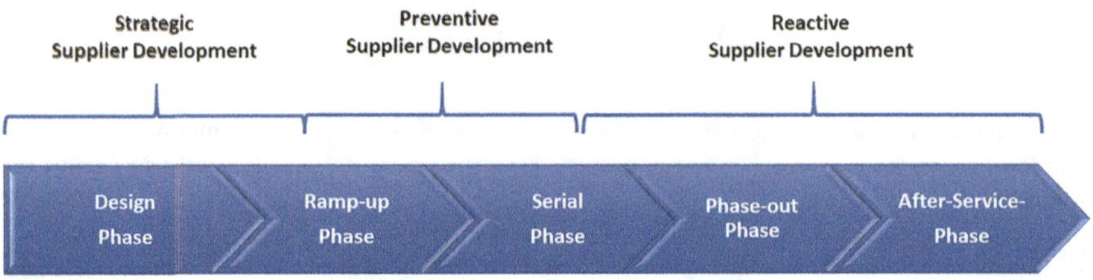

Fig. 3.18 Supplier development. (Source: Author's source)

of close, partnership-based and long-term relationships between customers and supplier networks within the value chain (Helmold & Terry, 2016). Describe supplier development as a continuous process to improve current or new suppliers. The basis of the development are the results of the supplier evaluation and key figures, which were described in the previous chapter. Emmett & Crocker (2009) define supplier development as a support process through direct or indirect measures. Here, too, the primary goal is to improve supplier performance (Emmett & Crocker, 2009). Figure 3.18 shows three categories, strategic, preventive and reactive supplier development, of supplier development in connection with the life cycle of a product. Product phases can be divided into development, start-up, series, phase-out and after-service phases.

Strategic Supplier Development

The strategic supplier development already takes place in the development phase. Measures are usually transferred to the start-up phase of a product. The strategic approach to supplier development aims at the long-term, conscious and continuous (further) development of the supplier's performance (potential). Strategic supplier development is initiated proactively to maintain competitive advantages over the long term. An essential difference to the merely reactive supplier development lies in the conscious search and selection of fields for development measures. The strategic supplier development is basically carried out through the direct participation of the buyer, who invests in supplier development measures and thus also in the suppliers themselves. An essential feature for the application of direct supplier development is a strategic partnership with the supplier, as amortization of the development activity over the relationship life cycle is required. The ability of a supplier to develop in the strategic sense means the creation of scope for action through options for the customer.

Preventive Supplier Development

Preventive supplier development aims at the early and forward-looking improvement of the suppliers on the basis of performance characteristics (performance characteristics) by the supplier management. Preventive measures are intended to prevent poor performance in the areas of quality, costs or delivery performance and usually have a longer time horizon. The need is not yet acute, but sensors and early alarm systems (audits, supplier evaluation, incidents) show deviations in the performance of the suppliers. In the best-case scenario, preventive measures are defined at the start-up of a product before series production.

Reactive Supplier Development

Supplier development includes measures taken by the customer as a merely reactive improvement in the event of short-term deterioration in performance of a supplier in series, discontinuation or after-service. It is usually caused by a current, specific problem in the exchange of services with the supplier (poor performance). The development measure has a short-term time horizon. The necessity arises from problems of the supplier, for example to deliver on time (security of supply in operations) as well as quality defects of the product or the service itself. With reactive supplier development, suppliers only become aware of the buyer when acute problems arise, so that are very short-term countermeasures (Troubleshooting). Often suppliers are encouraged to adhere to target agreements (based on key figures), the deficits of which have emerged from the supplier evaluation in the categories of quality, costs or delivery performance.

3.4.6 Supplier Integration

Supplier integration means the integration of the supplier into the company's corporate structures and processes so that processes and systems are synchronized in order to be able to work together more effectively and successfully, as Fig. 3.19 shows. In the case of supplier integration, independent companies work together to optimize their processes and structures in order to coordinate them as well as possible to increase success. This can sometimes be a difficult undertaking, not just for the purchasing department. With a goal-oriented implementation, however, ideally a win-win situation arises for the market partners involved. Supplier integration begins where the company's own boundaries end. A prerequisite for a functioning integration of external actors in one's own process chains is therefore an opening to the selected partners. Likewise, there must be a willingness to change internal work processes, ways of thinking and also the key figure/bonus systems. Depending on the industry, there are numerous opportunities for close, long-term cooperation with suppliers. Important processes that need to be taken into account when integrating suppliers include the following areas:

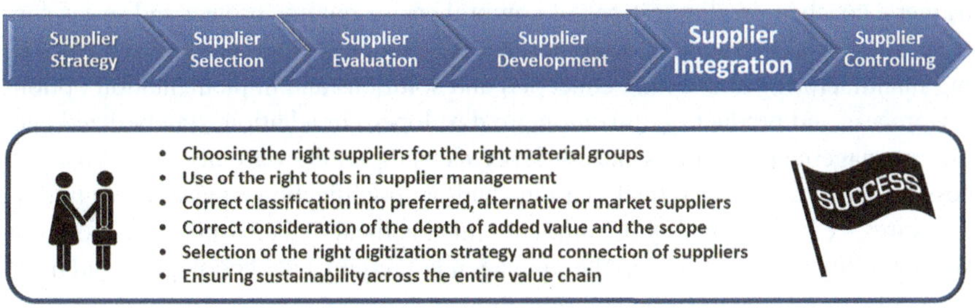

Fig. 3.19 Supplier integration. (Source: Author's source)

- Research & Development: Even further ahead in the value creation process, the involvement of external partners starts in the research and development area. In this way, suppliers and customers can each contribute their specific know-how in joint project teams, bundle knowledge and achieve synergy effects in the development of new products
- Purchasing: Often a supplier integration starts due to the naturally existing contacts in the purchasing area, for example with the agreement of specific delivery windows or packaging units up to the fully responsible warehouse management by the supplier. For example, this requires the forward-looking provision of medium to long-term production and sales plans
- Production: If supplier integration extends into the company's production processes, so-called supplier parks are often created in the direct vicinity of the customer, for example to implement just-in-time production
- IT: An optimal exchange of information can only be guaranteed through IT standards and the joint use of corresponding IT applications

Supplier Coaching

Supplier coaching is the systematic, collaborative improvement of supplier competencies through the measures carried out by supplier management together with the supplier. Coaching measures can be carried out with suppliers, distributors and sub-suppliers, with external providers, in a (supplier) academy or in the seminar room. Coaching measures require special coaching competencies of the employees in supplier management. Coaching activities usually cover a specific subject area within the supply chain (project management, quality management, methods of CSR production, etc.). No matter whether accompanying the project in the planning phase, accompanying series production or in the after-service phase, coaching measures lead to rapid improvements. In coaching, the focus of supplier management is on increasing product and process quality. Many companies have set up their own supplier academy (Porsche, ZF Friedrichshafen, Bosch). These help your own company to develop or coach new suppliers or high-risk suppliers to the required degree of maturity with regard to standards or quality requirements. The goal is the sustainable quality improvement of your suppliers. The most relevant factors are quality, time and costs; practical evidence e.g. B. the reduction of scrap and rework. CSR, flexible, efficient and future-proof. Experts and so-called supplier coaches (Eng.: trainers, coaches) in all questions of comprehensive quality, project and series support. Thereby u. a. Manufacturing processes of supplier parts are analyzed (including manufacturing and testing concepts) and solutions and implementation options for process and product optimization are developed. In addition, standardized supplier management programs and concepts also support the warranty target cost processes. The required requalification and/or qualification measures/upgrading measures – e.g. B. in quality or complaint management. All measures must focus on sustainability. Coaching in supplier management requires methodological and training skills through analysis and qualification.

International Purchasing Offices

International purchasing offices or global supplier management centers are part of internationalization and the change in the concept of supplier management. Multinational corporations such as Volkswagen, Daimler, Siemens, Bosch or Bombardier have purchasing offices in regions such as China, India or Eastern Europe that offer savings potential or are geographically distant from the parent company. Only in November 2015 did Deutsche Bahn open an international purchasing office in Shanghai. On the purchasing side, companies like Bombardier have more than six locations in China. Meanwhile, the added value share of Chinese products in sectors such as the automotive or rail industry is more than 20–30%. In terms of network-oriented supplier management, this is referred to as Best Cost Country Sourcing (BCCS). Traditional companies use terms like Global Sourcing (GS) or Low Cost Country Sourcing (LCCS). Of course, international purchasing or supplier management offices involve costs. For a purchasing office in China, you can get around EUR 50 thousand to EUR 80 thousand p.a. calculate, which makes up a full-time position in terms of full costs (1 full-time employee including salary and fringe benefits, office space, travel expenses, training, etc.). The costs for this have to be amortized through savings. It is not only large companies that benefit from international factor costs. Not only multinational corporations, but also medium-sized companies have the opportunity to move on the international stage. The German Centers in China provide i.a. Office space and production capacity in key industries/processes available. In addition, international purchasing cooperations can be set up in which the fixed costs for a purchasing office are shared. International offices in supplier management are centers of excellence and should not be confused here with the so-called "shared service" centers (SSC) that are increasingly emerging.

3.4.7 Supplier Controlling

Its origin has the controlling concept in practice. It was formed by Deyhle in analogy to the term marketing and is closely related to the tasks of controllers. The scientific discussion of the term controlling began on a broader scale in the 1970s. The first basic understanding of controlling in terms of time assigns it the task of providing business information for management purposes. In this sense, controlling should

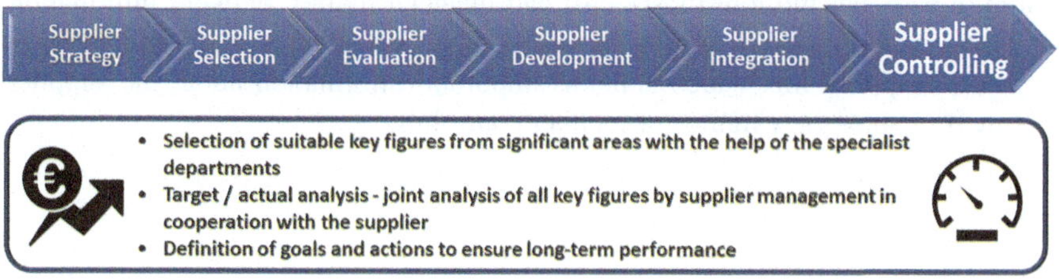

Fig. 3.20 Supplier controlling. (Source: Author's source)

fulfill a business transparency function. Controlling is then concerned with the systematic definition and assignment ("breaking down") of the goals to be pursued, measuring their achievement, determining deviations between target and actual values and developing measures to eliminate them. In other words, controlling aims to lead the company through and with the help of planning and the resulting plans. The latter run through the entire company, from strategic to operational planning. Controlling in this sense can also be understood as a cybernetic process that is illustrated with the control loop of planning and control.

As the last phase in supplier management, supplier controlling assesses supplier performance, forms the basis of objective key figures and forms the basis for supplier control and supplier management (Fig. 3.20). Typical key figures are the adherence to quantities and deadlines for the delivery of goods as well as the rate of complaints. Which key figures are used in individual cases depends on the selected supplier management scenario. There are differences, for example, between central, group-wide supplier control on the one hand and local, plant-related control on the other. The informative value of the key figures depends directly on the quality of the data that is included in the key figure calculation. In industries with little vertical integration, supplier controlling based on key figures is crucial for the success of your own products. The quality of supplier controlling is only as good as the quality of the underlying data. Four case studies from the automotive industry show the state of practice in supplier controlling and form the basis for an integrated architectural design. The architecture for data quality management in supplier controlling identifies the essential design elements and their relationships with one another.

The basis for performance measurement, the definition of goals and the review of results in strategic and operational supplier management is a traceable system of indicators for each supplier. A key figure system consists of various key figures from different areas, which on the one hand can be calculated from the "hard" factors available in the system and, on the other hand, are determined from objectified subjective assessments, i.e. "soft" factors. Excellent key figure systems enable the procuring company to carry out a 360 degree analysis through which preventive measures can be taken. The influence of the various key figures on an overall key figure results from their weighting. The key values determined in an evaluation cycle – and thus the degree of target fulfillment – form the basis for measures to further develop the supplier relationship in strategic and operational supplier management. The key figures that are calculated from automatically determined "hard" factors include quality data such as delivery quality, complaint rate, defects (measured in parts per million, PPM), cost and financial figures, delivery information, quantity reliability, sustainability factors or innovation figures. Key figures can be kept in a supplier file, which contains important information about the supplier. Figure 3.21 shows key figures in supplier controlling.

Supplier Controlling KPI Dashboard	Quarter 1 Actual-Plan	Quarter 2 Actual-Plan	Quarter 3 Actual-Plan	Quarter 4 Actual-Plan
CSR Data - Environmental Data (Emissions) - Social Improvements and Footprint (%) - Usage of Fair Practices (%) - ...				
Purchasing Spend - Frame Contracts (Euro) - Savings (%) - Usage of Frame Contracts (%) - ...				
Process KPI - Quantity of Orders (Euro and %) - Quantity of Frame Contracts (Euro and %) - Quantity of Deliveries (# and %) - ...				
Quality - Delivery Quality (%) - Field Quality (%) - Warranty Process and Cycle Time (Time/Case) - ...				
Cost - Material Cost (Euro) - Non-recurring Cost, e,g. Design (Euro) - Cost Saving Initiatives (Euro and %) - ...				
Dellivery - On-Time-Delivery (%) - Flexibility (Change of Quantity, Dates etc.) (%) - Additional Deliveries (%) - ...				
Financial KPI - Turnover (Euro) - Profitability (%) - Productivity (%) - ...				

Fig. 3.21 Supplier performance dashboard. (Source: Author's source)

3.5 Control Via Digital Supplier Dashboards and Cockpits

A supply or supplier dashboard (or cockpit) provides management with an at-a-glance awareness of the status of certain performance indicators such as inventory and supply operations (see Fig. 3.22). Thus, it is possible to respond to challenges before any incident is happening. The supplier dashboard is showing key operational indicators and trends like NCG, OTD, Outgoing Quality and sub-supplier performance. Indicators can vary from case to case. A supplier dashboard or supplier cockpit is a one-page summary of the supplier's critical performance indicators as shown in the example above. The dashboard is supposed to give managers a quick overview of detoriations and status on quality, delivery or other critical issues. It enables the supply manager to take immediate actions based on a graphs or a colouring. Many dashboard integrate also sustainability areas.

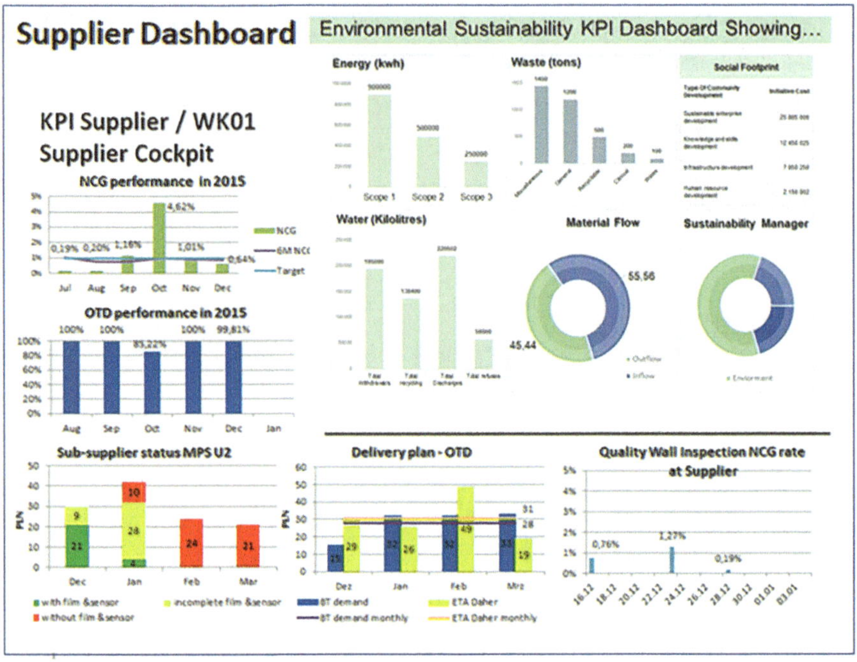

Fig. 3.22 Supplier dashboard. (Source: Helmold & Terry, 2016)

3.6 Case Study: Apple's Outsourcing Strategy

Apple's commercial triumph rests in part on the outsourcing of its consumer electronics production to Asia. Drawing on extensive fieldwork at China's leading exporter, the Taiwanese-owned Foxconn, the power dynamics of the buyer-driven supply chain are analysed in the context of the national terrains that mediate or even accentuate global pressures. Power asymmetries assure the dominance of Apple in price setting and the timing of product delivery, resulting in intense pressures and illegal overtime for workers. Responding to the high-pressure production regime, the young generation of Chinese rural migrant workers engages in a crescendo of individual and collective struggles to define their rights and defend their dignity in the face of combined corporate and state power. As the principal manufacturer of products and components for Apple, Taiwanese company Foxconn currently employs 1.4 million workers in China alone. Arguably, then, just as Apple has achieved a globally dominant position, described as 'the world's most valuable brand' (Brand Finance Global 500, 2013), so too have the fortunes of Foxconn been entwined with Apple's success, facilitating Foxconn's rise to become the world's largest electronics contractor. Apple is collaborating with the FoxConn company to secure sustainability and business ethics in terms of labour conditions, human rights, fair pay and other elements. Figure 3.23 shows the employees and the location of factories in China for Apple iPhone and iPad production.

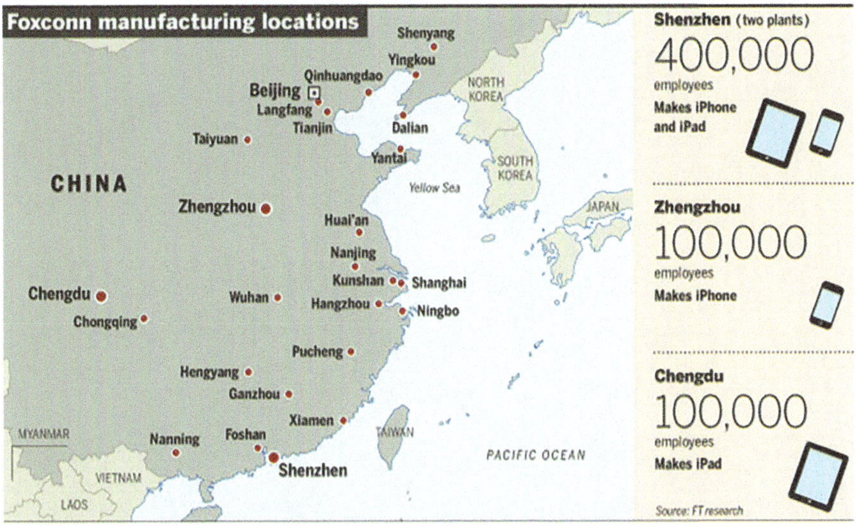

Fig. 3.23 Foxconn's manufacturing sites for Apple

References

Aberdeen Group. (2005). *Assuring supply and mitigating risks in an uncertain economy. Supply risk management Benchmark*. Aberdeen Group.

Emmett, St. & Crocker, B. (2009). *Excellence in Supplier Management. How to better manage contracts with suppliers and add value. Best practices in Supplier Relationship and Supplier Development*. Cambridge: Cambridge Academic.

Helmold, M. & Samara, W. (2019). *Progress in Performance Management Industry Insights and Case Studies on Principles, Application Tools, and Practice*. Springer Cham.

Helmold, M., & Terry, B. (2016). *Lieferantenmanagement 2030. Wertschöpfung und Sicherung der Wettbewerbsfähigkeit in digitalen und globalen Märkten*. Springer.

Helmold, M., & Terry, B. (2021). *Operations and Procurement 4.0. Industry insights, case studies and best practices*. Springer.

Helmold, M., Einmahl, R., Rassmann, K. & Carvalho, L. (2020). In IUBH discussion paper. Lessons from the COVID-19 situation: Rethinking global supply chain networks and strengthening procurement in public procurement in Germany. Abgerufen 31.10.2020. https://www.iubh-university.de/wp-content/uploads/DP_Logistik_Helmold_4_2020fin.pdf

Immerthal, L. (2017). Lieferantenmanagement im Wandel. Die Digitalisierung im Lieferantenmanagement beginnt mit guter Kommunikation. In Beschaffung aktuell. Abgerufen 31.10.2020. https://beschaffung-aktuell.industrie.de/einkauf/die-digitalisierung-im-lieferantenmanagement-beginnt-mit-guter-kommunikation/.

Kolev, G., & Obst, T. (2020). Die Abhängigkeit der deutschen Wirtschaft von internationalen Lieferketten. Institut der deutschen Wirtschaft. IW-Report Nr. 16. 23. April 2020. Abgerufen 31.10.2020. https://www.iwkoeln.de/studien/iw-reports/beitrag/galina-kolev-thomas-obst-die-abhaengigkeit-der-deutschen-wirtschaft-von-internationalen-lieferketten.html

CSR in Operations Management

4

Perfection is not attainable. But if we chase perfection, we can catch excellence.

Vince Lombardi (1913–1970)

4.1 Introduction to Operations Management

Operations management is the process and activity of planning, designing and controlling the process of production and redesigning business operations in the production of products or services. t involves the responsibility of ensuring that business operations are efficient in terms of using as few resources as needed and effective in terms of meeting customer requirements. Operations management is primarily concerned with planning, organizing and supervising in the contexts of production, manufacturing or the provision of services. It is concerned with managing an entire production or service system which is the process that converts inputs (in the forms of raw materials, labour, consumers, and energy) into outputs (in the form of goods and/or services for consumers). Operations management involves the systematic direction and control of the processes that transform resources (inputs) into finished goods or services for customers or clients (outputs) as shown in Fig. 4.1 Operations Management in the Context of the Input-Transformation-Output Process. Operations produce products, manage quality and create services. Operation management covers sectors like banking systems, hospitals, companies, working with suppliers, customers, and using technology. Operations is one of the major functions in an organization along with supply chains, marketing, finance and human resources. The operations function requires management of both the strategic and day-to-day production of goods and services. In managing manufacturing or service operations several types of decisions are made including operations strategy, product design,

T. Dathe et al., *Corporate Social Responsibility (CSR), Sustainability and Environmental Social Governance (ESG)*, Management for Professionals,
https://doi.org/10.1007/978-3-030-92357-0_4

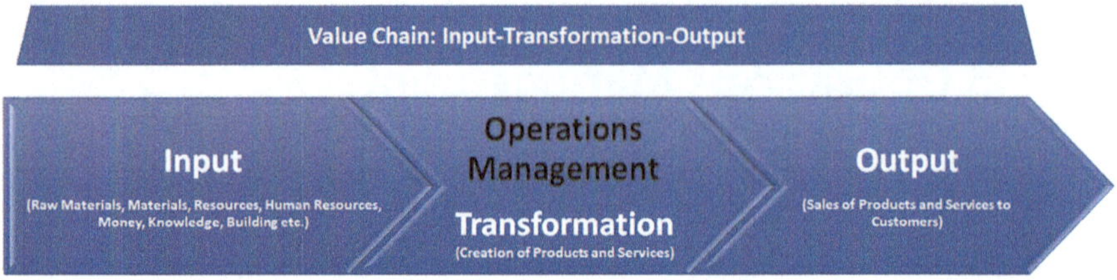

Fig. 4.1 Operations management in the context of the input-transformation-output process. (Source: Author's source)

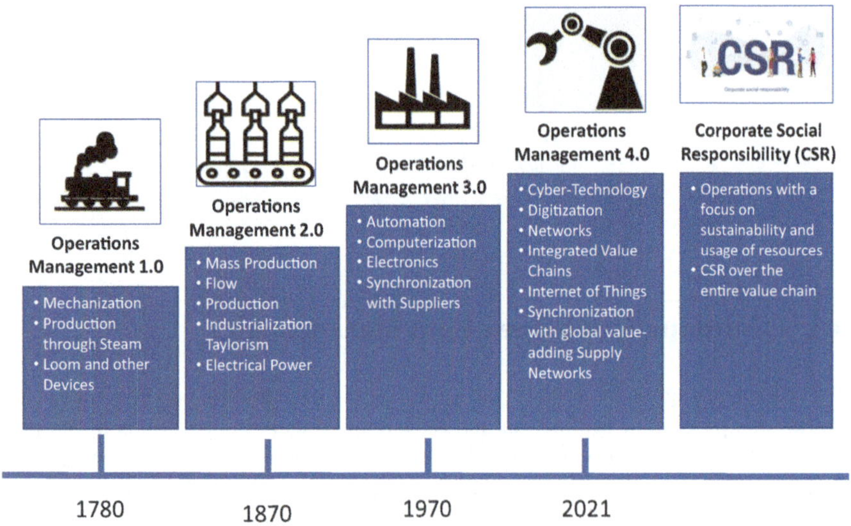

Fig. 4.2 History of operations management 4.0

process design, quality management, capacity, facilities planning, production planning and inventory control. Each of these requires an ability to analyse the current situation and find better solutions to improve the effectiveness and efficiency of manufacturing or service operations (Slack et al., 1995).

4.2 History of Operations Management

Operations Management is the ongoing digitization, automation of traditional manufacturing and industrial practices, using modern and smart technologies. Large-scale machine-to-machine communication (M2M) and the internet of things (IoT) are integrated for increased automation, improved communication and self-monitoring, and production of smart machines that can analyse and diagnose issues without the need for human intervention as shown in Fig. 4.2 History of Operations Management 4.0. Operations Management or Operations is not a new science. The

First Industrial Revolution and Operations management 1.0 was marked by a transition from hand production methods to machines through the use of steam power and water power. The implementation of new technologies took a long time, so the period which this refers to it the years around 1780 in Europe and the United States. Its effects had consequences on textile manufacturing, which was first to adopt such changes, as well as iron industry, agriculture, and mining although it also had societal effects with stronger middle class. The Second Industrial Revolution and Operations Management 2.0, also known as the Technological Revolution, is the around 1870 that resulted from installations of extensive railroad and telegraph networks, which allowed for faster transfer of people and ideas, as well as electricity. Increasing electrification allowed for factories to develop the modern production line. It was a period of great economic growth, with an increase in productivity, which also caused a surge in unemployment since many factory workers were replaced by machines. The Third Industrial Revolution, also known as the Digital Revolution, occurred in the late twentieth century, after the end of the two world wars, resulting from a slowdown of industrialization and technological advancement compared to previous periods. The global financial crisis in 1929 followed by the Great Depression affected many industrialized countries. The production of the Z1 computer, which used binary floating-point numbers and BooCSR logic, a decade later, was the beginning of more advanced digital developments. The next significant development in communication technologies was the supercomputer, with extensive use of computer and communication technologies in the production process; machinery began to abrogate the need for human power.

4.3 Elements of Modern Operations Management 4.0

Operations Management 4.0 refers to a new phase in the Industrial Revolution that focuses heavily on interconnectivity of the entire value chain, automation, machine learning, and real-time data. Corporate Social responsibility (CSR) is an integral part of the concept (Figs. 4.3 and 4.4).

4.3.1 Virtual Factory

Rapid product/process realization and enterprise integration have been identified among the major imperatives for enabling the next generation manufacturing paradigm. This paper proposes a virtual factory modelling approach to support these imperatives. A virtual factory is defined as an integrated simulation model of major subsystems in a factory that considers the factory as a whole and provides an advanced decision support capability. It seeks to go beyond the typical modelling of one sub-system at a time, such as the manufacturing model, the business process model and/or the communication network model developed individually and in isolation. A basic virtual factory model of a semi-conductor backend factory has been developed for concept demonstration. Application examples are used to

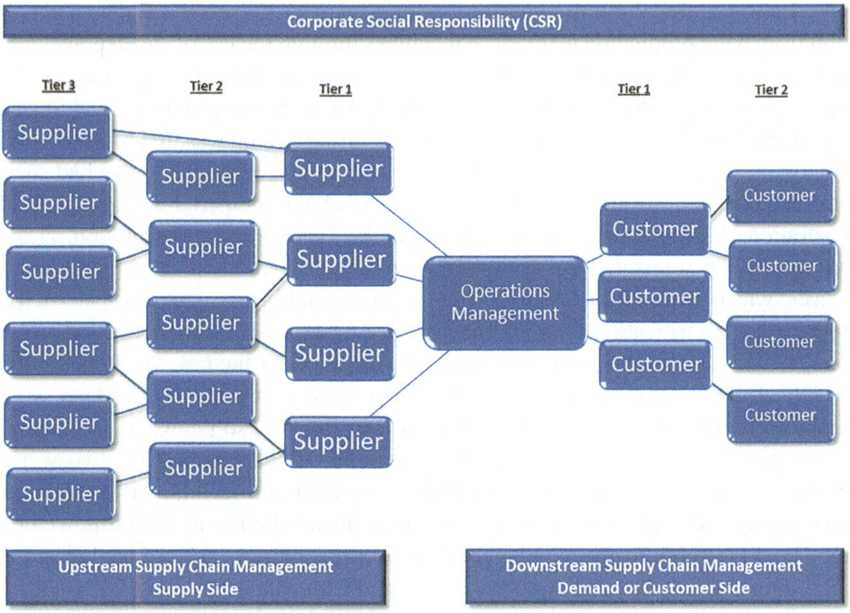

Fig. 4.3 Elements of operations management 4.0 in the value chain. (Source: Author's source)

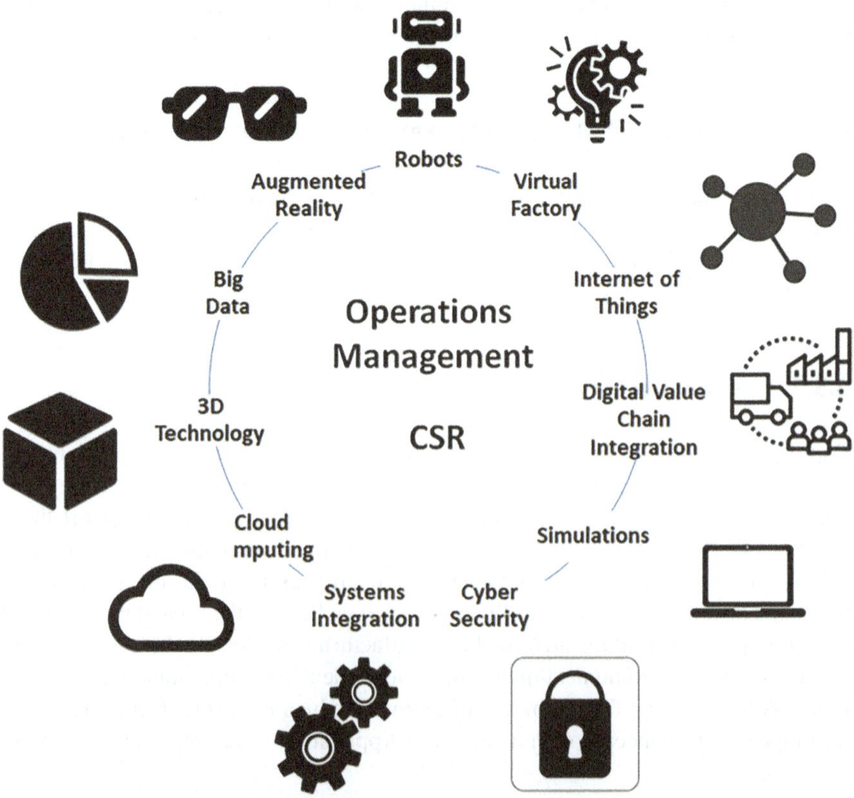

Fig. 4.4 Elements of operations management 4.0 in the value chain. (Source: Author's source)

demonstrate the integration between business processes and manufacturing system performance. Future work will move further towards the development of the complete virtual factory and its industry applications.

4.3.2 Digital Value Chain Integration

Virtual production tends to be used to help visualize complex scenes or scenes that simply cannot be filmed for real. In general, though, virtual production can really refer to any techniques that allow filmmakers to plan, imagine, or complete some kind of filmic element, typically with the aid of digital tools.

4.3.3 CSR Simulations

CSR simulations include a set of hands-on experiments to teach employees about systems and process improvement in all areas of the value chain. CSR simulations can focus on design, manufacturing, capacity planning or supply chain design. Purpose of simulations are to understand the implications of input variables and alternations of the value chain elements.

4.3.4 System Integration

CSR integration is a continuous improvement methodology for bringing disparate data and software systems together. The goal is to maximize customer value. CSR integration is a management system that emphasizes eliminating waste as a sustainable data integration and system integration practice.

4.3.5 Internet of Things

The Internet of Things (IoT) is a system of interrelated computing devices, mechanical and digital machines, objects, animals or people that are provided with unique identifiers (UIDs) and the ability to transfer data over a network without requiring human-to-human or human-to-computer interaction.

4.3.6 Cybersecurity

Cybersecurity is the protection of internet-connected systems, including hardware, software and data, from cyberattacks. In a computing context, security comprises cybersecurity and physical security – both are used by enterprises to protect against unauthorized access to data centers and other computerized systems.

4.3.7 Cloud Computing

Cloud computing is a type of computing that relies on shared computing resources rather than having local servers or personal devices to handle applications. In its most simple description, cloud computing is taking services ("cloud services") and moving them outside an organization's IT system and environment.

4.3.8 Additive Manufacturing

Additive manufacturing (AM) is the industrial production name for 3D printing, a computer-controlled process that creates three dimensional objects by depositing materials, usually in layers. The official industry standard term is the ASTM F2792 for all applications of the 3D-technology. It is defined as the process of joining materials to make objects from 3D model data, usually layer upon layer, as opposed to subtractive **manufacturing** methodologies.

4.3.9 Augmented Reality

Augmented reality (AR) is an interactive experience of a real-world environment where the objects that reside in the real world are enhanced by computer-generated perceptual information, sometimes across multiple sensory modalities, including visual, auditory, haptic, somatosensory and olfactory.

4.3.10 Big Data

Big Data is a phrase used to mean a massive volume of both structured and unstructured data that is so large it is difficult to process using traditional database and software techniques. In most enterprise scenarios the volume of data is too big or it moves too fast or it exceeds current processing capacity.

4.4 Principles of Operations Management

4.4.1 Digital Synchronization of Networks

To deliver on the benefits of digital supply chains, companies must synchronize every aspect of supply chain optimization, planning and execution throughout their supply chain network–bringing together previously disparate disciplines, departments, vendors and technologies into a single ecosystem that ties everyone and everything together. Information and departments that were previously siloed and disconnected become part of a synchronized digital supply chain, where all activities are orchestrated, information flows freely, and companies can easily adjust to changing demand signals. A synchronized supply chain has four distinct capabilities that can help drive increased sales and profits. The ultimate goal of a synchronized, digital supply chain, for one, is to quickly get product to consumers who want to buy it, and it's something that siloed, disconnected supply chains can't accomplish. Secondly, for a synchronized supply chain to work, companies have to position materials, capacity and finished goods to react to demand. To get there, it will take product development, where teams not only build the product to meet the line plan, but also over-develop in certain categories that are doing well, so they can quickly put new products into production when demand is strong. Vendors can then be evaluated based not only on price and quality, but also lead time and capacity. Companies may also choose to handle replenishment production closer to home to minimize delivery time, while using overseas vendors for basic goods and initial floor sets. With a synchronized supply chain, companies will closely forecast their raw material requirements, place commitments with multiple suppliers, and draw down the commitments as POs are issued and the materials are consumed. This reduces the risk of holding too much or too little inventory to meet demand. The other element of successful supply chain synchronization is to identify and execute the best supply/demand adjustment. As demand changes, companies must consider what they can do to quickly optimize their assortments. If sell-through on a new style is stronger than anticipated in New York, which means stores will be out of stock in three weeks, what are your best options to optimize profit? Do you ship by air freight, boat, or transfer goods from the warehouse, or from one store to another? With the current state of supply chains, it's difficult to sift through massive amounts of data to quickly determine the fastest, most profitable way to get the goods where they need to be. Synchronizing and digitizing the flow of information in a connected ecosystem is the only way to understand and react to changing demand signals. The fourth key to this better connected supply chain is the ability to predict future demand. As planning systems continue to advance, they are beginning to calculate demand based not only on historical sales, but also current POS data, external events, social sentiment, changing weather patterns, and other factors, each of which impacts demand. These capabilities provide a snapshot of what companies are hoping to accomplish by synchronizing and digitizing their supply chains. Machine learning and AI are increasingly being incorporated into the supply chain networks, since the massive amounts of data and various options for each opportunity are too vast for humans to quickly and accurately analyse.

4.4.2 7R Principle

Operations is concerned with managing an entire production system which is the process that converts inputs (in the forms of raw material, labour, energy and resources) into outputs (in the form of goods and/or services), as an asset or delivers a product or services. Operations produce products, manage quality and create service. Operation management covers sectors like banking systems, hospitals, companies, working with suppliers, customers, and using technology. Operations are one of the major functions in an organization along with supply chains, marketing, finance and human resources. The operations function requires management of both the strategic and day-to-day production of goods and services. Operations management involves the production, planning, organizing, and supervising processes of products or services and targets to meet customer demands by delivering the right product or service at the right quality, quantity, time, and place with right people at the right cost. This principle is called the 7R principle and targets the optimal satisfaction of the goal in the operations function. The Fig. 4.5 7R principle in operations management highlights the 7R principle with objectives and criteria behind the objectives (Helmold & Terry, 2016). In addition to the 7Rs, there are elements on quality, cost, delivery and other objectives important (Alpha). CSR is the most important part of the alpha objectives.

4.4.3 Gemba, Gembutsu und Genchi: Right Place of Happening

Gemba (現場) is also a Japanese term meaning "the real place." Japanese detectives call the crime scene gemba, and Japanese TV reporters may refer to themselves as reporting from gemba. In business, gemba refers to the place where value is created; in manufacturing the gemba is the factory floor. It can be any "site" such as a construction site, sales floor or where the service provider interacts directly with the customer. In CSR production and supply management, the idea of gemba is that the problems are visible, and the best improvement ideas will come from going to the gemba. The gemba walk, much like Management walk around (MWA), is an activity that takes management to the front lines to look for waste and opportunities to practice gemba kaizen, or practical shop floor improvement. In quality management, gemba means the manufacturing floor and the idea is that if a problem occurs, the engineers must go there to understand the full impact of the problem, gathering data from all sources. Unlike focus groups and surveys, gemba visits are not scripted or bound by what one wants to ask. Glenn Mazur introduced this term into quality function and supply management department (QFD, a quality system for new

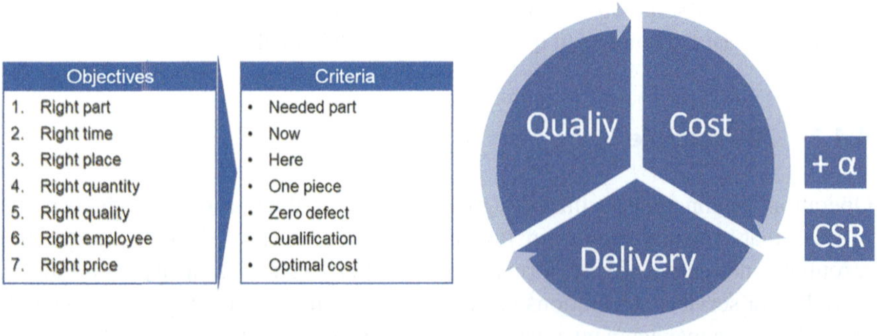

Fig. 4.5 7R principle in operations management

products where manufacturing has not begun) to mean the customer's place of business or lifestyle. The idea is that to be customer-driven, one must go to the customer's gemba to understand his problems and opportunities, using all one's senses to gather and process data.

Gembutsu (現地現物) is a Japanese word meaning "real thing". It is one of the components of the 'Three Reals' meaning go to the real place (gemba) to see the real thing (gembutsu) and collect the real facts (genjitsu). This term simply means that there is no substitute for seeing something with one's own eyes.

Genchi (現地) is the Japanese principle of going to and directly observing a location and its conditions in order to understand and solve any problems faster and more effectively. The phrase literally translated means "go and see for yourself" and is a part of the Toyota Way philosophy (Fig. 4.6).

4.4.4 Muda, Muri, Mura

In contrast to the traditional paradigm the objectives of CSR production are based on a reduction of throughput times and the elimination of non-value-adding activities. These activities are waste or so called "MUDA" (Japanese: 無駄). Both concepts, the traditional and the CSR concept, are directed towards customer satisfaction. Nevertheless, the CSR concept's foundation is based on the optimal reaction capability and not based on inventories or waste. Inventories increase the cost of capital and have negative impacts on the shareholder value, whereas short cycle times lead to small inventories. CSR manufacturing or CSR production, often simply "CSR", is a systematic method for the elimination of

Fig. 4.6 Bombardier Sifang transportation: Dr. M. Helmold and B. Lannoye. (Source: Author's Source)

waste ("Muda") within a manufacturing system. CSR also takes into account waste created through overburden ("Muri") and waste created through unevenness in workloads ("Mura"). Working from the perspective of the client who consumes a product or service, "value" is any action or process that a customer would be willing to pay for. Essentially, CSR is centered on making obvious what adds value by reducing everything else. CSR manufacturing is a management philosophy derived mostly from the Toyota Production System (TPS) (hence the term Toyotism is also prevalent) and identified as "CSR" only in the 1990s. TPS is renowned for its focus on reduction of the original Toyota seven wastes to improve overall customer value, but there are varying perspectives on how this is best achieved. The steady growth of Toyota, from a small company to the world's largest automaker, has focused attention on how it has achieved this success. There are three MU's including MUDA that support the elimination of waste within the philosophy of Toyota. In parallel to MUDA (Japanese: 無駄), there are MURA (Japanese: 無ら) and MURI (Japanese = 無理) which are the ground theory for the TPS. MURA means "in balance", MURI "overutilization". While certain capacities are too scarce (Bottleneck) there are other resources significantly below their capacity limits. The main objective of procurement and a strategic supplier management is to apply the JIT principle to the suppliers. Value-adding activities have to be rolled out to all suppliers from raw material to module and keiretsu suppliers. The keiretsu supplier is the closest relationship and connection to a supplier (Japanese: 系列子会社) Keiretsu is an integration of suppliers into the own organisation and system, there is in few cases partial ownership involved. There are four pillars for the CSR production system. These are the integral parts of a CSR production and JIT system as shown in Fig. 5.16. The four pillars consist of the flow, the tact, pull and zero-defect principle, which have to be introduced simultaneously. In the sense of an optimized supply chain, it is a fundamental activity to implement these four principles towards all areas. Practical examples by Porsche Consulting show that the introduction of the TPS led to radical improvements in terms of errors and defects per car (Quality), serial completion time (Cost and Productivity) and inventory (Logistics and Delivery). The study reveals that the reduction of defects per car was reduced by 63 percent. The throughput time could be improved by more than 53 percent. This caused a positive situation of inventory by 50 percent (Freitag, 2004). In the JIT approach, it is important that the right part comes in the right quantity in the right quality at the right time to the right place as shown in the 7R principle. This principle focuses on a zero defect as shown in the next figure. This principle was defined in the previous chapters as part of the objectives. The principles can be regarded as obtaining the right parts at the right quality and at the right time. This has to be in line with the right quantity in the right place by the right people at the right price (Helmold & Terry, 2016). Fig. 4.7 Mudi, Muri and Mura shows the concept of Muda, Muri and Mura.

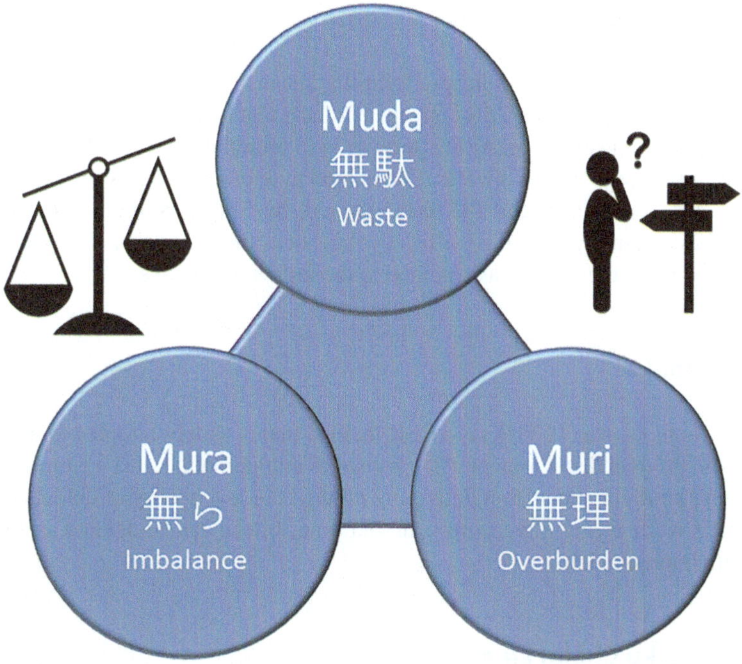

Fig. 4.7 Mudi, Muri and Mura. (Source: Author)

4.4.5 Heijunka

Heijunka (平準化) is a Japanese word that means "leveling." When implemented correctly, heijunka elegantly – and without haste – helps organizations meet demand while reducing while reducing wastes in production and interpersonal processes. The two main objectives are the standardisation of operations and the capability of flexible production of alternate derivatives on the same line (Ohno, 1990). Toyota defines Heijunka as the overall leveling, in the production schedule, of the volume and variety of items produced in given time periods and adds that it is a pre-requisite for just-in-time delivery.

Heijunka allows you to level your production in both volume and product diversity. CSR facilities that have implemented Heijunka, don't base their production off the actual flow of customer orders. Instead, the company will use the Heijunka methodology to calculate the total volume of orders place in a specific time frame and level them out. This allows the facility to produce the same amount and mix each day, without the ebbs and flows of demand cycles.

Balancing your workflow has many benefits to your organization. For instance, if you have an above average week of orders, followed by a below average week, you end up paying overtime the first week and sending employees home the following. This is waste in the simplest form, that could have been avoided with Heijunka.

4.4.6 Poka Yoke

Poka-yoke (ポカヨケ) is a Japanese term that means "mistake-proofing". A poka-yoke is any mechanism in a CSR concept a process that helps an equipment operator avoid (yokeru) mistakes (poka). Its purpose is to eliminate product defects by preventing, correcting, or drawing attention to human or other errors as they occur. The concept was formalised, and the term adopted, by Shigeo Shingo as part of the TPS. It was originally described as baka yoke, but as this means "fool-proofing" (or "idiot proofing") the name was changed to the milder poka yoke.

4.4.7 Jidoka

By definition, Jidoka (自働化) is a CSR method that is widely-adopted in manufacturing and product development. Also known as autonomation, it is a simple way of protecting your company from delivering products of low quality or defects to your customers while trying to keep up your takt time. Jidoka can be defined as automation with human touch.

4.4.8 Chaku Chaku Line

Chaku Chaku (Fig. 4.8) is a way to operate a semi-automated manufacturing line. One (or more) workers walk around the line, add parts to the processes, and then start the process. While the process works on the part automatically, the worker adds the next part to the next process, and so on. he word "Chaku Chaku" comes from Japanese. It can mean either "Load, Load" (着々), or it can simply be the sound the machine makes while unloading (ちゃくちゃく), similar to "Clack-Clack."

The basic principle of the Chaku Chaku line is very simple. The worker moves around the line from process to process and only loads the parts into the machine. After loading the part, the worker starts the machine and moves to the next process. At the end of the line, the worker starts again from the beginning.

4.5 Case Study: Mazda Operations Management Strategy

Mazda Motor Corporation is based in Hiroshima (Japan) and employees about 50,000 people. Mazda is dedicated to developing vehicles that are distinctive and innovative, using the latest and most advanced technologies to satisfy the diverse needs of customers worldwide. To accomplish this, Mazda created a global R & D network with operations in Japan, the United States, Germany and China. The

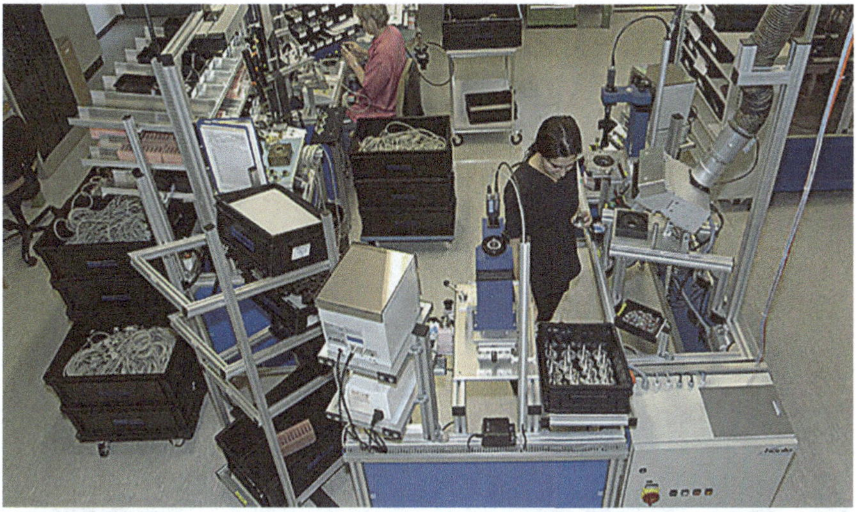

Fig. 4.8 Chaku Chaku Line. (Source: Author's Source)

Corporate Vision is: "We love cars and want people to enjoy fulfilling lives through cars. We envision cars existing sustainably with the earth and society, and we will continue to tackle challenges with creative ideas."

1. Brighten people's lives through car ownership
2. Offer cars that are sustainable with the earth and society to more people
3. Embrace challenges and seek to master the Do ("Way" or "Path") of creativity

Mazda's Brand Essence is "Celebrate Driving". "Celebrate Driving" delivered by Mazda is not just about driving performance. The aim of the branding is: Choosing a Mazda shall prize the customer and user with confidence and pride. Additionally, driving a Mazda is also leading up to urge to take on new challenges. Not just our products but every encounter with Mazda evokes the emotion of motion and makes customers' hearts beat with excitement. All of these are contained in our brand essence of "Celebrate Driving". This Marketing strategy targets not only existing users, but also new customers who are willing to change from existing brands (Mazda, 2019). Mazda is a company with the headquarters in Hiroshima (Fig. 4.9 Mazda Headquarters, Hiroshima; Japan) and uses Toyota methods in operations across the factories and supply chain. Toyota is all about the process about eliminating waste. Mazda is using CSR tools like 5S, Kanban cards, Andon and Poka Yoke. All of them are used to improve and optimise the processes through small changes (Kaizen). Mazda is all about making cars. Mazda's CSR Management starts with the design of each vehicle, in which engineers are brought together with

Fig. 4.9 Mazda Headquarters, Hiroshima. (Source: Author's Source)

experts from supply chain and manufacturing to make sure that the cars can be produced in the best and most ergonomic way as possible. Mazda states, that a car is not simply a bunch of products and metal, but it's a living creature with emotional bound to its driver. That is Mazda's ultimate goal of Kodo, the "Soul of Motion" design.

There are ten plants in Toyota city and just one with two assembly lines in Hiroshima. Toyota has another two plants in Japan and twenty-five over the world. Mazda has one more plant in Japan plus five manufacturing and four assembly plants worldwide. As a result, in 2016 Toyota produced over 10 million vehicles, where Mazda assembled over 1,5 million. With Toyota focus on process, there's no surprise their production system is made to be super effective. Cars were moving fast on the assembly line. Workers had precisely defined, simple tasks to perform within short cycle. Toyota's operators spend less than half a minute per station (Cycle times). Everything was packed in a small area, so the distances between workstations were minimal.

On the other hand, everything in Mazda was just slower. The cycle times for each operation in Mazda are longer and workers have more tasks to perform on single units. Mazda is using also CSR tools such as Kanban, Andon and Poka Yoke. There is less automation in Mazda. As a result, Mazda assembly line takes significantly more space. In Mazda, it takes 15 hours from stamping to final inspection in Mazda and 17 hours in Toyota's Takaoka Plant.

References

Freitag, M. (2004). *Toyota. Formel Toyota. Manager Magazin, 12*, 12–14.

Helmold, M., & Terry, B. (2016). *Global sourcing and supply management excellence in China. Procurement guide for supply experts*. Springer.

Mazda (2019). Mazda Headquarters. Retrieved 12.6.2019. https://www.mazda.com/en/about/.

Ohno, T. (1990). *Toyota production system. Beyond large scale production*. New York Productivity Press.

Slack, N., et al. (1995). *Operations management*. Pitman Publishing.

CSR in Marketing Management 5

You cannot buy engagement. You have to build engagement.

Tara-Nicholle Nelson

5.1 Introduction to Marketing

The Marketing promotes all activities of a company, sales through customer care, advertising, observation and control of the market as well as through appropriate control of own production as Fig. 5.1 Marketing Function in the value chain shows (Kuerble et al., 2016).

In times of change, constant internationalization, rapidly changing customer needs and increasing environmental and sustainability debates for companies as well as for end consumers, CSR plays an increasingly important role (Meffert et al., 2018). The interest of society in particular in ecological and socially acceptable behavior therefore urges companies to deal with CSR aspects along the entire value chain and to integrate them into entrepreneurial thinking and acting (Stibbe, 2019). In addition to the written elaboration and anchoring of these specifically defined areas of responsibility in the corporate strategy, these activities must ultimately be marketed and communicated to the end consumer in order to generate benefits and promote the purchase of a product. However, original marketing instruments can only be used to a limited extent, so that the areas of responsibility defined within the framework of corporate social responsibility must be part of an extended marketing strategy. From a marketing strategy point of view, this can result in a win-win situation for all actors involved, which leads to an increase in customer satisfaction, an increase in sales of the product and a general increase in prosperity could (Meffert et al., 2018).

T. Dathe et al., *Corporate Social Responsibility (CSR), Sustainability and Environmental Social Governance (ESG)*, Management for Professionals,
https://doi.org/10.1007/978-3-030-92357-0_5

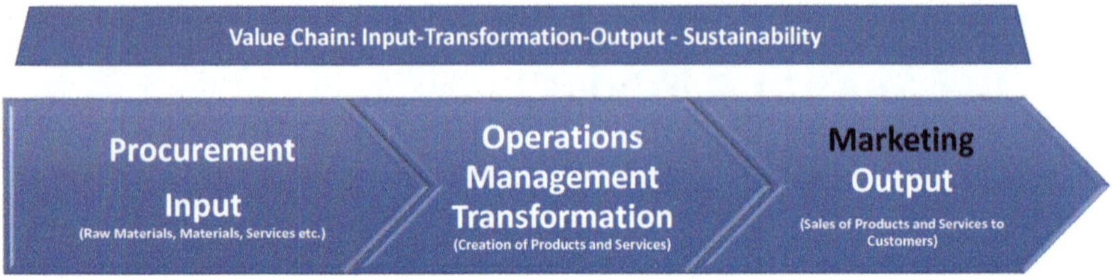

Fig. 5.1 Marketing function in the value chain

5.2 Marketing-Mix

In order to market a product or service efficiently, marketers follow very specific strategies. All decisions and actions that contribute to marketing are summarized in the so-called marketing mix. The instruments and measures defined therein help the company to create a structured marketing concept (for example in so-called 4P marketing).

The four marketing mix instruments:

- Product (product policy)
- Price (pricing policy)
- Place (distribution policy)
- Promotion (communication policy)

together result in a holistic marketing concept that has proven itself particularly for the marketing of products. However, when it comes to marketing services, the 4P marketing model has some weaknesses – nonetheless, it is a fundamental scheme that every marketer should know.

Numerous authors developed extended systems from the classic 4Ps of marketing. A common number is the 7Ps. They mostly relate to services. However, they are also used in the classic areas of product marketing, since service is becoming more and more important there and the aspects of services are also gaining in importance there. In the case of services and offers in service, further aspects are important for successful marketing:

- People or Person (see Personnel as a marketing mix area). The people who provide the service have a significant influence on the perception of quality by the customer. An unfriendly and badly dressed representative of a logistics company causes a negative quality perception of the transport service. Although the parcels reach the recipient punctually and undamaged, the client doubts it because of their appearance. See also Physical Evidence below.
- Process (see process policy for service provision). The service creation process also has a significant impact on customer satisfaction. Only satisfied customers will buy again and comment positively on the offer (see word of mouth).

Fig. 5.2 Marketing-mix

- Physical evidence or facilities (also called physical environment or equipment policy or physical evidence) aims to provide objective evidence of service quality. This includes the equipment policy. See physical evidence).
- The best food in an unpleasant environment doesn't taste good. The equipment of the restaurant affects the perception of the quality of a service. At the same time, the customer takes the equipment as a guide to conclude the quality in advance (physical evidence).

(Meffert et al., 2018) (Fig. 5.2).

5.3 Marketing Function as Driver for Implementing Triple Bottom Line

The control of corporate sustainability management can be mapped by the triple bottom line, which includes the three pillars of sustainability – economy, ecology and social issues. The economic area of responsibility initially includes securing the long-term competitiveness of the company. In addition to the design of efficient supply chain management, it is also important to secure liquidity and to be able to achieve long-term profit targets. Furthermore, the continuous acquisition of market shares and customers must not be disregarded, which must be implemented in particular by marketing management. The ecological responsibility is particularly reflected in the careful use of natural resources. Sustainable management is a success factor that needs to be expanded in the long term. As a result, companies have to recognize the urgency to dispute with regard to raw material procurement, waste management and recycling systems in order to meet changed customer requirements in the long term and to differentiate themselves from the competition. The third and final dimension deals with the area of social responsibility. In addition to the commitment to justice within society, the focus is on responsibility towards each individual employee. Life-long learning and the creation of a work-life balance should be cited as examples (Helmold et al., 2020).

5.4 Transformational Marketing Concept Towards CSR

The transformational transformative marketing concept or model towards CSR (synonym: sustainable eco-marketing) can be used for the practical implementation of CSR activities (Helmold et al., 2020). The basic idea of this approach is to constantly take up changed framework conditions in society and to transform these changes into already existing marketing activities. Furthermore, the objective is to implement all CSR efforts in all management areas and to communicate them to the stakeholders in a targeted manner. Last but not least, marketing is the function in the company with the strongest interfaces to external stakeholders. Therefore, marketing has to react to the changed driving forces. By analyzing these social changes and the resulting social needs, a company has to face a transformation in two ways: First of all, it is important to further develop its own business activities through marketing from an economic, ecological and social point of view and to position itself vis-à-vis its stakeholders. In the next step, stakeholders, especially customers, are to be informed about these sustainable approaches and at the same time encouraged.

5.5 Shared Value Marketing Concept Towards CSR

The shared value marketing approach elaborated by Porter and Kramer describes the interactions between the competitiveness of a company and the prosperity within the society in which the company operates. Particular attention must be paid to action and decision-making power, which ultimately Consistent need to ensure added value for consumers and companies. This phenomenon is often referred to in the literature as corporate societal marketing and, in addition to original economic marketing initiatives, also includes those that pursue social goals. The above model of transformative marketing can be confirmed to the extent that planet, profit and people are no longer additional marketing instruments are to be imagined without (Helmold et al., 2020).

Furthermore, the shared value approach explains the integration of social issues and problems in business processes in order to gain comparative competitive advantages. This integration begins with the analysis of points of contact between society and the company and can be expanded by identifying with social problems and grievances. If a company succeeds in picking up on precisely these points and strengthening them through product and communication policy, then there is, according to Porter "[…] no inherent contradiction between improving competitive context and making a sincere commitment to better society" (Helmold et al., 2020).

5.6 Cause-Related Marketing Concept Towards CSR

Cause-related marketing (CRM) is a popular form of marketing that is used particularly in connection with CSR, but is a purely voluntary measure by the company. Here, the sale of a product is advertised with the simultaneous support of a charitable cause. In corporate practice, certain percentages of the sales revenue of a product are usually defined in advance, which benefit a social project or a non-profit organization. The amount of the donation per product must, however, be in an appropriate relationship to the sales price and must not be set below or disproportionately. The amount of the total donation is based on the end consumer, who has a direct influence through frequency or sales volume (Helmold et al., 2020). By comparing it with a conventional, equally priced product, this marketing activity suggests an additional benefit to the customer, which can increase their satisfaction and long-term loyalty to the product. This philanthropy communicated to the customer ("doing something good for society") is also reflected in an increase in sales at the executing company. The mutual increase in social and economic benefits through CRM once again confirms the previous shared value approach (Helmold et al., 2020). A successful and targeted CRM is understood as the interaction of at least three involved participants, who all benefit from it: The actual product is marketed with a social benefit to the end consumer, it is highly likely that it intensifies the demand for this product and can thus significantly increase satisfaction. The company involved benefits from a strongly forecast. Particular caution is required with CRM with regard to allegations of greenwashing. In order to preventively avoid negative headlines "[…] CRM should not be used instead of, but only in addition to" real "CSR activities." the donation is not handed over properly and thus a distrust of the end consumer is caused.

5.7 Case Study: Apple's Design Strategy

CSR is optimising a process to preserve value with less work towards stakeholders and the society. CSR manufacturing is a management philosophy derived mostly from the Toyota Production System (TPS). CSR aims to eliminate waste in the entire value stream, by creating processes that need less human effort, less space, and less time to make products and services at lower cost, therefore CSR simply means creating more value for customers with fewer resources. However, how does this relate to Steve Jobs and iPod in particular or all Apple's iDevices in general? Steve Jobs used CSR in another way, instead of thinking of CSR as a way of minimising waste in the production process he looked at how to eliminate waste in the way the customer interacts with the iPod. For example, the volume up button could have different functions such as selecting a menu choice or taking a photo. This approach enabled Apple to produce mobile phones with just five buttons. Apple's (or perhaps Steve Jobs) innovation is by focusing on customers and how to offer them products without the un-necessary extras from design stage until displayed in an outlet.

There is a fine line between valuing the lessons demonstrated by great leaders and slipping into a blind devotion that masks the inevitable flaws to be found in every human personality. Steve Jobs had more than his share of flaws and he possessed more than his share of genius. Reading Walter Isaacson's recent and excellent biography of Jobs I am struck by the intuitive sense of CSR, of flow, of simplicity, that he demanded from both the aesthetics and the technical workings of every product. You would be hard pressed to find an executive with a better sense of the interaction between the social and the technical. When we think of CSR our mind first goes to the workings of the Toyota factory. However, the principles of eliminating waste and achieving interruption free flow may be found at an even more profound level in the design of Apple's breakthrough products and the intuition of Steve Jobs. Only nine percent of Americans today work in manufacturing and we might do well to turn our attention to the application of CSR principles to less obvious endeavours such as product design and the use of technology. From the design of the first Mac to the design of the iPad, Steve obsessed on their design. He understood what we wanted before we wanted it and that was his genius. We didn't know we wanted GUI's, an iPod or iPad, and even less did we think we would be attracted to a product by the elegance and simplicity of its packaging. He imagined the customer experience before we had experienced it. This is intuition, a zen appreciation for the movement of the hand and eye and the imperative to eliminate distractions to allow the mind of the user to flow from the first thought to the engagement in the utility of the device. As usual Jobs pushed for the purest simplicity. That required determining what was the core essence of the device. The answer: the display screen. So the guiding principle was that everything they did had to defer to the screen. 'How do we get out of the way so there aren't a ton of features and buttons that distract from the display? With the story of the development of each product it is easy to see why Jobs nearly drove those around him crazy. It was normal for him to walk around and look at the work of designers and engineers and immediately pronounce their work to be crap! And, a week later he would be gushing about the very same thing he labeled "crap" a week earlier. It was also normal that the work on the new product would be almost finalized, or finalized in the mind of others, and he would wake up in the middle of the night and realize why he was not comfortable with its design. The radius of the corners was wrong! Or, the ionized aluminum casing wasn't exactly right. He would stop everything and have the entire team working on the product go back and fix things based on his simple feel for the design. Inevitably he would be proven right. And in every case it was a matter of the flow, the movement of the eye and mind from one interaction with the product to the next. It was about "CSR" although he would not have felt the need to label it as such. It wasn't the CSR of the factory, but the CSR of the customer experience. It is doubtable that any CEO in the history of business has been as intimately involved in the design of breakthrough products. His contribution was not that of a traditional executive at all. It was total intimacy with the customer experience that was his contribution. The way CSR is implemented in many companies today it is viewed as primarily a cost reduction tool. Eliminating work-in-process, reducing the need for space, and increasing output per employee are all the natural results of CSR and all result in positive impact to the bottom line. Rarely was reducing costs the primary motivation behind Steve Jobs' decisions. The decision to open retail stores provides a telling example. Jobs obsessively wanted to control the entire flow of work from the design of chips to software, to the design of the case, the screen and the packing. This was the motivation for his decision to open Apple Stores. He and Ron Johnson spent many months designing the stores, developing prototypes and obsessing on every detail. From a traditional retailing perspective it made no sense. They didn't have enough different products to fill a store. Most analysts thought it would be impossible to push enough product through the stores to justify the cost of the space. Gateway was failing miserably in their retail stores and Dell was selling direct to customers. But that is not how Jobs was thinking at all. He was thinking about the brand, the customer experience, the joy that the stores would create. Larry Ellison, the CEO of Oracle was a close friend and Steve repeatedly invited him over to walk through his prototype store. "On each visit Jobs prodded Ellison to figure out ways to streamline the process by eliminating some unnecessary step, such as handing over the credit card or printing a receipt. 'If you look at the stores and the products, you will see Steve's obsession with beauty and simplicity – this Bauhous aesthetic and wonderful minimalism, which goes all the way to the checkout process in the stores,' said Ellison. 'It means absolute minimum number of steps. Steve gave us the exact explicit recipe for how he wanted the checkout to work. That is CSR thinking at its best.

Most experts predicted failure. "Maybe it's time Steve Jobs stopped thinking quite so differently," Business week wrote in a story headlines "Sorry Steve, Here's Why Apple Stores Won't Work." The retail consultant David Goldstein declared, "I give them two years before they're turning out the lights on a very painful and expensive mistake." Gateway's stores were averaging 250 visitors per week. On May 19, 2001 the first Apple Store opened in Tyson's Corner Mall, one of the most expensive retail properties in the country. By 2004 Apple stores were averaging 5400 visitors per week! That year they had $1.2 billion in revenue, setting a record in the retail industry. In July 2011, a decade after the first store was opened, there were 326 Apple stores. The average annual revenue was $34 million, and the net sales in 2010 were $9.8 billion. They were not only profitable, but they boosted the brand and reinforced everything else that Apple did. The development of Apple stores and Apple products demonstrated an aspect of CSR thinking that is not understood by most CSR practitioners. It is not simply about cutting costs. It is about creating value in the customer experience by optimizing flow. Many CSR writers and practitioners have not been willing to step up to the plate and address the issues of organizational structure and systems. But, if you don't you are not likely to be CSR. The story of Sony's lost opportunity and the development of the iPod proves the point. Sony had a music division and contracts with a large number of the most popular bands and artists. They were a dominant force in the music business. They had another division that had created the Walkman, a personal device to carry and play music. They had a computer division producing personal computers. They even had software to sell music online. And, at the time, they realized that Napster and other free music download websites were destroying the profitability of their business. It was out of control. Within the Sony brand they had every piece required to solve the problem. However, the three big and powerful divisions fought among themselves and could not collaborate to develop a solution. At Apple Computer there was a leader who understood disruptive technology. It wouldn't be unfair to call Steve Jobs the Crown Prince of disruptive technologies. At that time Apple was merely a personal computer company. They produced no personal or portable devices. But, Jobs loved music. He understood that the personal computer could be the music hub. He personally led the charge to develop the iPod and there were no warring divisions within Apple. Jobs personally met with music royalty including Bob Dylan, Bono, the head of Universal, Sony and other music studios. He went to Japan and found the disc drive at Toshiba that could hold a thousand tunes. He developed an end-to-end solution that met the needs of the artists, the music studios, his own company, and most important, the customers who loved music! He practically lived with Jony Ive, the chief designer, whose aesthetic sense of elegant simplicity for not only the device, but even the packaging, created a unique brand image and advantage. The combination of iTunes software for your computer, the iTunesstore, and the iPod, met the needs of all key stakeholders. It was a victory of seamless integration. It eliminated waste in every component of the music delivery process. It could only have been achieved by an organization devoid of silos and a leader who understood the advantage of a seamless experience by the end user. In every instance of product development and marketing, Steve Jobs understood and demonstrated how eliminating waste from the flow of work and the flow of the customer experience results in the creation of value. Perhaps more than any other executive in our lifetime he understood the interdependence of the human and technical factors in product development and in their use. This is the CSR that needs more of our attention.

References

Helmold, M., et al. (2020). *Corporate Social Responsibility im internationalen Kontext. Wettbewerbsvorteile durch nachhaltige Wertschöpfung*. Springer.

Kuerble, P., Helmold, M., Bode, O. H., & Scholz, U. (2016). *Beschaffung-Produktion-Marketing*. Tectum.

Meffert, H., Burmann, C., Kirchgeorg, M., & Eisenbeiß, M. (2018). *Marketing: Grundlagen marktorientierter Unternehmensführung Konzepte – Instrumente – Praxisbeispiele* (13th ed.). Springer.

Stibbe, R. (2019). *CSR-Erfolgssteuerung. Den Reformprozess verstehen, Reporting und Risikomanagement effizient gestalten*. Springer.

6 Innovation Management

Innovation distinguishes between a leader and a follower.

Steve Jobs

6.1 Introduction to Innovation Management

"Innovation" comes from the Latin word "innovare" and stands for renewal or reformation. From an economic point of view, innovation is something complex and new that brings economic benefits for an organization or and for the company. Innovation management includes elements such as ideas, inventions and diffusions (Müller-Prothmann & Dörr, 2019). Innovations include the generation of ideas and the constant validation and review of these ideas as part of a structured innovation process (Nelke 2016). Innovation Management comprises three levels, as shown in Fig. 6.1. In addition to the operational level, the working level, there are the strategic and normative levels (Stibbe, 2019). Innovations are decided on the normative and strategic level and put into practice on the operative level (Helmold & Samara, 2019). Terms that are often used in connection with innovation are ideas, collections of ideas and inventions. An invention or invention must be differentiated to the extent that it has not yet been exploited and used as a creative achievement of a new problem solution compared to innovation. It is the same with the idea, which is a creative thought of something new. In all cases, "new" can always be seen relatively. It can be new for this situation, the company or the world. In particular new developments such as New Work, Industry 4.0 or increasing globalization have an important impact on innovations and innovation management (Granig et al., 2018). Of central importance are the collection of ideas, the selection and the decision which ideas are implemented. This process must be managed by the higher management (Helmold & Samara, 2019).

T. Dathe et al., *Corporate Social Responsibility (CSR), Sustainability and Environmental Social Governance (ESG)*, Management for Professionals,
https://doi.org/10.1007/978-3-030-92357-0_6

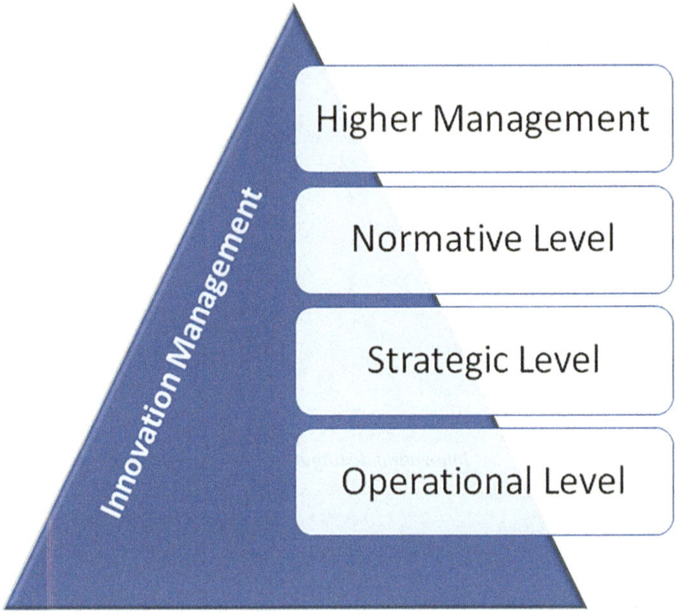

Fig. 6.1 Innovation management levels. (Source: Author's Source)

Management is a term that is used constantly in companies. It stands for the management of a task and for the coordination of activities in order to achieve a defined purpose and goals. Accordingly, innovation management is the structured promotion of innovations in companies and includes tasks in the planning, organization, management and control of these innovations. Innovation management deals with all measures to favour innovations in organizations and to generate benefits, for example:

- New products and services to conquer new markets
- Improved products and services to stand out from the competition
- Improvement of internal processes in order to strengthen the company
- Innovations to from the inside or to save costs
- Development of new business models to use new sources of income
- New Work Styles that enable Employees to achieve a better Performance

6.2 Technical Relevance and Attractivity

Innovations are usually complex undertakings with a high expenditure of technology, use of resources and therefore usually cause very high costs and investments. It is therefore imperative that the company management sustainably evaluate every innovation with regard to its prospect of success, and this with regard to strategic relevance, technology expenditure, benefits and resource intensity. Ideas and possible innovations always require a strategic and resource-based review (Zahn, 1995;

Pfeiffer et al., 1991). Figure 6.2 Relationship between strategy and resources shows the relationship between strategy and resource use.

6.3 Strategic Relevance of Innovation Management

The strategic relevance and attractiveness of the innovation is the sum of all technical and economic advantages that can be gained by exploiting the strategic development opportunities in a technology area. The technology attractiveness depends on the one hand on the technology properties (potential side) and on the other hand on the requirements of (future) users (demand side).

The two sizes of the technology portfolio, technology attractiveness and resource strength, each represent a (highly) aggregated evaluation result in relation to deeper individual factors. Experts envisage the following things to check and determine technology attractiveness (Helmold & Samara, 2019):

- Further development potential: To what extent is a technical further development and thus performance increases and/or cost reductions possible?
- Range of application: How can the number of possible areas of application of the technology and the quantities per area of application be assessed?
- Compatibility: What negative or positive effects can be expected in user and surrounding systems (innovation obstacles, drivers)?

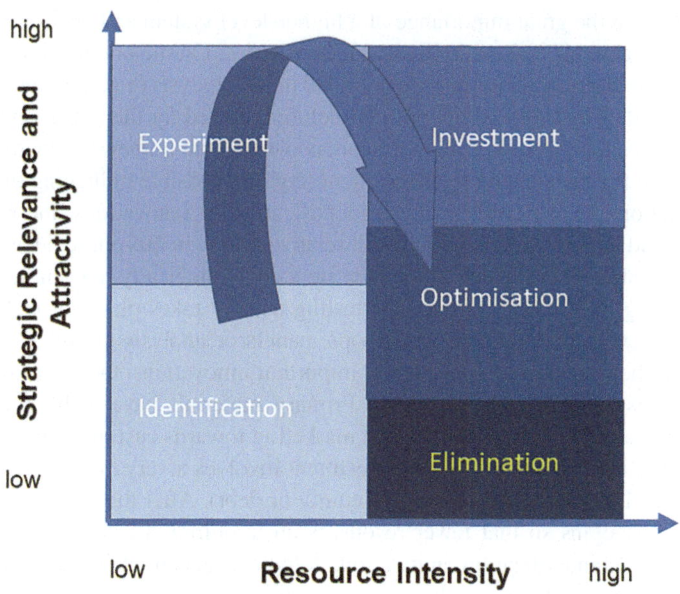

Fig. 6.2 Relationship between strategy and resources. (Source: Author's Source)

6.4 Resource Intensity

The strength of the resources expresses the extent to which the assessed company has the prerequisites in comparison to its potential competitors to make the considered technological alternative successful, i.e. H. in a timely manner and in the form of marketable products. In other words, it is a measure of a company's technical and economic strength or weakness in relation to a technology relative to its competitors. Experts in tourism propose the following three indicators to determine the strength of resources (Helmold & Samara, 2019):

- Technical-qualitative degree of mastery: How is our technology-specific know-how to be assessed in relation to the competition, is there a lead or lag in development?
- Potentials: To what extent are financial, human and material resources available to exploit the existing further development potential of the technology?
- (Re) action speed: How quickly can the evaluating company exploit the further development potential of the technology compared to the competition?

6.5 Future Potential of Innovations

In addition to the studies described above with regard to strategic relevance and use of resources, innovations must be subjected to a future prognosis in which the future prospects of success are evaluated. Scenario analyses can be used to forecast the development of the user side (Pfeiffer et al., 1991) [155]. Pfeiffer and his co-authors also emphasize the great importance of a higher-level system and environment perspective that extends beyond individual technologies. On the one hand, this means that technical peripheral systems are included in the analysis (e.g. the establishment of a methanol or hydrogen supply infrastructure required for the implementation of fuel cell drives for cars). On the other hand, non-technical framework conditions are also decisive for the technology assessment (e.g. the possible tightening of exhaust gas legislation). In the context of the identification of innovations, the necessary resources and strategic relevance are still relatively low. In this phase, ideas are collected, evaluated and selected. In the next step, the strategically relevant ideas must be tested (Fig. 6.3: Experiment). This testing usually takes place through experiments. However, observations, workshops, panels or analysis groups can also be used. With the selection of strategically important innovations, the use of resources in companies automatically increases. Primary materials have to be bought, the products have to be mass-produced and marketing towards customers requires proactive marketing. This phase of the investment involves a very high expenditure of resources and thus financial resources (equity or debt). After the investment phase, optimization begins so that fewer resources are required. The optimization takes place through standardization, unification, volume effects or technical innovations. In the last step, if it turns out that the innovation no longer has any strategic relevance, all activities are eliminated and shut down (Helmold & Samara, 2019).

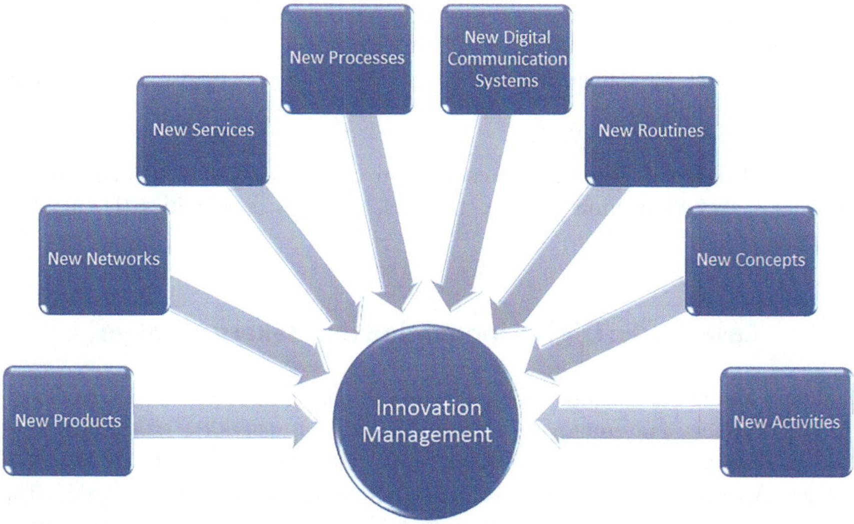

Fig. 6.3 Innovation elements. (Source: Author's Source)

6.6 Fields and Tasks of Innovation Management

Innovation management forms two key pillars. On the one hand, innovation management includes the creation of suitable and structured framework conditions so that ideas arise everywhere in the company and are implemented into successful innovations. It is very much about organizational development activities (Helmold, 2021). And secondly, the actual innovation, the active search, development and implementation of ideas. This requires creativity and appropriate project management, for example. Innovation management is very versatile and multifaceted. The fields of action of innovation management include the following elements:

- Future management: Identification of trends and future opportunities and risks
- Development of the innovation strategy and planning of the innovation activities, for example with an innovation roadmap
- Organization and distribution of roles in innovation management, such as decision-making structures and process ownership
- Idea management for finding, developing and evaluating ideas
- Innovation process for transforming an idea into a successful innovation: concept development, business plan, solution development, prototypes, implementation and marketing
- Creating an innovation culture that promotes innovation
- Portfolio management and innovation controlling (e.g. innovation indicators) to control innovation activities
- Dealing with patents and property rights.

- Open innovation and innovation networks to use external innovation sources and resources.
- Management of change (change management) in the course of innovation projects

Figure 6.3 depicts innovations in several areas like products, networks, services, processes, communication systems, routines, concepts or activities (Helmold & Terry, 2021).

6.7 Case Study: Digital Innovation in a Bakery in Tokyo

Figure 6.4 shows an example of New Work in a bakery store in Tokyo. The device helps customers and employees to focus on relevant activities, rather than non-adding value processes. The customer can place the selected goods on the scanning device. A camera is identifying the goods purchased and showing the price. The customers can pay easily with cash or credit card. The device helps employees to

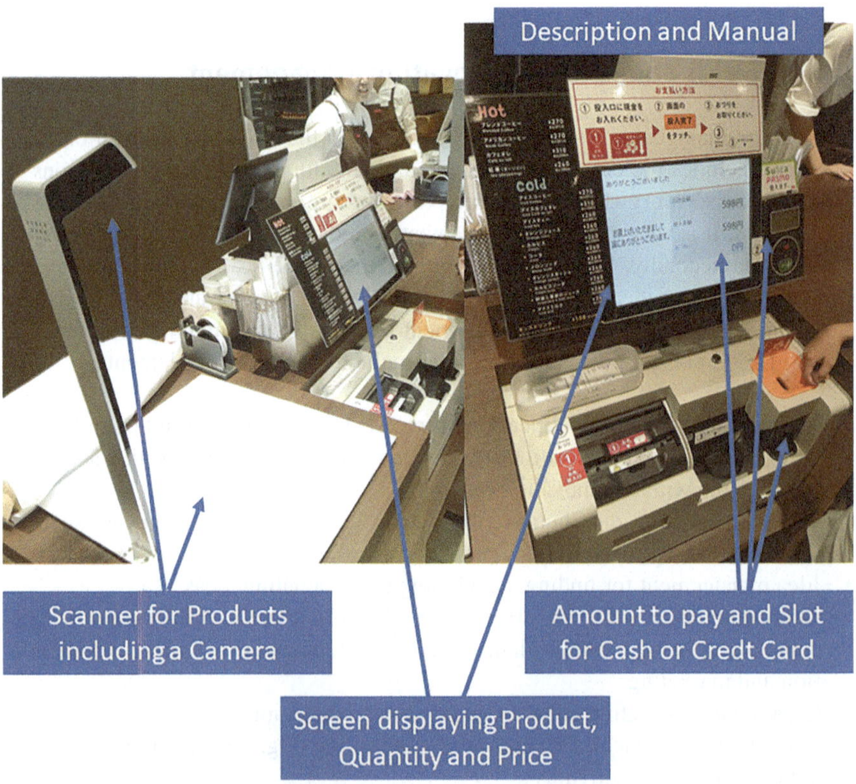

Fig. 6.4 New work innovation in a bakery in Tokyo. (Source: Author's Source)

focus their activities on giving advice to customers rather than payment execution. Additionally, the process improved the transaction time significantly. There is no waiting time anymore for customers. Thus, an innovation helped to create more added value to customers.

References

Granig, P., Hartlieb, E., & Heiden, B. (2018). *Mit Innovationsmanagement zu Industrie 4.0: Grundlagen, Strategien, Erfolgsfaktoren und Praxisbeispiele*. Springer.

Helmold, M. (2021). *Kaizen, CSR Management und Digitalisierung. Mit den japanischen Konzepten Wettbewerbsvorteile für das Unternehmen erzielen*. Springer.

Helmold, M., & Samara, W. (2019). *Progress in performance management. Industry insights and case studies on principles, application tools, and practice*. Springer.

Helmold, M., & Terry, B. (2021). *Operations and supply management 4.0. Industry insights, case studies and best practices*. Springer.

Müller-Prothmann, T., & Dörr, N. (2019). *Innovationsmanagement: Strategien, Methoden und Werkzeuge für systematische Innovationsprozesse*. Hanser Verlag.

Nelke, A. (2016). *Kommunikation und Nachhaltigkeit im Innovationsmanagement von Unternehmen: Grundlagen für die Praxis (Wirtschaftsförderung in Lehre und Praxis)*. Springer.

Pfeiffer, W., Metze, G., Schneider, W., & Amler, R. (1991). *Technologie-Portfolio zum Management strategischer Zukunftsgeschäftsfelder* (6th ed.).

Stibbe, R. (2019). *CSR-Erfolgssteuerung. Den Reformprozess verstehen, Reporting und Risikomanagement effizient gestalten*. Springer.

Zahn, E. (1995). *Handbuch Technologiemanagement* Stuttgart. Schäffer-Poeschel

Ethical Theories 7

Do not be embarrassed by your failures, learn from them and start again.

Richard Branson

7.1 Ethics and Laws

The term ethics is derived from the Greek language (Greek ἔθος = habit, custom; ἦθος = an accustomed place) (Liddell Scott Joines Greak-English Lexicon, 2021) and means in modern English "a study of what is morally right and wrong, or a set of beliefs about what is morally right and wrong" (Cambridge Dictionary, 2021a, b). In practice, the terms "moral" and "ethical" are often used anonymously. According to Cambridge Dictionary, "morals" are "standards for good or bad character and behaviour" or "relating to the standards of good or bad behaviour … that each person believes in" (Cambridge Dictionary, 2021a, b).

In summary, ethical norms or morals are personal believes and social standards that regulation the interpersonal relationships in a society. Ethics is the science that deals with the ethical norms by investigating, questioning and evaluating such standards. The study of ethics delivers ethical theories which are behavioural principles based on various ethical norms. The ethical theories, as the results of investigating, questioning and evaluating moral views in reality, may provide guidelines for decision-making in complex ethical situations (see Fig. 7.1).

Similar to ethical norms, there are also legal norms that regulate interpersonal behaviours. An essential difference between the ethical and the legal norms is that the legal norms (laws) are legally binding and are enforced by the authority of the state. In addition, ethical norms are usually higher standards than legal norms. Since

T. Dathe et al., *Corporate Social Responsibility (CSR), Sustainability and Environmental Social Governance (ESG)*, Management for Professionals,
https://doi.org/10.1007/978-3-030-92357-0_7

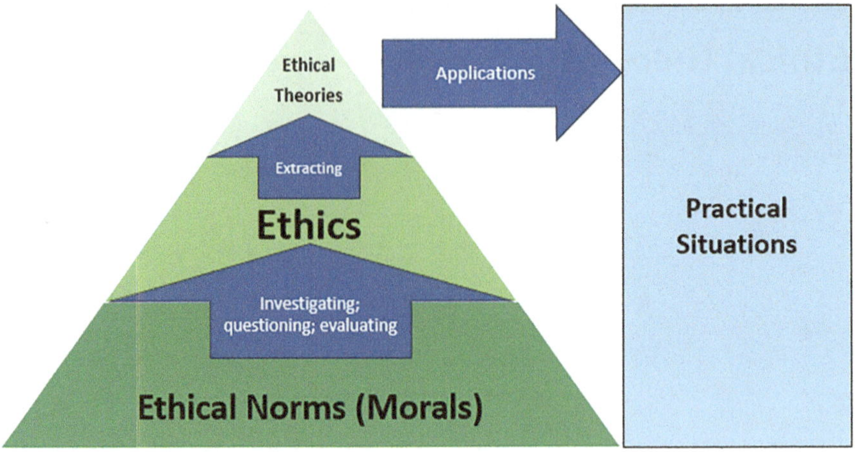

Fig. 7.1 How ethical theories help to solve practical problems

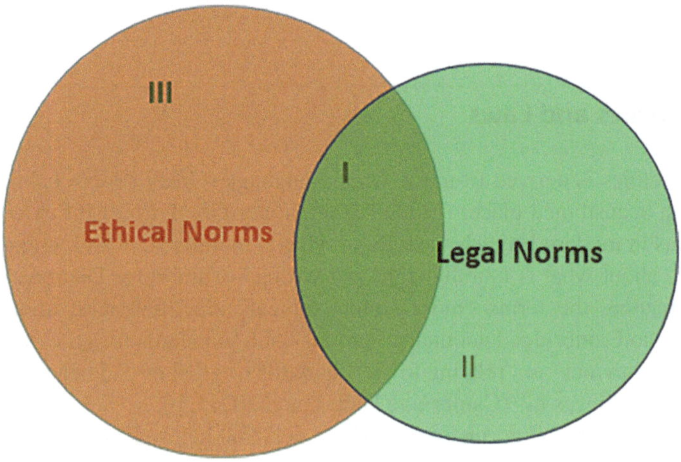

Fig. 7.2 Ethical norms and legal norms

the legal norms are developed based on social expectations, there is an essential overlap between the ethical and the legal norms.

In general, the areas of application for the above standards can be divided into the following three areas (See Fig. 7.2):

I. Behavioural rules in accordance with both legal norms and ethical norms.
II. Legal norms that differ from ethical norms.
III. Ethical norms that differ from legal norms.

II & II mark the areas where there are value conflicts arising from the differences between the two sets of norms. The discussions on corporate social responsibility mainly focus on Category III situations, dealing with ethical dilemmas beyond legal standards.

There are the following branches of the study of ethics dealing with ethical behaviours:

- Normative ethics: examines and evaluates the principles and criteria of moral behaviours as a yardstick for morally correct actions.
- Descriptive ethics: empirically describes the application of norms and value systems. In other words, how the ethical decisions are made in practice.
- Applied ethics: provides recommendations for action based on the theories of normative ethics. The practical areas of application for applied ethics are v. a. the social areas as well as political challenges.
- Metaethics: focuses on the methods of moral argumentation and the applicability of ethical theories.

7.2 Selected Approaches in Normative Ethics

Normative ethics provides the theoretical basis for applied ethics. The aim of normative ethics is to determine the norms and values in a certain situation in order to distinguish the "right" from the "wrong" especially in complex situations.

This section introduces some main approaches to normative ethics.

7.2.1 Consequentialist Versus Non-consequentialist Ethics

The ethical values of a society usually come from the philosophical theories or the religions. Regional differences can be observed in the approach to normative ethics. While the North American researchers often concentrate on the applicability of the theories from the individualistic perspective in a capitalist society, their European colleagues are more concerned with the question of justice and the ethical legitimation of norms in state or economic institutions and also question the ethical Legitimacy of capitalism (Crane & Matten, 2016). In other regions (e. g. the Arab countries) the ethical norms are strongly influenced by the religion.

The business activities in the international environment in our time are dominated by Western ethical ideology, which are characterized by some philosophical positions that can be traced back to the age of the Enlightenment in the eighteenth century. The core object of the Enlightenment is rational thinking with reference to human reason or the distancing from prejudices and religious intolerance of middle age. The resulting modernized theories are known as Western modernism. Western modernism continues to shape Western civilization with regard to the state, the understanding of law and the development of science. The philosophical currents egoism, utilitarianism ethics of duty and the concept of justice are particularly influential for today's business ethics.

The process of ethical action may be divided into three steps: the motivation, the action and the consequence of the action. Depending on the focus on the consequences of the action in the evaluation of the action, a basic distinction is made between consequentialist and non-consequentialist theories (Fig. 7.3).

Non-consequentialism evaluates actions according to their intrinsic characters. Non-consequentialist ethical theories include egoism and utilitarianism. Consequentialism judges if human actions are right or wrong according to the consequences. An example of non-consequentialist theories is the ethics of duty.

7.2.2 Egoism

In the colloquial language, the term "egoism" is often used synonymously as "ruthlessness" with a rather negative connotation. The opposite of egoism is altruism, meaning ways of thinking and acting that are intended to maximize the benefit of others, regardless of the consequences for oneself. The ethical egoism, however, is from of negative connotation.

Ethical egoism means self-centeredness. The objective of egoism is to maximize the self-interest in ways of thinking and acting. A good decision must be voluntary and serve one's own interests. Ethical egoism represents the basic assumptions for the theoretical model Homo Economicus in economics. This economic model is based on economic rationality, which aims to maximize the economic benefits with the available means or to minimize the inputs for a specific goal.

As early as the eighteenth century, Adam Smith recognized that the egoism of individuals in the market economy promotes competition and information transparency, so that ultimately all market participants benefit from it. This view is shared by the American economist Milton Friedman, who argues that individuals, as actors in the economy, do not have sufficient information at their disposal to make optimal

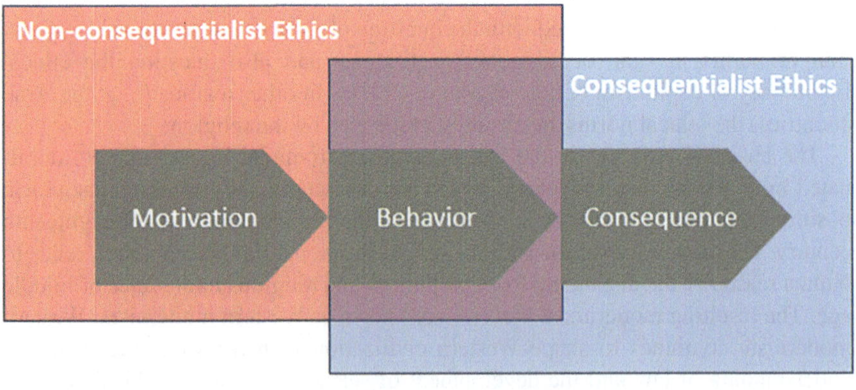

Fig. 7.3 Consequentialist vs. non-consequentialist ethics

decisions for society. The optimal result is achieved when each actor acts solely for his own benefit, because the market mechanisms would optimize the overall economic process like an invisible hand (Friedman, 1970, S. 2–11).

The failure of the planned economy experiments in the last century seems to substantiate the above theses. However, the unequal distribution of resources and wealth is often criticized as a negative effect of egoism. For example, while the current generation can benefit economically at the expense of environmental pollution, the damage will mainly affect the life of future generations, who have no way of influencing today's market events. The egoistic behavior of the current generation could thus lead to a systematic environmental destruction of the planet. The current environmental activist movements are trying to make society aware of the long-term impacts of our actions, so as to find a solution to this problem in the current time.

7.2.3 Utilitarianism

Utilitarianism is based on the so-called "utility analysis" according to the "principle of greatest happiness". An action is morally correct if the sum of happiness (= presence of joy and absence of pain) for all concerned - the aggregate total benefit - is maximized. This happiness is called "utility" in the language of utilitarianism and represents the core concept of utilitarianism.

Utilitarianism finds wide applications in economics and in politics. Alternative actions are evaluated according to the basic principles of utilitarianism, i.e. the sum of utility of all relevant stakeholders or participants is to be maximized (Rogers, 2010). According to the concept of utilitarianism, a complex investment project can be assessed according to the aggregated value of its economic, ecological and social impact.

The theory of utilitarianism calls for the common good, i. e. the well-being of a group of people. Like the other consequentialist theories, utilitarianism is often criticized for its subjectivity and inaccuracy, since, for example, the pleasure or pain felt is individual and subjective, and thus difficult to measure.

To the advocates of utilitarianism, all individuals are rational and capable of evaluating the consequences of an action, measured by the value of utility. Thus, the value of the consequences of the action is independent of the observers (Schroeder, 2006). However, since the evaluation deals with future consequences of actions, the result of the utility analysis is never be free of subjectivity of the observer in his speculation of the future.

Another weakness of utilitarianism is the disadvantages of minority interests. For example, if a passenger plane is hijacked by terrorists and is likely to be used for a terrorist attack, utilitarian analysis would suggest unambiguously that the plane be shot down to protect a large number of innocent citizens at the expense of a minority (the passengers and crew on board). Such a result could, however, contradict the generally accepted moral standards of the society. In 2006, the Federal Constitutional Court of Germany ruled out the shooting down of an aircraft in the above fictitious situation on the grounds of human dignity (Bundesverfassungsgericht, 2006).

7.2.4 Ethics of Duty

Ethics of duty is also called deontological ethics (Greek: δέον (deon) = the duty). The focus of ethics of duty lies primarily in testifying if an action is being conducted based on an obligatory rule.

Immanuel Kant is generally seen as a representative of ethics of duty. He understands duty as the necessity of an act out of respect for the moral norms, which can be recognized by men through reason. According to him, the absolute good is based solely on good will and the human motive for action should only be a duty, not an increase of joy or a reduction of harm (Kant, 1900). Kant describes the basic principle of ethics as a categorical imperative with the following formulations (Kalscheuer, 2017, S. 16 ff.):

I. Formulation of universality: "Act only according to that maxim whereby you at the same time will that it should become a universal law."
   (a) Formulation of natural law: "Act as if the maxims of your action should become the universal natural law through your will."

In other words, the moral maxim should be universal like the laws of nature. It should be transferable to all people (including oneself) and independent of the situation.

Based on this principle, the death penalty would unacceptable, since the approval of the killing by the state would imply that the killing or murdering would be generally approved.

II. Formulation of humanity: "Act in such a way that you treat humanity, both in your person and in the person of everyone else, at all times as a means to an end, never just as a means."

"Purpose in itself" is to be understood as general intention to act, which all reasonable beings must take into account when acting (absolute purpose). Desires or striving for objects or conditions of life, on the other hand, can only serve as a means to an end (relative end). The intended action should aim at an absolute purpose.

In business life, this rule means above all that other people who offer their services for a fee should not be treated merely as a tool, but with respect.

III. Formulation of autonomy: "(Act) only in such a way that the will through its maxim can at the same time regard itself as universally legislating."

In contrast to things that can only have a relative purpose (price), humans have an intrinsic value (dignity). Human dignity is based on the autonomy of human beings to independently recognize, establish and abide by ethical laws.

We may use the example of an airplane hijacked by terrorists to illustrate the difference between duty ethics and consequentialist utilitarianism.

According to the utilitarian criteria, killing is a wrong act because it causes pain to the people concerned. However, if the lives of many potential victims of a terrorist attack can be saved by giving up on fewer innocent people (the passengers and crew), the decision to kill (shooting down the aircraft with a fighter jet) could well become an option worth considering. The judgment of the action is subjective and depends on the viewer's point of view.

In the ethics of duty, the killing of a person is fundamentally wrong and is at no time an option for action. This assessment does not change according to different circumstances and is therefore consistent.

The ethics of duty is often criticized for neglecting the consequences of actions. In addition, the formulation, like Kant's categorical imperative, is so complex that the rules are often difficult to implement in practice. The assumption of a rational sense of duty of all human beings is often viewed as overly optimistic. Compared to the ethics of duty, the assumptions of ethical egoism (e. g. concept of homo economicus) seem to be a more realistic description of the human society (Crane & Matten, 2016, S. 104).

7.2.5 Theories of Justice

The concept of justice plays an essential role in normative ethics. The systematic definition and justification of the term justice, as well as its effectiveness in the social order, are among the core objects of the theories of justice.

The nature of justice has been debated controversially from ancient Greece to our present time. In general, justice is to be understood as the simultaneous fair treatment of individuals in a given situation, with the result that everyone gets what he deserves (Crane & Matten, 2016, S. 109). The American philosopher John Rawls made an important contribution to theories of justice by postulating two principles of justice in his book A Theory of Justice (Rawls, 1979):

1. "Each person is to have an equal right to the most extensive total system of equal basic liberties compatible with a similar system of liberty for all."
2. "Social and economic inequalities are to be arranged so that they are both:
   (a) to the greatest benefit of the least advantaged, consistent with the just savings principle, and.
   (b) attached to offices and positions open to all under conditions of fair equality of opportunity.

Rawls attributes a number of unrestricted fundamental rights to every individual, including protection from abuse, the right to vote and hold public office, freedom of speech and assembly, freedom of thought and the right to property (Rawls, 1979).

Today, the term "human rights" is commonly expanded to include freedom of speech, freedom of conscience, the right to privacy and the right to a fair trial etc. A worldwide consensus on the content of human rights in our presence was formally recorded by the Universal Declaration of Human Rights of the United Nations (adopted in 1948) and the Charter of Fundamental Rights of the European Union (adopted in 2000).

The increasing gap between rich and poor around the world gives rise to discussions on the unequal distribution of wealth. With his theories, Rawls advocates a fundamental correction of redistribution in favour of the socially disadvantaged. The environment-friendly politics can also be justified by theories of justice in protection of the future generations.

7.2.6 Pragmatic Application of Ethical Theories

The ethical theories are useful instruments for assessing complex ethical situations. However, the investigation of a given situation depends on the choice of the theoretical grounds and the subjectivity of the observer which may lead to different results.

Furthermore, theories are abstract reductions of real worldly situations. In the practical application, additional important aspects such as interpersonal relationships and emotions of the stakeholders must be taken into account. In an international environment, the different cultures may have immense influence on ethical decisions. Out of various perspectives, there is often a spectrum of opinions, instead of a uniform assessment of a given situation. For the determination of an optimal solution for a complex practical situation, the ethical theories are to be applied in a pragmatic manner. That is, the solution to a dilemma should be worked out based on a holistic view of all relevant considerations (Baumann, 1993).

7.3 Decision-Making Based on Ethical Theories

Normative ethical theories provide guidelines for the identification of morally right behaviours in a given ethical situation. In order to develop successful CSR strategies in a multi-cultural environment, it is also important to understand how ethical decisions are made in different cultures/societies. Ethical decision-making process and the ethical norms of different cultures/societies are subjects of the empirical research of descriptive ethics.

The ethical decision-making process may be described in four steps (Craft, 2013):

1. To identify a moral situation.
2. To make judgement on the situation (The normative ethical theories are often used as fundamental instruments for this step).
3. To determine the intention to act based on the judgment.
4. To act according to the intention.

The decision-making process in business practice is under influence of various factors which can be divided into two groups (Ford & Richardson, 1994) (Fig. 7.4):

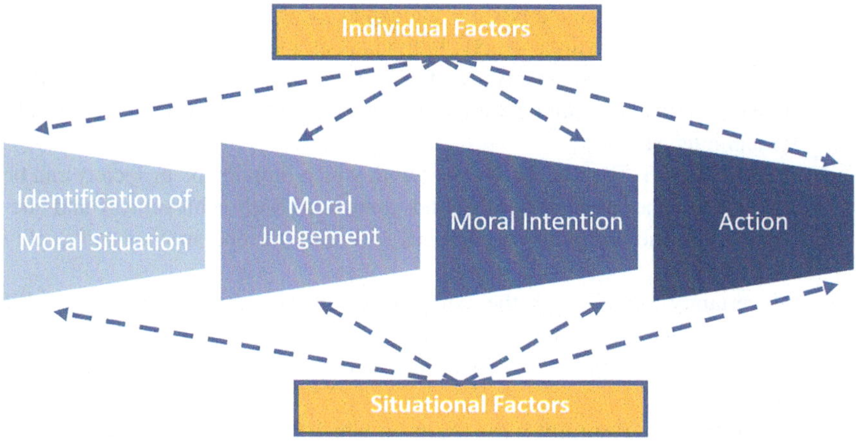

Fig. 7.4 Ethical decision-making process under influence of individual and situational factors based on (Crane & Matten, 2016)

(i) Individual factors: influencing factors that are rooted in the person of the decision maker.
(ii) Situational factors: influencing factors coming from the environment.

Some of the typical individual factors are:

- Age (Craft, 2013). The influence of age is the main consideration in Kohlberg's theory of cognitive moral development. Kohlberg defines three phases of cognitive moral development. According to him, ethical behaviour of the individuals is largely influenced by the status of the decision-maker in terms of the phase he is in (Kohlberg, 1969):
  - Phase 1. The individual behaves in his own interests according to external rewards and punishments.
  - Phase 2. The individual behaves according to the expectations of others.
  - Phase 3. The individual behaves according to his own principles of rights and justice rather than external influences.
- Gender. Overall, women are more likely to make ethically "right" decisions, while men are more consistent in their decisions (Craft, 2013).
- Nationality or cultural background of the decision maker. A well-accepted instrument for culture-related research is the VSM model by Hofstede with the following cultural dimensions (Dathe & Helmold, 2018):
  - Power Distance = the gap in the power position of individuals in a society that is accepted by those with little influence. This shows in which extent inequality is generally accepted in a society. In a society with high power distance, the unethical behaviours of an individual are unlikely to be questioned by his subordinates.

  - Individualism vs. Collectivism = the extent to which individuals are dependent on one another in a society. Individualism means that individuals in the group only care for themselves and their immediate families, while in collectivism, mutual care among the group members are more important than individual interests.
  - Masculinity vs. Femininity = values with which individuals in society can be motivated. The masculine values are associated with achievement and success, while the feminine values focus on caring for one another and quality of life.
  - Uncertainty Avoidance = the extent to which individuals feel threatened if things are unclear or in unknown situations.
  - Long-Term Orientation = the willingness to forego values in the present for future profits.
  - Indulgence vs. Restraint = the extent to which individuals control their own desires and impulses.

- Occupational fields. Empirical studies show a higher rate of immoral behaviour in some occupational fields (De George, 1999) and that ethical training has a positive effect on employee behaviour (Trevino & Nelson, 2014).
- Personal integrity. For example, to what extent the decision maker is willing to uncover unethical behaviour in the immediate environment ("whistleblowing"), despite the probable impairment of his own life as a result of his action (Rothschild & Miethe, 1999).
- Moral imagination. To what extent is the decision maker able to recognize the variety of possible actions and the likely consequences of the actions, in order to develop possible solutions. Individuals with a high moral imagination are more likely to recognize potential ethical conflicts under the prevailing ethical rules (Werhane, 1999).

The situational factors can be further divided into two subgroups:

- The topic-related factors and.
- The contextual factors.

"Moral intensity" and "moral framing" are two examples of topic-related factors.

Moral Intensity describes the intensity of an ethical dilemma perceived by the decision-maker. The intensity of an issue may vary according to six factors (Jones, 1991):

- Magnitude of consequences: The expected harms/benefits impacted by the situation/action (for example, health issues as a result of a faulty product).
- Social consensus: The degree to which people are in agreement over the ethics of the situation/action (for example, the certainty that an act will be deemed unethical by the majority).
- Probability of effect: The likelihood that the harms/benefits will actually take place.

- Temporal immediacy: The amount of time it will likely take for the consequences to occur (for example, long-term effects of smoking).
- Proximity: The feeling of (e. g. social, cultural, psychological, or physical) nearness the decision-maker has for those impacted by the decision (for example, poor working conditions in the neighborhood may be experienced as a more intense moral issue than those in a faraway country).
- Concentration of effect: If the consequences of the action are largely concentrated on a few or spread lightly on many (for example, stealing 100 EUR from a single person is felt more intensive than taking the same amount from a large multinational company).

Moral framing is to be understood as the formulation of an ethical situation. The language used can suggest a decision and thus influence the decision-making process (Crane & Matten, 2016, S. 162).

Some common contextual factors are:

- Reward or punishment mechanisms for moral behaviour (Craft, 2013). For example, how far can the decision-maker can expect a reward or punishment and what is the expected reward or punishment.
- Power distance in the organization. The more power the supervisor has, the less likely that his ethical decision will be questioned by his subordinates.
  - Individual role in the organization. The role may be defined with the hierarchical level or the technical function, as well as one's views (Buchanan & Huczynski, 1997).
- Organizational culture. The organizational culture includes the ethical norms, values and assumptions that are generally accepted in the organization (Anhand et al., 2004).

(Compare (Crane & Matten, 2016, S. 134 ff.).

References

Anhand, V., Ashforth, B., & Joshi, M. (2004). Business as usual: The acceptance and perpetuation of corruption in organizations. *Academy of Management Excutive, 18*(2), 39–53.

Baumann, Z. (1993). *Postmodern ethics*. Blackwell.

Buchanan, D., & Huczynski, A. (1997). *Organizational behavior* (3rd ed.). Prentice-Hall.

Bundesverfassungsgericht. (2006). Von https://www.bundesverfassungsgericht.de/SharedDocs/Entscheidungen/DE/2006/02/rs20060215_1bvr035705.html abgerufen.

Cambridge Dictionary. (2021a). *Ethics*. Von https://dictionary.cambridge.org/de/worterbuch/englisch/ethic abgerufen.

Cambridge Dictionary. (2021b). *Moral*. Von https://dictionary.cambridge.org/de/worterbuch/englisch/moral abgerufen.

Craft, J. (2013). A review of the empirical ethical decision-making literature: 2004–2011. *Journal of Business Ethics, 117*(2), 221–259.

Crane, A., & Matten, D. (2016). *Business ethics. Managing corporate citizenship and sustainability in the age of globalization* (4th ed.). Oxford University Press.

Dathe, T., & Helmold, M. (2018). *Erfolgreich im Chinageschäft: Strategien und Handlungsempfehlungen für kleinere und mittlere Unternehmen (KMU)*. Springer Gabler.
De George, R. (1999). *Business ethics* (5th ed.). Prentice Hall.
Ford, R., & Richardson, W. (1994). Ethical decision making: A review of the empirical literature. *Journal of Business Ethics, 13*(3), 205–221.
Friedman, M. (1970, September 13). The social responsibilty of business is to increase its profits. *New York Times Magazine*.
Jones, T. (1991). Ethical decision making by individuals in organizations: An issue-contigent model. *Academy of Management Review, 16*, 366–395.
Kalscheuer, F. (2017). *Autonomie als Grund und Grenze des Rechts: Das Verhältnis zwischen dem kategorischen Imperativ und dem allgemeinen Rechtsgesetz Kants (Kantstudien-Ergänzungshefte, Band 179)*. De Gruyter.
Kant, I. (1900). *Kritik der praktischen Vernunft, Grundlegung zur Metaphysik der Sitten, Erster Teil, Erstes Buch, 1. Hauptstück, § 7 Grundgesetz der reinen praktischen Vernunft*. Ausgabe der Preußischen Akademie der Wissenschaften.
Kohlberg, L. (1969). Stage and sequence: The cognitive development approach to socialization. In D. G. (Ed.), *Handbook of socialization theory and research* (pp. 347–380). Rand McNally.
Liddell Scott Joines Greak-English Lexicon. (2021). *The online Liddell-Scott-Johnes Greak-English Lexicon*. Von http://stephanus.tlg.uci.edu/lsj/#eid=48064 abgerufen.
Rawls, J. (1979). *Eine Theorie der Gerechtigkeit*. Suhrkamp Verlag.
Rogers, J. (2010). In defense of a version of satisficing consequentialism. *Utilitas, 22*(2), 198–221.
Rothschild, J., & Miethe, T. (1999). Whistle blower disclosures and management retaliation: The battle to control information about organization corruption. *Work and Occupations, 26*(1), 107–128.
Schroeder, M. (2006). Not so promising after all: Evaluator-relative teleology and common-sense morality. *Pacific Philosophical Quarterly, 87*(3), 348–356.
Trevino, L., & Nelson, K. (2014). *Managing business ethics: Straight talk about how to do it right* (6th ed.). Wiley.
Werhane, P. (1999). The role of self-interest in Adam Smith's wealth of nation. *Journal of Philosophy, 86*(11), 669–680.

Corporate Social Responsibility (CSR) and Ethical Management

8

If everyone is moving forward together, then success takes care of itself.

Henry Ford

8.1 CSR as Strategic Framework for Ethical Management

Despite the worldwide overwhelming interests for the social role of business organisations, there is no generally accepted definition for the term Corporate Social Responsibility (CSR). In this chapter, we will introduce a few theories relevant to the CSR strategy and Ethical Management in the real-world business practice.

The term Corporate Social Responsibility (CSR) was first mentioned by Howard R. Bowen in his book *Social Responsibilities of the Businessman* in 1953. In his book, Bowen demands a greater contribution to the civil society by the large corporations in the United States, on the grounds of their significant economic power and the major influence of their business endeavours on lives of the ordinary people (Bowen, 1953, S. xi). The concept of Corporate Social Responsibility (CSR) evolved continuously alongside the social movements in the following decades, e. g. the civil rights movement, the consumer movement, the environmental movement and the women's movements (Carroll, 2016).

Today's Ethical Management as a part of the business practice often applies CSR framework when dealing with the maintenance of customer and supplier relationships, as well as environmental management and other ethical issues. However, the CSR concept is filled with difference nuances of contents in various organizations.

In the following sections, some alternative approaches for the development of Ethical Management strategies will be introduced.

T. Dathe et al., *Corporate Social Responsibility (CSR), Sustainability and Environmental Social Governance (ESG)*, Management for Professionals,
https://doi.org/10.1007/978-3-030-92357-0_8

8.2 Carroll's CSR Pyramid

The 4-step-pyramid developed by A. Carroll in 1979 is one of the most widely used CSR-models. The clear structure of this model facilitates CSR communication, even if the demarcation of the different CSR categories is not ways easy in practice.

In this model, Carrol describes the social responsibility of companies in four hierarchical levels (see Fig. 8.1):

1. **Economic responsibilities;**
2. **Legal responsibilities;**
3. **Ethical responsibilities; and**
4. **Philanthropical responsibilities.**

Economic Responsibility

The society demands from the companies to be profitable over time. Only when a company is economically successful, will it be able to offer useful products and services to the market, to provide secure jobs and to contribute to the society with tax payments. Economic responsibility forms the basis for corporate social responsibility.

Legal Responsibility

Furthermore, the society demands that companies do not use illegal means in their endeavours for value creation. The business organisations, like all other members of the society, are subject to the laws and official regulations. Some recent incidents (e.

Fig. 8.1 Carroll's 4-step CSR pyramid. (Based on Carroll, 1979)

g. the diesel scandal of Volkswagen, where the German automaker was caught by the US Environmental Protection Agency for manipulating the emission tests from 2009 through 2015 to forge low pollution level of their diesel vehicles) highlight the necessity for continuous monitoring by the society.

Ethical Responsibility
Ethical responsibility is the contribution beyond legal standards that is expected by the society. A company is considered to assume its ethical responsibility when it e. g. implements environment-friendly technologies in the production process or ensures decent working conditions and fair pay for employees in foreign production sites.

Philanthropical Responsibility
Philanthropic responsibility is a voluntary contribution that represents the highest level of corporate social responsibility. A company may assume its philanthropical responsibility by improving the quality of life for their employees (e. g. providing family-friendly working time model, providing childcare facilities) and/or the local community (e. g. making voluntary donations for art projects).

Carroll's pyramid model is sometimes criticized for failing to address conflicts of interest. For example, in the course of the globalization process, many production sites have been relocated to low-wage countries. As a result, while the developing countries benefit from the new investments (job creation, new sources of tax revenues etc.), the industrial countries suffer from a rising unemployment rate and the deteriorating social division. The pyramid model does not offer a way of presenting a practical CSR strategy with a differentiated focus on the four types of corporate social responsibility.

8.3 Two-Dimensional Model of Quazi & O'Brien

The strength of the 2-dimensional CSR model by Quazi and O'Brien lies in the clear definition of the corporate CSR strategy. In this model, the CSR decisions in business practice, regardless of the cultural environment or the market constellation, are determined by two factors:

- The understanding of CSR concept: broad vs. narrow responsibility;
- The benefits vs. costs of CSR activities.

Subsequently, the possible CSR strategies may be divided into the following four groups (Quazi & O'Brien, 2000) (see Fig. 8.2):

- Classic view: The company has a narrow understanding of social responsibility, while the costs outweigh the benefits of CSR activities in the strategic assessment. The focus is on the economic considerations.

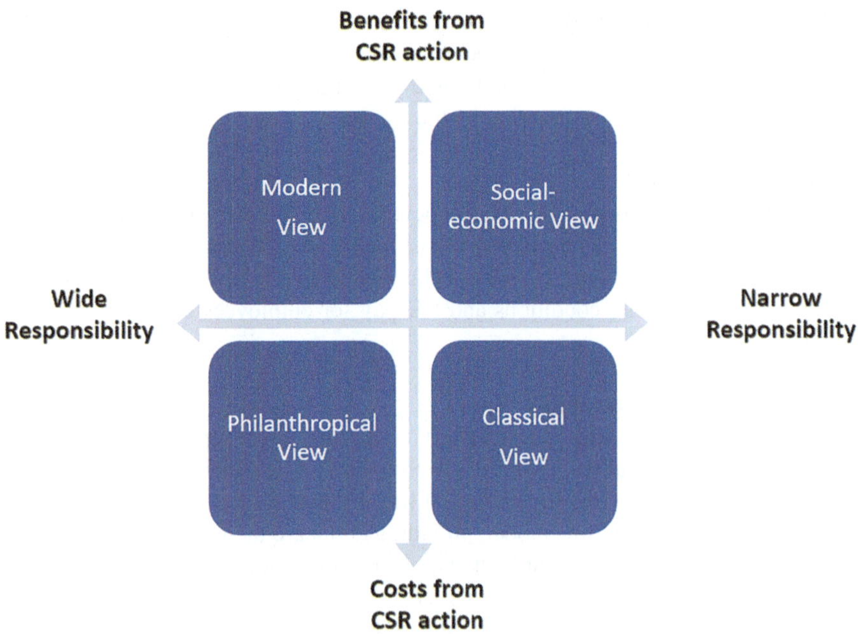

Fig. 8.2 Two-dimensional model of Quazi & O'Brien. (Based on Quazi & O'Brien, 2000)

- Socio-economic view: The company has a narrow understanding of social responsibility, while the benefits of CSR activities outweigh the costs in the strategic assessment. Economic benefits are expected from the CSR activities.
- Modern view: The company has a wide understanding of social responsibility while the benefits of CSR activities outweigh the costs in the strategic assessment. The economic impact of the CSR activities on the shareholders are taken into account when defining the strategy.
- Philanthropic view: The company has a wide understanding of social responsibility, while the costs outweigh the benefits of CSR activities in the strategic assessment. The overall impact of the CSR activities on the shareholders are taken into account when defining the strategy.

Although this 2-dimensional model is practical in strategy development based on the corporate understanding of CSR concept, it fails to provide any possibilities to connect the strategy to the individual CSR activities.

8.4 Three-Domain Model by Carroll & Schwartz

This model is intended to be a further development of the original 4-step pyramid model according to Carroll. In order to overcome the weakness of the pyramid model that the pure form of the four levels of corporate social responsibility can be

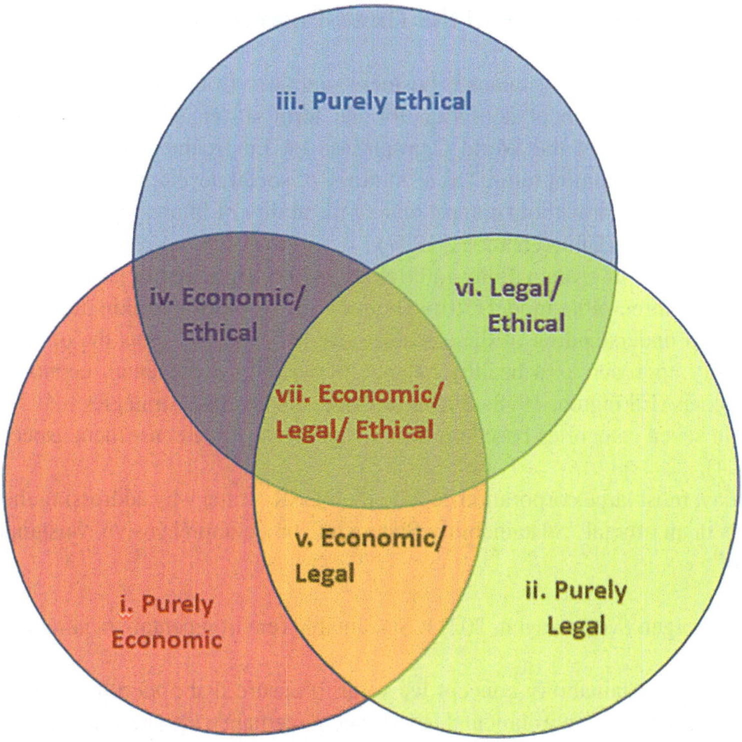

Fig. 8.3 Three-domain model by Carroll und Schwartz. (Based on Schwartz & Carroll, 2003)

rarely found in the business practice, this model offers several additional mixed forms of strategic orientations. Altogether, the 3-domain model contains 7 categories of CSR contributions (See Fig. 8.3)

I. Purely economic;
II. Purely legal;
III. Purely ethical;
IV. Economic-ethical;
V. Economic-legal;
VI. Legal-ethical; and
VII. Economic-legal-ethical.

Due to the public interests for the environmental impact of the business activities, some researchers suggest splitting the ethical perspective in this model into an ethical and an additional environmental perspective (for example (Welzel, S. 262).

8.5 Sustainability and the Three-Pillar Model

The society demands sustainable business practices from the corporations to be sustainable. A prominent definition for the term sustainability comes from the Brundtland report of the World Commission on Environment and Development (WCED) "Our common future" as a "strategy of social development that meets the needs of the present without compromising the ability of future generations to meet their own needs" (United Nations, 1987).

The concept of sustainability intertwines with Corporate Social Responsibility (CSR). The three-pillar model ("triple bottom line") coined by Elkington represents a common understanding of the sustainability concept. It depicts the optimal sustainability approach as a healthy balance between environmental, economic and social goals (Elkington, 1998a, b). In practice, the business strategies may be classified in seven categories based on their focus on the three constituent aspects (see Fig. 8.4).

Today, most large corporation declare their CSR-strategy by addressing the three aspects in an official "Sustainability Statement" or a comprehensive "Sustainability Report":

- Volkswagen (Volkswagen, 2021): Sustainable (environmental-social-economic)

With our sustainability concept we want to ensure that opportunities and risks associated with our environmental, social and governance activities are identified as

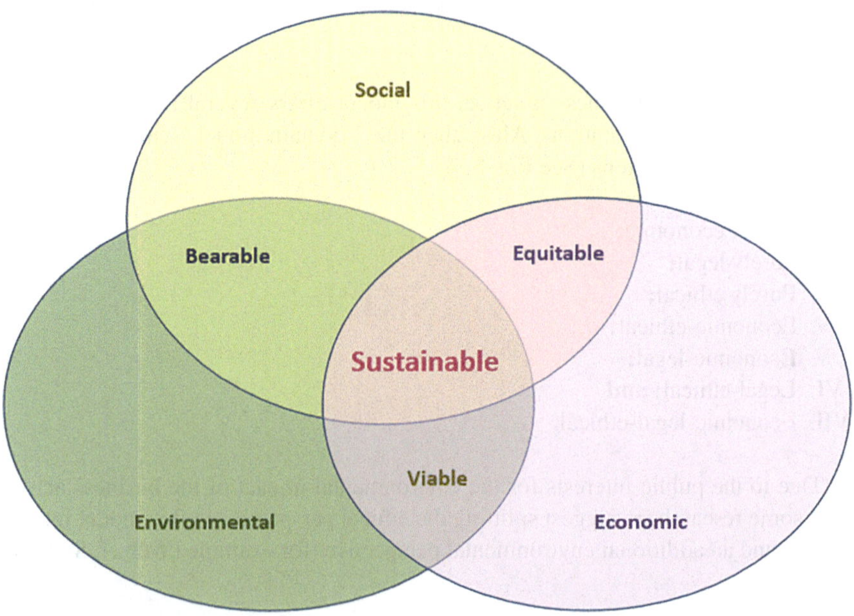

Fig. 8.4 Three-dimensional model of Sustainability. (Based on Elkington, 1998a, b)

early as possible at every stage of the value creation process. In keeping with this aim, we are determined that our corporate social responsibility (CSR) activities will have a lasting, positive impact on the Company's value and reputation.

- Deutsche Bahn (Deutsche Bahn, 2021): Environmental

Being green is not just some kind of act. It's the future. Sustainability at Deutsche Bahn.

- Louis Vuittons (Louis Vuittons, 2021): Bearable (social-environmental)

Our committed journey:

- Sourcing responsibly;
- Acting on climate change;
- Committing to circular creativity;
- Fostering diversity and inclusion; Supporting communities;
- Developing savoir-faire.
- SAP (SAP, 2021): Social

With a global network of customers, partners, employees, and thought leaders, SAP helps the world run better and improve people's lives.

- Siemens (Siemens, 2021): Bearable (social-environmental)

Sustainability is an integral part of our business – it's in our DNA. We empower our customers to drive sustainable growth and transform their industries. With our DEGREE framework, we set strategic ambitions for the benefit of all our stakeholders on the key topics of environment, social and governance.

8.6 Corporate Citizenship (CC)

The expression "Corporate Citizenship (CC)" has sometimes been used synonymously with "Corporate Social Responsibility (CSR)" to describe the social role of companies. Overall, this term in the literature is filled with different nuances of content (Crane & Matten, 2016, S. 69):

- CC in the narrower sense: equal to the philanthropic level of corporate social responsibility.
- CC in the equivalent sense: equal to CSR.
- CC in the broader sense: including the additional aspect of large corporations using their dominant power to take political influence, especially in terms of (see Fig. 8.5 The concept of corporate citizenship in the broader sense. Custom depiction.):

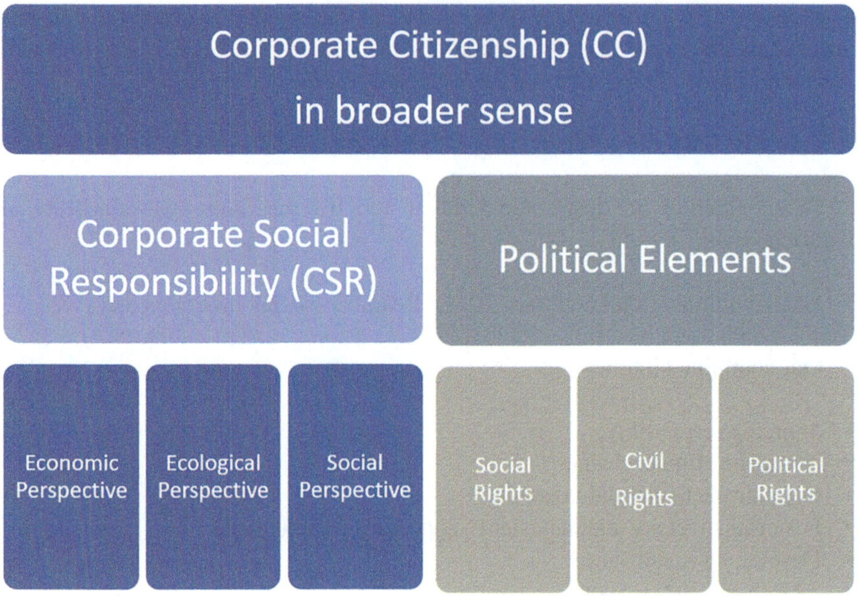

Fig. 8.5 The concept of corporate citizenship in the broader sense based on (Crane & Matten, 2016). Custom depiction

- Social rights: The rights of individuals to participate in society, e.g. the right to education, medical care and other social welfare.
- Civic rights: Freedom from abuse and interference (especially by the government), freedom of speech, right to property, etc.
- Political rights: the right to vote, the right to hold public office or in general, the right to participate in the civil political process.

For decades, the multinational corporations (MNCs) from the industrialized countries were encouraged to use their power to actively influence domestic politics in the developing countries. With the rise of the emerging economies, however, such attempts are being increasingly challenged by the complexity of cultural conflicts and geopolitics. To many critics, such political responsibility rests solely with the state institutions and shall not be misused for public relations measures.

8.7 ESG Rating

The corporations' violations against common ethical values increase the investment risks for the investors. To deal with the public image risks, some rating agencies (e.g. MSCI, FTSE4Good, IMUG, Inrate, Oekom Research, Sustainalytics etc.) are offering special ESG-rating services to evaluate the CSR performance of the companies, industry sectors and countries. The ESG approach creates a new dimension for the evaluation of financial investments, in addition to the classic criteria of profitability.

The ESG rating covers the following aspects of sustainable investments:

1. Environment (E). The ecological performance of a business is often measured by emissions, share of renewable energy etc. in the production process. A company is considered particularly sustainable if, for example, the main product uses environment-friendly technologies (e. g. electronic vehicles).
2. Social (S). The social performance can be reflected by the diversity and inclusion measures, production safety and workplace design, as well as human rights issues such as prohibition of child labor.
3. Governance (G). Governance stands for the inspection bodies or processes that are intended to ensure compliance with ethically sustainable standards in the company.

The ESG ratings are sometimes criticized for lack of information transparency, since the rating result is largely based on the self-declaration of the corporations themselves. More details on the ESG concept are presented in the following chapter.

References

Bowen, H. (1953). *Social responsibilities of the businessman*. Harper & Row.

Carroll, A. B. (1979). A three-dimensional conceptual model of corporate social performance. *Academy of Management Review, 4*, 497–505.

Carroll, A. B. (2016). Carroll's pyramid of CSR: Taking another look. *International Journal of Corporate Social Responsibility 1*(3), 1–3.

Crane, A., & Matten, D. (2016). *Business ethics. Managing corporate citizenship and sustainability in the age of globalization* (4th ed.). Oxford University Press.

Deutsche Bahn. (2021). *Sustainability*. Von https://gruen.deutschebahn.com/en abgerufen.

Elkington, J. (1998a). *Cannibals with forks: The triple bottom line of 21st century business*. University of Michigan: New Society Publishers.

Elkington, J. (1998b). *Cannibals with forks: The triple bottom line of 21st century business*. University of Michigan, S. New Society Publishers.

Quazi, A., & O'Brien, D. (2000). An empirical test of a cross-national model of corporate social responsibility. *Journal of Business Ethics, 25*(1), 33–51.

SAP. (2021). sustainability. Von https://www.sap.com/corporate/de/company/sustainability-csr.html abgerufen.

Schwartz, M., & Carroll, A. (2003). Corporate social responsibility: A three-domain approach. *Business Ethics Quarterly, 13*, 503–530.

Siemens. (2021). Sustainability. Von. https://new.siemens.com/global/en/company/sustainability.html abgerufen.

United Nations. (1987). *Our common future*. Retrieved from Report of the World Commission on Environment and Development. Von http://netzwerk-n.org/wp-content/uploads/2017/04/0_Brundtland_Report-1987-Our_Common_Future.pdf abgerufen

Volkswagen. (2021). *Von sustainability*. https://www.volkswagenag.com/en/sustainability.html abgerufen.

Louis Vuittons. (2021). *Sustainability*. Von https://us.louisvuitton.com/eng-us/magazine/sustainability abgerufen.

Corporate Social Responsibility (CSR) Versus Environmental Social Governance (ESG)

9

We cannot change what we are not aware of, and once we are aware, we cannot help but change.

Sheryl Sandberg

This section compares the similar concepts of Corporate Social Responsibility (CSR) and Environmental Social Governance (ESG) from the perspective of business practitioners. Both concepts have become common in business practice, not only for the large multinational corporations (MNCs), but also for the small to mid-sized enterprises (SMEs).

In a nutshell: CSR describes how a company shall behave ethically and ESG deal with the appropriate metrics to measure the ethical performance (Gupta, 2021a, b).

9.1 Definition of ESG

The Mankind is focusing more and more on environmental and social aspects to support our blue planet Earth for the next generation (see Fig. 9.1 Baltic Sea beach.).

With this understanding for Climate change and Carbon free industry needs, Green thinking, ESG is becoming a mainstream corporate initiative to save and maintain our resources.

ESG is the abbreviation of Environmental Social Governance and is seen as part of a further wording and familiar description of Corporate Social Responsibility to evaluate one's company's social responsibility (Euramco, 2021). It is seen as voluntary efforts of corporate companies and not driven by country's law or global regulations. Further, it is a part of the CSR setup for sustainability and ecological

T. Dathe et al., *Corporate Social Responsibility (CSR), Sustainability and Environmental Social Governance (ESG)*, Management for Professionals,
https://doi.org/10.1007/978-3-030-92357-0_9

Fig. 9.1 Baltic Sea beach

behaviours in connection of corporate values, etiquettes and investment decisions (Euramco, 2021).

An important baseline of the overall ESG discussion is the kind of products, the respected company is offering to their customers and how those products are manufactured in regarding of climate and environmental protection especially the carbon footprint is more and more a critical element in corporate evaluations. Many corporate companies and Non-profit organisations are targeting CO_2 neutral operations in the next decade or even till 2030 with reducing of plastic components, green efficient electricity like wind, water or solar energy supply and sol heating. Also, E-Mobility like electric cars, using shared public transportation and avoiding petrol-based cars and kerosine-based planes are part of this development of demonstrating ESG.

Further items are to be considered are:

- Environment management with renewable energy
- Environment regulation for manufacturing and services
- Criteria for Human capital
- Product regulation and responsibility
- Equal payment and tariff payment
- Anti-discrimination efforts
- Diversity and inclusion
- Managing fluctuation of employees (Euramco, 2021).

Those aspects shall provide an understanding of the Quality of Corporate Social Responsibility of the companies and how those companies are executing and living its voluntary standards (Euramco, 2021). To underline this, the United Nations Principles for Responsible Investing standard was established. To be signed by companies to enforce their commitment of working against corruption, bribery, money laundering (Euramco, 2021).

9.2 UN Initiative: Who Cares Wins

The storyline of Environmental Social Governance ESG was initiated by former UN Secretary Kofi Annan who started the reform of the United Nation in 2003 and wrote a letter at the beginning of the year 2004 to more than 50 Executives to join forces to enhance ESG topic and raise an understanding for protecting our planet with incorporating Corporate Financials (Kell, 2018). As a first result of Kofi Annan's initiative: there was a paper: "Who Cares Wins" by Ivo Knoepfel (United Nations, 2004; Kell, 2018).

The report "Who Cares Wins" is connecting markets especially financial markets to a changing world, environment behaviours and committed recommendation by the corporate financial industry like banks, investment trusts and insurance companies. The overall frame is the recommendation for the specific integration of environmental, social and governance aspects in asset management strategies and brokerage investments (United Nations, 2004).

Therefore, ESG is also today mainly driving by investment companies like Blackrock, MSCI and Standard & Poor's and less by regulators and single states, governments, or political organizations. Moreover, CEOs and board of directors seen ESG standards and ratings as a crucial item to satisfy investor and maintain the stock price for its company. Therefore, more and more companies are driving to reshape their business to environmental friendlier outcomes to satisfy customers and stakeholders also driven by social media pressure and finally its shareholder. However, the main goal is to be a preferred investment by ETF and indices like Dow Jones, MSCI, DAX 50 ESG etc. where ESG are becoming more and more prominent as a soft standard in the future in comparison to looking only on market share and market capitalization (QONTIGOX, 2021).

The commitment for "Who Cares Wins" was given by the following companies:

- ABN Amro
- Aviva
- AXA Group
- Banco do Brasil
- Bank Sarasin
- BNP Paribas
- Calvert Group
- CNP Assurances
- Credit Suisse Group

- Deutsche Bank
- Goldman Sachs
- Henderson Global Investors
- HSBC
- IFC
- Innovest
- ISIS Asset Management
- KLP Insurance
- Mitsui Sumitomo Insurance
- Morgan Stanley
- RCM (a member of Allianz Dresdner Asset Management)
- UBS
- Westpac
- World Bank Group (United Nations Department of Public Information, 2004)

The list of committed companies indicates a rich diversity of different regions who intend to drive ESG forward as a new standard.

The initiative is supported by 20 monetary companies from 9 different countries with total assets of US$ 6 trillion under their responsibility. A look closer, the swiss banks like UBS and Credit Swiss are part as same as the US based Morgan Stanley and Goldman Sachs. A special aspect is that Lehman Brothers and Merrill Lynch as well as Bear Stearns, all known as the investment banks who were massive struggling in the Financial Crisis in 2008 have not signed and work on those initiative to invent ESG as such. As we all known Lehmann Brother filled bankruptcy (Wiggins et al., 2014), Merrill Lynch were acquired by the Bank of America (Campbell, 2013) and Bear Sterns was bailout by the US Federal Reserve FED and sold to JPMorgan Chase (White, 2008). Therefore, it's interesting that those three financial long-term and up to the 2008 financial crisis well-financed institutions have not considered to be part of Kofi Annan's initiative of Environmental Social Governance ESG and failed in the end to manage their company overall quality approach to be successful in line of risk management in their investments. It's unclear and not investigate, if the three companies would have joined the ESG discussion at the beginning to allow them to think about new and enhancing ESG and risk standards and not betting against the American Housing market, American homeowners and finally against the American economy as described in the book and movie "The Big Short" (Lewis, 2011; McKay & Randolph, 2015).

In retrospective, today ESG is popular for new and old investment company like Blackrock and Vanguard which are dominating the Exchange-traded fund investments but also did not sign the UN initiative from 2004. Nowadays they are offering a range of ESG financial investments in this area same as MSCI and Standard & Poors and using ESG as a positive channel to support world-wide green initiatives in combination of their shares selecting strategy. Blackrock uses its new ESG strategy more and more actively and did not discharge around 53 supervisory boards resp. supervisory board members in 2020 of many international companies e.g.:

- Daimler
- Lufthansa
- Uniper
- Heidelberger Zement
- Exxon
- Volvo (Köhler & Landgraf, 2020)

This is part of Blackrock CEO Larry Finks strategy announcement in January 2020 to consider environment, social and Good Governance aspects more and more and understand it as a risk mitigation tool since the understanding is: climate risk is also an investment risk in form of less divided payments or less share price increasing with no or limited ESG consideration by the public-traded Companies (Köhler & Landgraf, 2020). This was also the intention of the 20 companies who initiated the ESG together with the UN to reduce investment risks and enhance shareholder value in focusing on risk mitigation e. g. Brand reputation, supporting regulations and driving market access in new areas and technologies within their overall ESG investment strategies (United Nations, 2004).

The understanding of Big Money in brand reputation is one of the key success factors along the value chain in a globalized and internet-connected world, especially today with fast on demand social media updates via Twitter, Facebook, and YouTube where negative publicity like shitstorm is more frequent, faster, and intensive in brand damaging and destroying customer loyalty (see Fig. 9.2 ESG and brand reputation connection (United Nations, 2004).).

In the end, the 2004 ESG proposal consists of 9 elements for more superior investment decision and sustainability in terms of society questions:

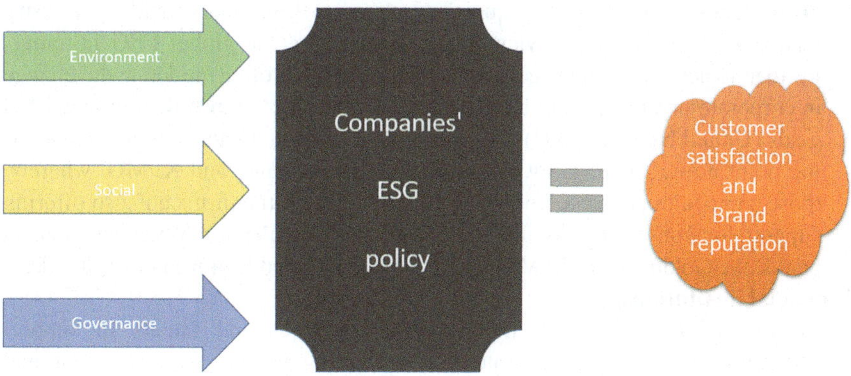

Fig. 9.2 ESG and brand reputation connection. (United Nations Department of Public Information, 2004)

Analysts.

- Employees are requested to think more and more often about Environmental Social Governance chances, influence, and trends and to incorporate the learnings in their daily operational work. Next, passion to gain knowledge and develop working models for ESG to further strengthen the algorithm of investment decisions. For the assets class of emerging markets, for which is more difficult to develop ESG figures shall be part of the research to support investment decision on the entire global supply chain. Since usually manufacturing is part of the journey of developing countries coming a developed country which is seen in the history of the industrialisation in Europe and in new developing countries today as well: environmental focus and social aspects like labour security and green energy is to be considered and developed from right the beginning. To develop the ESG benchmark also academic linkage is to be enhanced as well as the connection between industrial and academic research (United Nations, 2004). For investment analysts, the portfolio theory for investment classes is an essential part of their daily operational work in compilation of a risk-based approach to ensure the right decision making at the right time. Those fields are now being supported by ESG.

Companies.

- In Corporate Organizations, ESG shall be driven by information. To build, to research, to understand, to process and to distribute information about Environmental Social Corporate Governance is the key responsibility for companies. Especially in quarterly reports, annual reports and shareholder or stakeholder communication: progress but also areas of improvement need to be communicated to establish the critical thinking and critical mass for ESG. Those communication needs to be simple and standardised to have an opportunity to see differences in the ESG implementation and progress in the different firms for investors (United Nations, 2004).

Consultants and independent financial adviser.

- To be focused on answering question related to ESG and providing industry feedback from an outside view related supporting the global ESG initiative. Further, to act as a change agent to navigate and more often moderate the change in corporate organization to help executive to receive the overall company ESG goals (United Nations, 2004). The big 4 Consulting companies might be a starting point nowadays e. g. PwC, Deloitte, Ernst & Young and KPMG, whereby those companies are more known as the Big 4 accounting firms but also offering support for consulting. As financial advisers particular for M&A are seen in banks like Goldman and JP Morgan, which have signed Kofi Annan's ESG ideas.

Financial institutions.

- Institutions are committed to invest in structures and talents to support Environmental Social Corporate Governance pioneering in investment and research aspects. Further, building up the capacity of people and department is a crucial step into a change management process today and in the future. As an essential factor, it is seen that executives, senior management and board of directors are committing to the ESG launch and driving it with their leadership skills forward. Finally, learning as an organization is one of the elements of this cultural and social change (United Nations, 2004).

Investors.

- To invest in ESG Key Performance indicators (KPI) and Key Quality Indicators (KQI) to measure success, failure and trends of the respected ESG strategy by the invested companies is the task of Brokers and Asset managers to support the overall environmental and social change in the investment branch. It's important to recognize well-positioned companies which are role models for ESG. The ESG KPI as a working model based on academic and industry research is to be customized to provide service to investors and help them to execute and defend their investment decision. (United Nations, 2004).

Non-profit organisation (NGO).

- As all other market participants, also NGO are invited to accelerate and promote the ESG model (United Nations, 2004), which is from today's experiences well-managed and visible in the ecosystem of most of the stock-listed companies. They are focusing on CSR or ESG aspects and monitoring progress within its own company, by analysing competitors and within its branch.

Pension funds and Pension trusts.

- Being a trustee means to ensure and establish decision-making models and risk-based approaches regards its own common tasks and to the commitment to its clients and customers to invest their money safely. In this asset class, ESG criteria needs to be established to support environmental and social investment standards in the role as fiduciary (United Nations, 2004).

Regulators.

- Global governments and related institution e.g., Central Banks like the US Federal Reserve or the European Central Bank or the Bank of England regulating the financial system and are requested to support the voluntary ESG approach which are driven by banks, corporate financial institution, analysts and brokers. As a voluntary approach, regulators looking initially into the approach and coming with a draft guideline or regulation up later. With ESG, it is intended to be voluntary, but a minimum environment and social insight is also welcomed by the regulators for this UN proposal (United Nations, 2004).

Stock exchanges.

- Stock exchange are places to trade stocks e.g., New York Stock Exchange NYSE, Nasdaq, and Euronext. Further, those institutions creating more well-known indices for example Wall Street icon Dow Jones and S&P 500or German DAX or Shanghai composite and others. In ESG aspect, the companies are invited to issue ESG indices like DAX 50 ESG (QONTIGOX, 2021). The start was of course with active communicating ESG behaviors of their listed company and work with rating agencies like Standard &Poor's, Moddy's and Fitch which are also well-known as the Big Three in the rating world to include not just financial figures but more often also ESG aspects into their rating KPIs (United Nations, 2004). MSCI is also playing an important role with its MSCI indices e.g., MSCI World or ESG derivates nowadays.

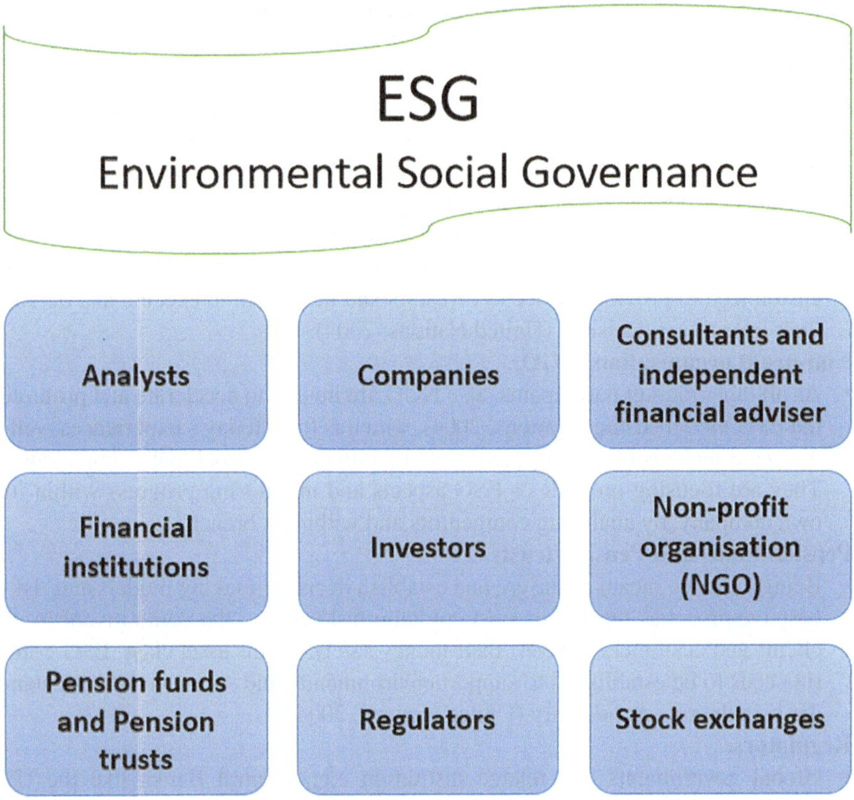

Fig. 9.3 Nine proposed elements of collaboration making ESG successfully. (United Nations Department of Public Information, 2004)

The nine elements are the key aspects of the "Who Cares Wins" report (see Fig. 9.3 Nine proposed elements of collaboration making ESG successfully (United Nations Department of Public Information, 2004).)

To sum up, the voluntary initiative is well recognized in the world and more and more companies using ESG as a standard to convince investors on an investment in their own company. However, the drive was coming after the 2008 Financial crisis since social aspects are coming more imported at least on short-term and long-term due to more and more influence of ETF index funds. Those ESG aspects were from a traditional point of view not part of the investment decision making process. Nowadays, the focus is on:

- Climate change management
- Company culture policy
- Diversity and Inclusion
- Labour work condition
- Health management

- Innovation performance
- Safety and security management
- Supply chain management
- Water management (Kell, 2018).

In 2008, the ESG investment is estimated with US$ 20 trillion in the world and is further increasing since pressure by banks and investment firms is enhancing. In retrospective, share price evolving was higher with strong ESG focus instead of low ESG engagement by the stock exchange listed companies (Kell, 2018). Companies on the short-list with negative ESG terms are:

- Alcohol
- Firearms
- Tobacco firms (Kell, 2018).

In addition, coal-mining companies, nuclear energy firms, long-haul and point to point airline carriers as well as traditional car makers might be considered with a negative ESG rating for investments. Well, the point is that in developed countries, ESG standards can be easily adapted. However, the old pollution-based industry is further part of our global supply chain and a certain level of manufacturing processes is always need. The alternative to outsource everything or using only recycle materials cannot be the only way of our solution for the moment. The question is how fast can the world-wide production process can be adapted to a clean manufacturing process and which technologies are needed? Moreover, developing countries need to have access to ESG as well like low-cost manufacturing countries otherwise it's just greenwashing of the developed countries stock-listed companies and not a change of our blue planet.

With the new ESG rating standards, additional new jobs are arriving and generated like ESG analysts or ESG trainings specialist. Such ESG talents are highly requested as same as ESG certificates or masterclasses (Fidelity, 2021; Kell, 2018).

9.3 UN Initiative: Freshfield Report

Next to "Who cares who wins" by swiss advisor consultant Ivo Knoepfel, the United Nations Environment Programme Finance Initiative (UNEP FI) and the British law firm Freshfields Bruckhaus Deringer developed and issued the Finance Initiative: Innovative financing for sustainability. A legal framework for the integration of environmental, social and governance issues into institutional investment – also known as the Freshfield Report (United Nations, 2005; Kell 2018). The 2005 Freshfield report indicates that most of the asset management and pension funds are conducted by a handful of firms and key people. To influence and support those decision makers of estimated US$ 14 trillion global mutual funds in 2003 and in the overall context of the world-wide investment industry of US $ 42 trillion, ESG training and knowledge needs to be established to be able to navigate the way how investments are conducted (Nations, 2005). Because changes on this level have a great impact on environmental and social aspects (Nations, 2005). One aspect is to identify potential ESG risks that leads to neglecting of ESG criteria in the investment criteria of decision makers. In addition, company policies need to undergo a transforming process to cover the thoughts of the Asset Management Working Group (AMWG) of the established United Nations Environment Programme (United Nations, 2005). The baseline of the Freshfield report is to answer the questions shall the implementation of ESG into investments be voluntary, legally required or regulation by law, especially for pension funds both private and public, insurance companies reserves and mutual funds (United Nations, 2005).

While the 2004 Who Cares Wins paper by the United Nations Department of Public Information is more focused on voluntary initiative by companies like banks, funds, and insurance companies (see Fig. 9.4 Who Cares Wins Paper vs. Freshfield Report; (United Nations, 2005).).

The 2005 Freshfields report by the United Nations Department of Public Information focusing on regulations and current laws of the single countries in Asia-Pacific, Europe, and North America.

Asia-Pacific: Australia – Japan
Europe: France – Germany – Italy – Spain – United Kingdom
North America: Canada – United States of America (United Nations Environment Programme, 2005).

From a financial and investment point of view, the US-New York driven stock exchange with its worldwide influence on other markets needs to be considered as benchmark for other stock exchanges in the world. The NYSE with its blue-chip

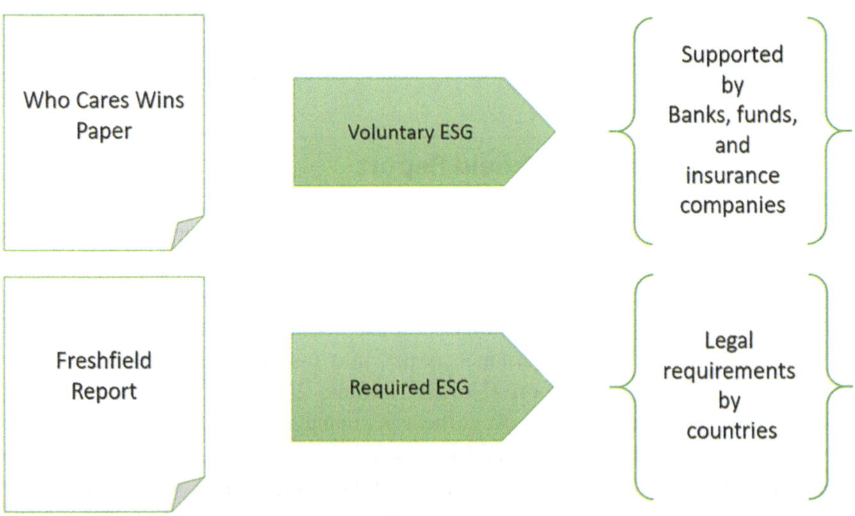

Fig. 9.4 Who Cares Wins Paper vs. Freshfield Report. (United Nations, 2004, 2005)

index Dow Jones and the technology driving standalone Nasdaq is seen despite many global crises like:

- Dotcom crisis in 2001,
- Financial crisis in 2008,
- Corona crisis in 2020.

still as the leading market for investments for all investors in the world.

The US have the leading stock exchanges and influence trends how to invest money likewise with trends like CSR and ESG. Next to New York, London is the key financial marketplace in Europe despite the 2020 Brexit, it is driver seat for other EU markets like Paris or Frankfurt.

With this in mind, we see an interesting gap in regulations, that in the US there was no need to consider ESG aspects in the day-by-day investment for pension funds as a tool to support its investment decision (United Nations, 2005). Most of European countries have established an obligation to consider ESG-like aspects in investment decision of pension funds in 2005 including Germany, France, and UK (United Nations, 2005), which is seen that from environmental, social and Governance point of view, the European legislation in single countries is more restrict than in the US. However, since most of the investments in public traded stocks are made from or in the US, the overall consideration and need to look on ESG aspects in the decision-making process by stockbrokers or Investment analysts is low from legislative and more on voluntary basis in this timeframe. But the voluntary commitment of one of the largest US investment banks as described in the Who Cares Winss paper by the United Nations Department of Public Information shows the interest and drive also from the US investment point of view (United Nations, 2004). With Blackrock's ETF portfolio and its ESG care, the US investment companies are even more seen as the new ESG benchmark drivers nowadays. The legal ESG requirement of each single country is mixed at 2005 (see Table 9.1 ESG demands from single countries law perspective.):

Table 9.1 ESG demands from single countries law perspective

Region	Country	ESG incorporate in countries 'law in 2005
Asia-Pacific	Australia	Yes
	Japan	Not now (2005)
Europe	France	Yes
	Germany	Yes
	Italy	In discussion (2005)
	Spain	Not now (2005)
	United Kingdom	Yes
North America	Canada	Not now (2005)
	United States of Amerika	Not now (2005)

United Nations (2005)

In the Freshfield analysis, there are no Emerging countries like BRIC or Next Eleven listed. BRIC is described as Brazil, Russia, India, and Peoples Republic of China (O'Neill, 2001). Next Eleven N-11 is a term to summarize the developing countries: Bangladesh, Egypt, Indonesia, Iran, Mexico, Nigeria, Pakistan, Philippines, South Korea, Turkey, and Vietnam (O'Neill et al., 2005). The Goldman Sachs research team by O'Neill developed those abbreviations to demonstrate the future power of those economies and markets.

As conclusion of the Freshfield report it is visible that ESG KPIs, financial KPIs and figures are coming together and are recognized by more and more countries in their legal framework (United Nations, 2005). The discussion about integrating ESG standards was still under discussion and the well-known financial numbers first approach is still essential in many countries and organisation in early 2000s (United Nations, 2005). Finally, investment decisions depending on facts and the information available currently, with more ESG KPI available other decision-making process might be follow soon.

9.4 Creating of the Principles for Responsible Investment

The outcome of the two discussed journals, created the Principles for Responsible Investment PRI approach, which was on the top of that introduced on the New York Stock Exchange in 2006 (Kell, 2018; PRI Association, 2021a, b).

PRI is based on Kofi Annan's initiative to empower world largest institutional investors to develop a Principles for Responsible Investment approach for the world in connection with United Nation value and behaviours (PRI Association, 2021a, b). PRI set its goal to:

1. Driving investment decision and engagement for ESG Environmental Social Governance.
2. Supporting Investment owners in their decision for ESG and support networking of PRI supporters (also known as signatories who signed the Principles for Responsible Investment PRI charter) on long term basis.
3. Acting in the interests of economy and financial markets regards to ESG investment standards from operational point of view (PRI Association, 2021a, b).

Principles for Responsible Investment PRI organisation describes itself as not being part of the United Nation but supported by the UN and not related to any country or government. It's a non-profit organisation (NGO) who indent to freely encourage members to support the Principles for Responsible Investment PRI and to use ESG standard for their investment decision and leverage their risk in daily operational activities but is also in contact with politicians for exchanges (PRI Association, 2021a, b).

To support investor: a recipe for investors were developed to have a hands-on guide for environmental social investments with the goal of a sustainable and global finance system (PRI Association, 2021a, b). However, the 2008 financial crisis on

Table 9.2 Principles for responsible investment

Principles for responsible investment	Wording
Principle 1 – Analysis and decision	Incorporating of the environmental social governance ESG into the investment decision making processes
Principle 2 – Ownership	Owning ESG standards in policies and practices and live those ESG values within investment decision process
Principle 3 – Disclosure	Requesting and seeking disclosure of ESG issues in invested companies in annual reports and quarterly analyst calls
Principle 4 – Promotion	Promoting the overall acceptance and implication of ESG principles in the entire investment industry on banks, funds, and pension funds etc. in short-, mid- and long-term.
Principle 5 – Effectiveness	Strengthening the effectiveness of implementation and living the ESG principles in the investment process within the investment industry.
Principle 6 – Reporting	Reporting and tracking of the enhancement and progress of ESG principles implementation for companies and stock exchanges

PRI Association (2021a, b)

subprime real estate market and the creating of CDO Collateralized Debt Obligation as a kind of structured Asset-Backed Security ABS has not proven that the market three years after the creation of the PRI initiative is focused more on social aspects, because the subprime crisis was a bet against the world economy in the end of 2008 (Vink & Thibeault, 2007; Lewis, 2011; McKay & Randolph, 2015). Therefore, the robustness of the ESG aspect into volatile markets and in upcoming crisis needs to be investigated in the future since the Corona market downturn was so short to analyze ESG influence and stock indices market were outperform after a few months again.

The support for investor is documented in Six PRI principles for investments with responsibility by the PRI Association (see Table 9.2 Principles for Responsible Investment (PRI Association, 2 PRI Association, 2021a, b):

The Six Principles are a good starting point to implement ESG standards, however there is no guidance what are ESG standards and how to work getting clean water out of the manufacturing cycle and living with limited resources, talking about green energy and many more. With this, more training is needed for people who need to implement those standards in the financial cooperation's and stock-listed and private-owned companies.

For Principle 3b as add on providing solution for invested companies would be beneficial to support stock-listed companies in the journey of zero emissions, wate reduction or water neutral manufacturing.

For Principle 5b as add, the developing of the right ESG KPIs would be essential to compare different stock listed and private owned companies as well as to make the right investment decisions in an efficient way.

Further, the questions are how to treat institutions which are not following the process, also the process of disinvestment is not clear provided as a principle. Brokers are forced to disinvest in a company, but potential known the market capitalisation and Return of Investment might be further increasing. How to disconnect further negative bonus payment by Brokers but also by executives which are not following ESG standards in invested companies would be helpful.

Another point is how to deal with Military companies who are based on weapon manufacturing for national armies. Those might not be able to change its business model because Police and Defence forces need weapons like to support recuse mission for refuges around the world like in Afghanistan in August 2021.

Next, how is the situation for ethical support of cyber security for countries and governments. There are new elements which coming into the game and need to be analysed and understood same as mining raw materials as rare earth for IT, electro cars or smart phones. 100% Recycling might be option like Apple it's targeting since recent years on the long-term but also short-term and mid-term solutions would be essential to meet today's and future ESG standards to rescue our Earth.

One concern is that members need to pay a fee for the PRI membership to be part of the network. The fee is paid on annual basis PRI Association, 2021a, b). It looks like to join an organisation and with this all ESG aspects are fulfilled. Further, payments and funding from other organisation like government shall be avoided since governments are responsible for judication and creating new laws and be able to change laws easily. Therefore, an independency might not be given which is part of ESG vision to be independent as such. On the other hand, a positive transparent aspect is that all corporate sponsorships and governmental payments are listed in the annual report of the PRI association (PRI Association, 2021a, b).

Since the creation of the PRI is linked and driven by the United Nation and Kofi Annan's initiative. There is a relationship to the UN as partner of Choice. Two UN suborganisation collaborating with the PRI and have a seat in the Board of Directors of the PRI association.

First, with the UN Environment Programme Finance Initiative UNEP FI. The UNEP FI is based on over 200 Financial organisations like bank and insurance companies who are collaborating in sustainability and financial questions together. The activities compile promotion, creating ideas around environmental and social lesson learned and best practise sharing under the community of all members of listed financial institutions in the PRI (PRI Association, 2021a, 2021b).

Second, with UN Global Compact. Global compact is a policy and corporate network for politicians and corporate executives to share a common understanding of responsible and sustainable business decisions (PRI Association, 2021a, b). Over 7.000 corporate organisation and 135 countries which means executives, governments and politicians have signed the initiative on voluntary values and behaviours with focus on (PRI Association, 2021a, b):

- Anti-corruption
- Environmental Protection
- Human rights
- Labour rights
- Supporting UN goals.

In total, the mission of PRI is to foster the understanding of an economically efficient and sustainable as well as global financial investment system to support the long-term monetary value creation for customers in liaison with Environmental, Social and Governance structures (PRI Association, 2021a, b). Participants are inspired to contribute commonly designed ESG aspects in (PRI Association, 2021a, b):

- Adopt ESG Principles and Principles of the PRI
- Drive collaboration and networking
- Promote ESG Governance compositions
- Drive integrity
- Enrich accountability
- Address concerns to the sustainable economy and the financial system in regards of lesson learned, market practices and market regulations

9.5 Launch of the Sustainable Stock Exchange Initiative

The next step in the history of ESG was the launch of the Sustainable Stock Exchange Initiative SSEI in 2007 (Kell, 2018).

> "I call on stock exchanges around the world to join this effort" Ban Ki-moon 20017 – 2016 UN Secretary-General (Sustainable Stock Exchange Initiative, 2019)

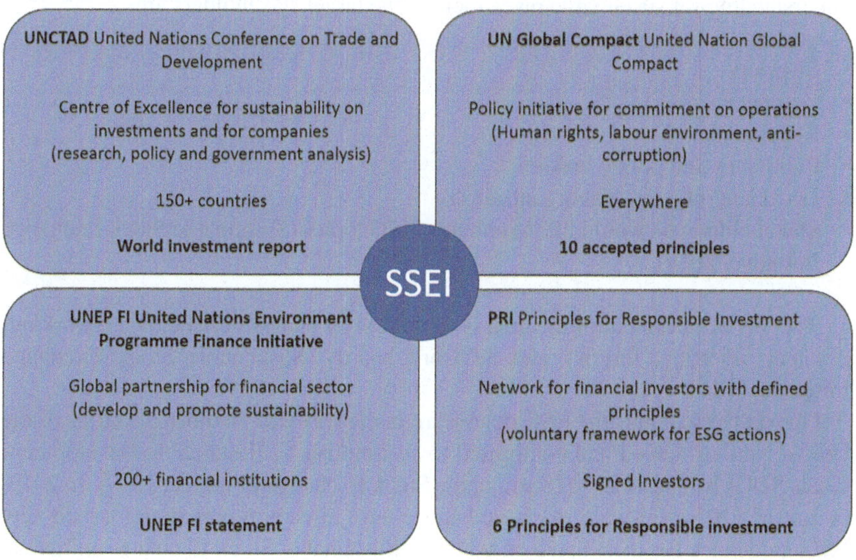

Fig. 9.5 Comparison of the different UN organisation and related organisation for ESG aspects within the Sustainable Stock Exchange Initiative SSEI. (Sustainable Stock Exchange Initiative, 2019)

The Sustainable Stock Exchange Initiative is a partner program by different UN collaboration platforms:

- UNCTAD United Nations Conference on Trade and Development: Division on Investment and Enterprise
- UNEP FI United Nations Environment Programme Finance Initiative
- UN Global Compact United Nation Global Compact
- PRI Principles for Responsible Investment (Sustainable Stock Exchange Initiative, 2019)

All ESG aspects are driven by the United Nation and its sub organisation, which is remarkable, because the common understanding is that the UN is usually blocked by Veto countries or other political discussions, but here it seems due to the need of understanding the climate change and the need to react from a mankind point of view, the United nation is on the driver seat. Further, in the aspect of dealing with big money and investors like stock exchanges, banks, investment trust and other it's a positive signal for a green economy and green finance future.

A comparison of the different UN organisations and related organisations described the different focus and stakeholder management of the related foundation in targeting ESG aspects (see Fig. 9.5 Comparison of the different UN organisation and related organisation for ESG aspects within the Sustainable Stock Exchange Initiative SSEI (Sustainable Stock Exchange Initiative, 2019).).

The mission of the SSEI is correlating with the four-supporting organisation of the UN to provide a framework to enhance Environmental Social Governance ESG understanding for sustainable investments. The target stakeholders are:

- Investors
- Companies
- Regulators
- Politicians and policy makers
- Local and international organisation
- Stakeholder who would like to enhance ESG topics (Sustainable Stock Exchange Initiative, 2019).

The UN achievement of the goal is supported by analysis elements, networking, efficient reporting, forums, and advisory boards (Sustainable Stock Exchange Initiative, 2019).

One delivery item is the ESG disclosure in the way that member countries of the United Nations agreed and committed to accomplish 17 Sustainable Development Goals SDGs by end of 2030 (Sustainable Stock Exchange Initiative, 2019). In 2019, 60 out of 110 world-wide stock exchanges have already reported and issued new ESG guidelines for their listed companies (Sustainable Stock Exchange Initiative, 2019). Therefore, the pressure on listed companies on stock exchanges is increasing to publish their own ESG guidelines and establish department to deal with ESG aspects. As an initial starting point, it is common to incorporate this into the HSE

Fig. 9.6 Four key elements of SSIC action plan. (Sustainable Stock Exchange Initiative, 2019)

Health Safety and Environment departments, if available as a stand-alone department.

Another delivery item is the climate action (Sustainable Stock Exchange Initiative, 2019). Initially sees as a tool to understand the risk management of climate change for investors, but nowadays seen as an opportunity for new investments like Solar panel and eMobility like the well-known electro car pioneer Tesla. Many investors have seen this as an additional growing item in their portfolio and the sky-rocking shares of Tesla and NIO are proven this concept in comparison to tractional petrol car manufacturer is working.

For investors, the outperforming of green or ESG driven companies and indicis is given in the last years with higher return on investment (share price increasing and divided payments) than in traditional non-green and non-ESG standard focusing markets and companies. By this effort, the SSEI is supporting with training material for stock exchanges as well as analysts to provide guidance how climate KPIs shall be listed in annual reports (Sustainable Stock Exchange Initiative, 2019; Kell, 2018).

The SSEI action plan is compiling of 4 key elements: Promote green products and services, strengthen environmental disclose of data, develop green financial markets, grow green network dialogue (see Fig. 9.6 Four Key elements of SSIC action plan.).

The 4 elements are a path forward in comparison to the other initiative with an action plan how to solve and educate the market participants on ESG topics. However, a ESG Project Management Office would be accelerate the process and implementation of standards, timelines and resources within the initiative and the companies who joined. Another improving aspect is Quality to ensure that standards and regulations are understood in the right matter and to have an independent department to ensure all employees up to the Sr. Management are applying the common ESG approach. Moreover, the global supply chain is common in our globalized economy and therefore ESG standards shall be applied by third party supplier or Contract Manufacturing Organisation CMO. To ensure tracking and reliable collaboration, a Quality department is a useful approach to be implemented to ensure the ESG standards are applied through the entire global supply chain.

In total, the Sustainable Stock Exchange Initiative has enhanced not only the focus on ESG factors within the companies. It has further enhanced the issuing of green bonds and ESG indicis because 42 of 110 stock exchange have already implemented it (Sustainable Stock Exchange Initiative, 2019).

9.6 COP21 Paris UN Climate Conference 2015

In 2015, the United Nation Climate change conference in Paris also known as COP21 or CMP11 took place. It was the 21st annual conference of parties COP and the 11th meeting of the party's CMP to the 1997 Kyoto Protocol (United Nations, 2021). The outcome of the COP21 was the Paris agreement which is a world-wide agreement of reacting on the climate change to reduce global greenhouse gas emission. The key result of the agreement was that global warming must be limited to below 2 °C in comparison to pre-industrial levels. Further, the net greenhouse gas emissions in the second half of the twenty-first century shall be zero (United Nations, 2021). In adoption of the Paris agreement, the 174 signed countries agree to target only 1.5 °C temperature increase, which might mean zero emissions between 2030 and 2050 according to scientists (Sutter & Berlinger, 2015; UNFCCC, 2015).

With the low pace of the implementation of the agreed COP21 results especially in Europe but also in other parts of the world, Greta Thunberg started a school strike in Sweden in 2018 which accelerated over the year to a global on the street Friday for Future movement (Hecking, 2018). The social and mobilization impact it quite high which is seen first by the European parliament election in 2019 due to massive interaction of new voters and vote for climate campaign by green parties and Friday for Future activism (Ulrich, 2019).

9.7 ESG as a New Factor for Investments

In 2018, the PRI has more than 1.600 members and represents US$ 70 billion investment assets which is a strong increase from the starting point of the overall UN ESG initiative. The support tools like leadership trainings and guidance's supported the engagement in decision making process for ESG investments (Kell, 2018). ESG is today a mainstream approach whereby many investors still see the only responsibility for itself to maximize the shareholder value for its clients in the way to pick the right stocks which are promising the maximum of the combination in share price increasing and dividend payment or ensure for private equity fully owned companies the maximum profit. Maximizing Return on investment and the

Markowitz's portfolio theory is the base line for those investors, and they argue that CSR and ESG are not the right tools for investment decisions (Markowitz, 1952, Kell, 2018). Further, the lack of reliable data and compilations like in quarterly figures are breaking the trend to apply ESG as a tool (Kell, 2018).

Although there is a certain amount of investors which see ESG as a negative item, the trend goes in the direction of ESG as a new factor for investments which is also summarized by Al Gore (Kell, 2018). 80% of the companies using Global Reporting Initiative GRI standards for ESG reporting. In addition, there were new standards with higher quality launch recently:

- International Integrated Reporting Initiative IIRC
- US-based Sustainability Accounting Standard Board SASB (Kell, 2018).

To unlock the potential of ESG: Artificial intelligence, machine learning, block chain, Big Data and the global trend of digitalization might be additional factors that ESG is coming more and more a simpler tool and user-friendly and not rocket-science in 2020s (Kell, 2018).

For entrepreneurs, the challenge is to circumnavigate the twentieth century thinking of free CO2 emission, cheap labour, and economy of scale. Today, green products and green services are the key feature for investors and customers (Sustainable Stock Exchange Initiative, 2019; Kell, 2018).

9.8 CSR and ESG as Two Entrepreneurial Tool Sets for Sustainability

Corporate Social Responsibility CSR and Environmental Social Governance ESG are both tools to support corporate companies and Non-Profit Organisations NGOs to have a positive picture of them in the world as well as underline their claim to make the world better from a society point of view.

Fig. 9.7 Comparison of corporate social responsibility CSR and environmental social governance ESG. (Gupta, 2021a, b)

With this claim companies are focusing on social and environmental aspects from inside but also more and more from outside of the organisation. Nowadays both concepts are using interchangeable by companies, stakeholders, and financial analysts. However, both theories are different: CSR was first and ESG was followed and developed based on CSR. Without CSR, no ESG would be going to be happened (Gupta, 2021a, b).

CSR is the tool to make companies accountable where ESG is a tool to make work and efforts measurable (see Fig. 9.7 Comparison of Corporate Social Responsibility CSR and Environmental Social Governance ESG.).

The comparison illustrates that CSR is not being measurable with hard numbers for stakeholders outside of the respective companies. To support social projects in the community is a positive factor for the society and helps companies to build up a long-term relationship in the area which the companies are operating. However, for financial analysts which are number, and data driven where looking for a comparable tool like ESG where you can compare carbon emission in tons on different companies in the same sector or branch of operation. On the other side, CSR and ESG embrace our society in a way that both initiatives support our society, people's well-being and our climate ecosystem.

CSR:

- Driver for sustainable projects
- Philanthropic and charitable approach on voluntary basis
- Enhancing visibility and marketing strategy for companies to support our society
- ISO 26000 standard supports to transfer CSR activities of companies into an action plan (Gupta, 2021a, b).

ESG:

- Big data and digitalization will help to calculate transparent sustainable and social KPIs
- Contribution as a compliance and risk tool with incorporating into companies' decision-making process for future investments
- Financial KPIs, social KPIs, environmental KPIs coming together in providing a bigger picture for financial analysts and the society about a company and its competition situation
- Return on investment, ethical and moral KPI as a joint effort to understand a company risk profile next to quality and cost of goods (Gupta, 2021a, b).

Greenwashing of KPIs is a sometimes-common practice and does not support sustainable solutions. Therefore, the combination of ESG and CSR as a two-way approach of voluntary CSR and data driven ESG is an interesting combination to support individuals, our society, and the ecosystem around us for a more sustainable future.

9.9 Regulations, ISO Standards and ISO Certification on ESG

In Europe and the US, the regulation is increasing on the topic of CSR and ESG. The EU has intensified its ESG Non-Financial Reporting Directive (Directive 2014/95/EU), and the United States Securities and Exchange Commission SEC is thinking to enhance its ESG aspects on financial reporting soon (Gupta, Understanding and Adopting ESG – An Overview [Part II: ESG Reporting as a Genesis of Fiduciary & Other Legal Obligations], 2021).

The International Organization for Standardization ISO based in Geneva issued several ISO standards regarding ESG (ISO, 2021; Certification Italy, 2021; Connexis, 2018; QMS Certification, 2020):

- ISO 14001:2015 Environmental management systems – Requirements with guidance for use
- ISO 50001:2018 Energy management systems – Requirements with guidance for use
- ISO 45001:2018 Occupational health and safety management systems – Requirements with guidance for use
- ISO 26000:2010 Guidance on social responsibility
- ISO 22000:2018 Food safety management systems – Requirements for any organization in the food chain
- ISO 37001:2016 Anti-bribery management systems – Requirements with guidance for use
- ISO 9001:2015 Quality management systems – Requirements
- ISO 19600:2014 Compliance management systems – Guidelines
- ISO/IEC 27001:2013 Information technology – Security techniques – Information security management systems – Requirements
- ISO 56002:2019 Innovation management – Innovation management system – Guidance
- ISO/TC 322 Sustainable finance
- ISO 14007:2019 Environmental management – Guidelines for determining environmental costs and benefits
- ISO 14008:2019 Monetary valuation of environmental impacts and related environmental aspects
- ISO 14030-1 Environmental performance evaluation – Green debt instruments – Part 1: Process for green bonds
- ISO 14030-2 Environmental performance evaluation – Green debt instruments – Part 2: Process for green loans
- ISO 14030-4 Environmental performance evaluation – Green debt instruments – Part 4: Verification program requirements
- ISO 14097:2021 Greenhouse gas management and related activities – Framework including principles and requirements for assessing and reporting investments and financing activities related to climate change
- ISO 37000 Governance of organizations – Guidance
- ISO 45000 FAMILY OCCUPATIONAL HEALTH AND SAFETY (ISO, 2021; Certification Italy, 2021; Connexis, 2018; QMS Certification, 2020).

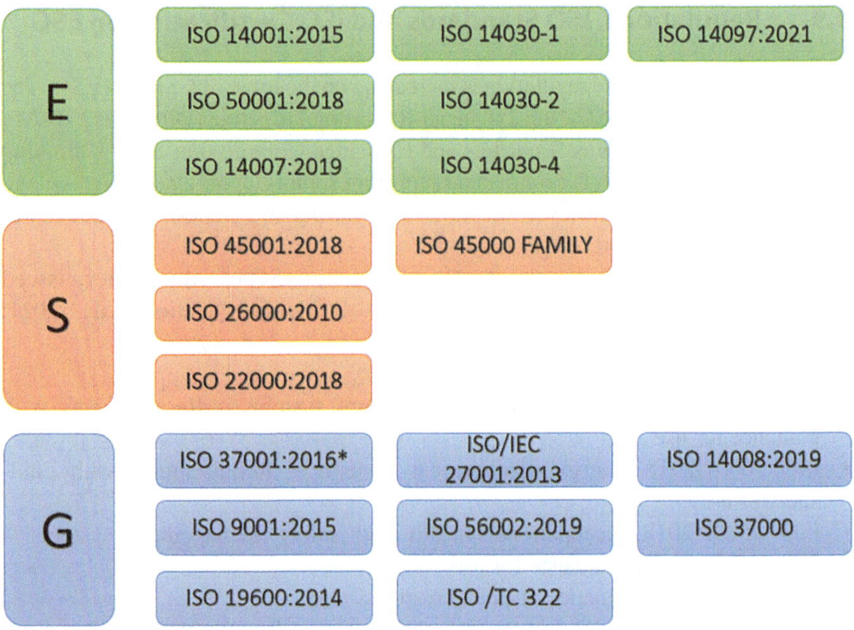

Fig. 9.8 Proposed linkage to ESG ISO standards for each single item: Social, Environmental and Governance, *in (Certification Italy, 2021) grouped as social item. (ISO, 2021; Certification Italy, 2021; Connexis, 2018; QMS Certification, 2020)

With the increasing number of ISO standards for ESG activities, the numbers of different non-ISO certificates might be increasing as well. Therefore, to establish an overall ISO certification for ESG in the future like ISO 9001:2015 for Quality Management Systems or ISO 13485:2016 for Quality Management systems regarding Medical Devices, where a certification by a notified body is being issued would be beneficial for the entire industry to follow the same approach as the other ISO Certificates examples has proven. A notified body e.g., BSI or TÜV Süd or TÜV Rhineland is needed for such a certification as a partner of choice for the manufacturing and service industry as well as for EU regulators.

On the other side for the US regulators such concept is supported but is not part of their Quality Management System. Thus, a common US solution, a dual approach, or a global-like solution like Basel III in the way that the global banking regulations was endorsed by G20 countries and is proven as a useful approach (BIS, 2011).

With many different ISO standards as listed, there is a better granularity for each single ESG aspect possible to underline the different environmental, social and governance functions (see Fig. 9.8 Proposed linkage to ESG ISO standards for each single item: Social, Environmental and Governance, *in (Certification Italy, 2021) grouped as social item (ISO, 2021; Certification Italy, 2021; Connexis, 2018; QMS Certification, 2020).

The grouping of the different ISO standard was conducted after an initial assessment and needs to be understood as a proposal and contribution to the ongoing discussion in corporate and scientific communities about ESG standardization and potential certifications.

ISO as a global organization started to discuss a new standard ISO/TC 322 on sustainable finance to connect environmental and social aspects together for the corporate financial market in 2020 (ISO, 2021). The aim is to understand the local national regulations and develop one standard for the whole market. Further, it's supported the overall UN ESG initiative and is a reaction of the 2019 World Economic Forum Sustainable Development Impact Summit in New to foster a higher implementation pace of a more sustainable finance world (ISO, 2021).

The elements are (ISO, 2021):

- Develop global sustainable ESG terminologies, principles, and standards for the financial markets incl. Banks, investors, and insurance companies
- Reduce confusion and unnecessary efforts of market participants on ESG aspects as well as preventing green washing or sustainability washing
- Facilitator role for developing innovation regards ESG sustainable products within the financial market
- Support standards for third party evaluation for sustainable financial products and global supply chain
- Define standard KPIs for ESG performance to be measurable by market participants on financial products (ISO, 2021).

The overall approach of ISO/TC 322 is supporting the initial idea of the United Nations to roll out the ESG benchmarking from the stock exchanges to the listed companies included investors and bank and finally convince all companies to be part of the ESG journey to supporting sustainable product and services for us and planet earth.

The need of guidelines from independent organizations was seen in the DWS case – the investment arm of the Deutsche Bank – with its former employee Desiree Fixler and discussed in the Wallstreet Journal (Frühhauf, 2021; Finanzen.net., 2021; Die Zeit, 2021). The case was a discussion about ESG approaches and ESG investment figures in DWS financial documentation (Frühhauf, 2021; Finanzen.net., 2021; Die Zeit, 2021). The discussion also proved the ongoing uncertainty and the need of reliable KPI figures for ESG investments. Especially the reputation of such investment companies can be damaged like the 14% drop of DWS shares price in the end of August 2021 has shown (Frühhauf, 2021; Finanzen.net., 2021; Die Zeit, 2021).

Therefore, ESG is being understood as risk management tool to support the value of a company and its performance (Gillan et al., 2021), but currently ESG is still a risk itself since the standards from regulations are not clearly enough. However, on a long-term goal and strategy, ESG-focused companies will be more successful (Cini & Ricci, 2018).

References

BIS. (2011). *Basel III: A global regulatory framework for more resilient banks and banking systems* – Revised version June 2011. Von https://www.bis.org/publ/bcbs189.htm abgerufen.

Campbell, D. (2013). *Bank of America finishes merger of Merrill lynch into parent.* Von https://www.bloomberg.com/news/articles/2013-10-01/bank-of-america-finishes-merger-of-merrill-lynch-into-parent-1-abgerufen

Certification Italy. (2021). *Sustainability certification's ESG rating 2020.* Von https://www.certificationsrl.it/en/certifications/sustainability-esg-rating2020/ abgerufen

Cini, A. C., & Ricci, C. (2018). CSR as a driver where ESG performance will ultimately matter, Symphonya. *Emerging Issues in Management* (symphonya.unimib.it), *1*, 68–75.

Connexis. (2018). *ISO: ESG standards & development.* Swiss. Von http://www.connexis.ch/files/product_sheet_iso_esg_standards.pdf abgerufen.

Die Zeit. (2021). *US-Börsenaufsicht ermittelt wegen Greenwashings gegen DWS.* Von https://www.zeit.de/wirtschaft/unternehmen/2021-08/deutsche-bank-tocher-dws-url-dws-fondsanbieter-deutsche-bank-tochter-us-boersenaufsicht-ermittlungen-nachhaltigkeitsa abgerufen.

Euramco. (2021). *EURAMCO asset management Glossar/Wissensdatenbank.* Von https://www.euramco-asset.de/glossar/environmental-social-governance-esg/ abgerufen.

Fidelity. (2021). *ESG masterclass.* Von https://www.fidelity.de/nachhaltigkeit/?ef_id=EAIaIQobChMIpc-Cm9uw8gIVmLp3Ch0Uvw5JEAMYAiAAEgKohvD_BwE:G:s&s_kwcid=AL!8201!3!517572569424!p!!g!!esg&utm_source=google&utm_medium=cpc&utm_campaign=Wholesale_Acquisition_ESG_ESG&utm_term=esg&utm_content=searcha abgerufen.

Finanzen.net. (2021). *DWS-Aktie mit Kursrutsch: US-Börsenaufsicht untersucht wohl Nachhaltigkeitsangaben der Deutsche Bank-Tochter.* Von https://www.finanzen.net/nachricht/aktien/beschoenigte-angaben-dws-aktie-mit-kursrutsch-us-boersenaufsicht-untersucht-wohl-abgerufen

Frühhauf, M. (2021). *DWS weist Vorwürfe entschieden zurück.* Frankfurter Allgemeine Zeitung. Von https://www.faz.net/aktuell/finanzen/dws-weist-vorwuerfe-entschieden-zurueck-17505019.html abgerufen.

Gillan, S. L., Koch, A., & Starks, L. T. (2021). Firms and social responsibility: A review of ESG and CSR research in corporate finance. *Journal of Corporate Finance*, Elsevier Vol. 66(C).

Gupta, P. (2021a). *Understanding and adopting ESG – An overview [Part II: ESG reporting as a genesis of fiduciary & other legal obligations].* Von https://www.rhtgrace.com/understanding-and-adopting-esg-an-overview-part-ii-esg-reporting-as-a-genesis-of-fiducia abgerufen.

Gupta, P. (2021b). *Understanding and adopting ESG – An overview part I: The evolution of ESG from CSR.* Von https://www.rhtlawasia.com/wp-content/uploads/2021/03/ESG-Part-I-The-Evolution-of-ESG-from-CSR.pdf abgerufen.

Hecking, K. (2018). *Globale Klimakrise: Gretas Aufstand.* Der Spiegel. Von https://www.spiegel.de/wissenschaft/natur/greta-thunberg-das-gesicht-der-globalen-klimabewegung-a-1241185.html abgerufen.

ISO. (2021). *International organization for standardization.* International standards. Von https://www.iso.org/home.html abgerufen.

Kell, G. (2018). The remarkable rise of ESG, Forbes. Von https://www.forbes.com/sites/georgkell/2018/07/11/the-remarkable-rise-of-esg/?sh=54e411821695 abgerufen.

Köhler, P., & Landgraf, R. (2020). *ESG-KRITERIEN: Blackrock greift beim Klimaschutz durch.* Von https://www.handelsblatt.com/finanzen/banken-versicherungen/banken/esg-kriterien-blackrock-greift-beim-klimaschutz-durch/26000222.html?ticket=ST-6001466-RZdGOqF26LWR7seH0bhG-ap5 abgerufen.

Lewis, M. (2011). *The big short: Inside the doomsday machine* (Reprint ed.). Norton & Company.

Markowitz, H. (1952). Portfolio Selection. *The Journal of Finance, 7*(1), 77–91.

McKay, A., & Randolph, C. (2015). *The big short.* Regency Enterprises Plan B Entertainment.

O'Neill, J. (2001). *Building better global economic BRICs* (Global economics paper no. 66 (66)). Goldman Sachs & Co. Von https://www.goldmansachs.com/insights/archive/archive-pdfs/build-better-brics.pdf abgerufen.

O'Neill, J., Wilson, D., Purushothaman, R., & Stupnytska, A. (2005). *Global economics paper no: 134: How solid are the BRICs? Goldman Sachs economic research.* Von https://www.goldmansachs.com/insights/archive/archive-pdfs/how-solid.pdf abgerufen.

PRI Association. (2021a). *Principles for responsible investment brochure 2021*. PRI Association.

PRI Association. (2021b). *Principles for responsible investment.* PRI association. Von https://www.unpri.org/pri/about-the-pri abgerufen.

QMS Certification. (2020). *ISO 14001 boosted by ESG companies.* Von https://qms-certification.com/blog/iso-14001-boosted-by-esg-companies-2/ abgerufen.

QONTIGOX. (2021). *DAX® 50 ESG (PR) EUR.* Von https://www.dax-indices.com/index-details?isin=DE000A0S3E04 abgerufen.

Sustainable Stock Exchange Initiative. (2019). *About the SSE initiative.* Von https://sseinitiative.org abgerufen.

Sutter, J., & Berlinger, J. (2015). Final draft of climate deal formally accepted in Paris. *CNN*. Cable News Network, Turner Broadcasting System, Inc. Von https://edition.cnn.com/2015/12/12/world/global-climate-change-conference-vote/ abgerufen.

Ulrich, B. (2019). *Europawahlergebnis Angriff aus dem Kinderzimmer, Die Zeit.* Von https://www.zeit.de/politik/deutschland/2019–05/europawahlergebnis-klimapolitik-fridays-for-future-protestwahl-gruene?utm_referrer=https%3A%2F%2Fwww.google.com%2F abgerufen.

UNFCCC. (2015). *Adoption of the Paris agreement – By the president – Draft decision -/CP.21.* Von https://unfccc.int/resource/docs/2015/cop21/eng/l09r01.pdf abgerufen.

United Nations. (2004). *Who cares wins. The global compact, connecting financial markets to a changing world.* United Nations Department of Public Information.

United Nations. (2005). *Innovative financing for sustainability a legal framework for the integration of environmental, social and governance issues into institutional investment.* Asset Management Working Group: United Nations Environment Programme.

United Nations. (2021). *Framework convention on climate change.* Von Paris climate change conference – November 2015. https://unfccc.int/process-and-meetings/conferences/past-conferences/paris-climate-change-conference-november-2015/paris-clim abgerufen.

Vink, D., & Thibeault, A. (2007). ABS, MBS and CDO compared: An empirical analysis. *The Journal of Structured Finance, 14*(2), 27–45.

White, B. (2008). Bear Stearns passes into Wall Street history. *Financial Times.* Von https://www.ft.com/content/d42c01d2-2d8d-11dd-b92a-000077b07658 abgerufen.

Wiggins, R., Piontek, T., & Metrick, A. (2014). *Yale program on financial stability case study: The Lehman brothers bankruptcy A: Overview.* Yale University.

Stakeholder der CSR

10

Before you react, think. Before you spend, earn. Before you criticize, wait. Before you quit, try.

Ernest Hemingway

10.1 The Concept of Stakeholder

In context of economic theories, the term "stakeholder" was used as early as 1963 in an internal memo of the Stanford Research Institute (SRI), defined as "those groups without whose support the organization would cease to exist") (Freeman, 2010). In the classic form of stakeholder theories, the typical stakeholders in a business organisation are especially the financiers, the customers, the suppliers, the employees and the society, to whom the business owes its success (see Fig. 10.1).

This term was later on expanded by Edward Freeman into "any group or individual who can affect or is affected by the achievement of the firm's objectives"). Thus, Freeman includes a number of further stakeholders, including the government, competitors, consumer advocates, the media, and other stakeholders, while emphasizing the interaction between the company and the stakeholders (Freeman et al., 2007, S. 3). In addition, employees and managers are often portrayed as two separate stakeholder groups, since they often represent very different perspectives due to their roles in the organization. In general, Freeman divides the stakeholders into two subgroups: the primary (direct) stakeholders and the secondary (indirect) stakeholders (see Fig. 10.2 Stakeholder according to Freeman. Based on (Freeman et al., 2007, S. 7)).

Freemann contradicts Friedman's shareholder value approach, which asserts that the responsibility of the manager consists solely of the responsibility towards the

T. Dathe et al., *Corporate Social Responsibility (CSR), Sustainability and Environmental Social Governance (ESG)*, Management for Professionals,
https://doi.org/10.1007/978-3-030-92357-0_10

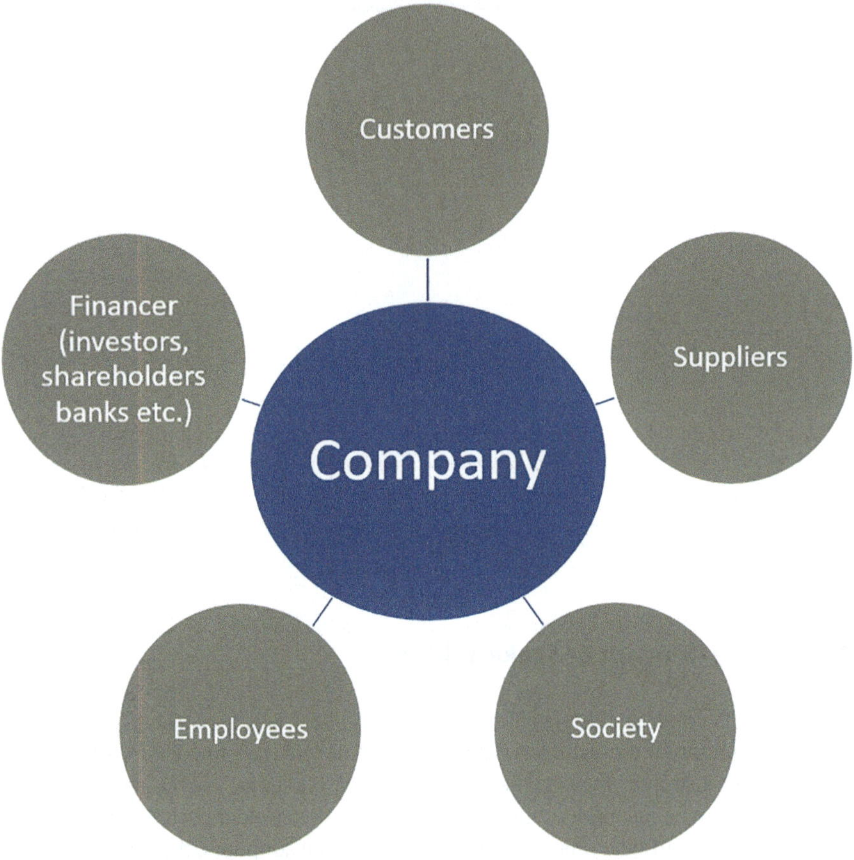

Fig. 10.1 Stakeholders in the classic stakeholder theory. (Interpretation of Freeman et al., 2007, S. 3)

shareholders (Friedman, 1970). According to Freemann, the company's added value is a result of interactions between relevant stakeholders, thus the companies, represented by the managers, has a social responsibility towards all stakeholders. Based on contractual agreements and statutory provisions, those stakeholder groups have a legitimate interest in the business process (Freeman et al., 2007, S. 7).

Other researchers point out that the shareholders are not always interested in long-term ownership of the company, but potentially rather focused on short-term profit maximization through speculation at the stock market (Crane & Matten, 2016, S. 63). Sumantra Ghoshal observes dazu (Ghosthal, 2005): "Most shareholders can sell their stocks far more easily than most employees can find another job."

For applications in business practice, the stakeholders are often defined according to the individual business model and the purpose of the stakeholder analysis. The stakeholders are often grouped by internal and external stakeholders according

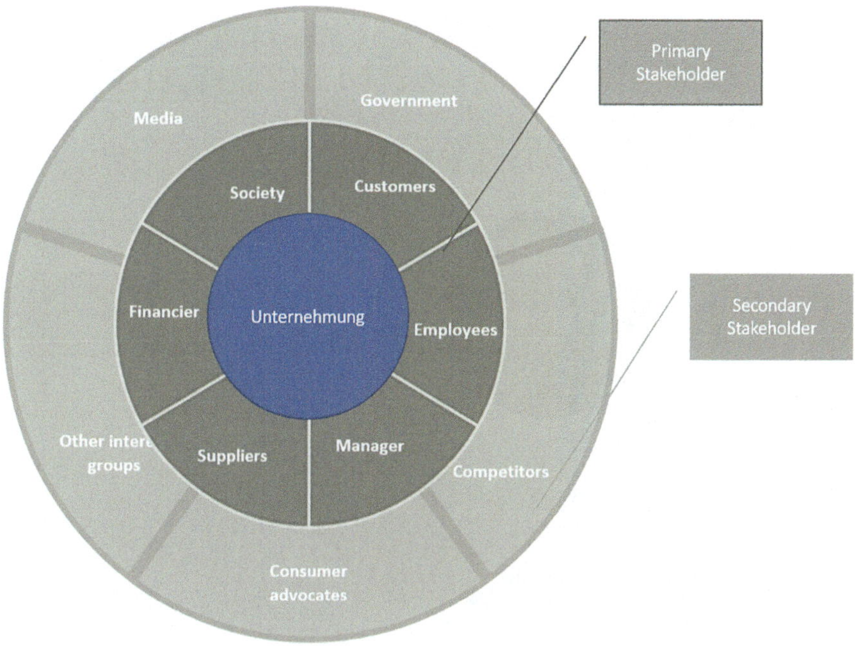

Fig. 10.2 Stakeholder according to Freeman. (Based on Freeman et al., 2007, S. 7)

to their legal relationship with the business organisation (see Fig. 10.3 Internal and external stakeholder groups. Based on (Helmold et al., 2020)).

Later on, Rowley proposes a network model of stakeholders. In his opinion, the stakeholders have stakeholders of their own who have an indirect impact on the company through the network (Rowley, 1997). The network theory improves the classic stakeholder framework by implementing the indirect stakeholder groups. Due to the large number of stakeholders involved, however, this model is criticized for lack of clarity.

10.2 Corporate Governance

The managers are obliged to organize the business operations in interest of the shareholders. The main duties of the managers toward the shareholders include the following aspects (Parkinson, 1993, S. 76–100):

- Duty to act for the benefit of the company, both in terms of short-term financial performance and the long-term survival of the company;
- Professional duty. Managers are obliged to run the company in the most professional and effective manner;
- Duty of care. The managers are legally bound to conduct corporate affairs with the expected level of commitment.

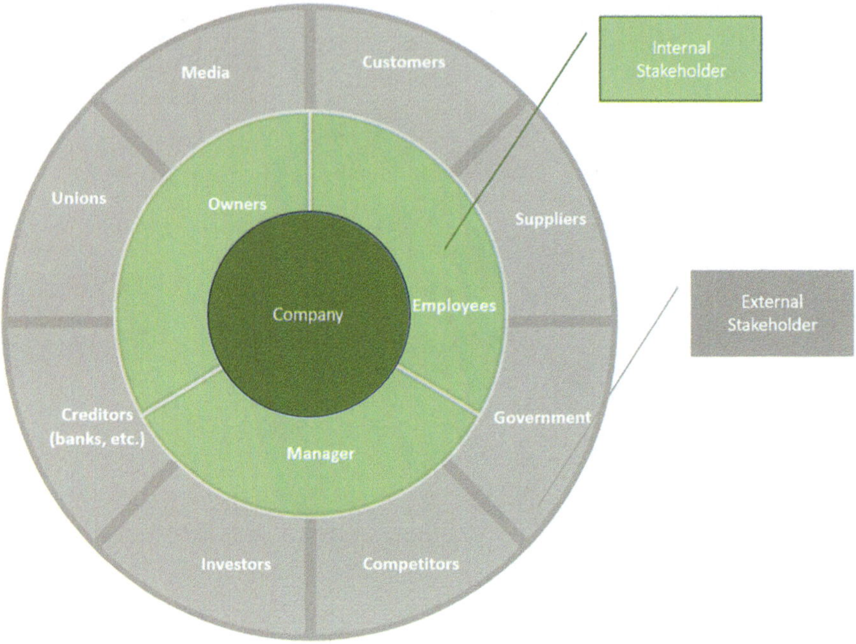

Fig. 10.3 Internal and external stakeholder groups. (Based on Helmold et al., 2020)

The shareholders' control of the company over the business executives is referred to as "corporate governance" in narrower sense. "Corporate governance" in a broader sense stands for the entirety of rules, processes and organisational structures through which the stakeholders can exercise their rights to monitor and control the business through the managers. Typically, the stakeholders practise the control through participation in the determination of the strategic goals, the exercise of supervision and the reward or reprimand of the management (Parkinson, 1993, S. 157).

Unfortunately, the managers in the practice don't always act in interest of the stakeholders as they are supposed to. For example, in September, 2015, the US Environmental Protection Agency (EPA) accused Volkswagen AG of illegal manipulation of emissions tests for the diesel vehicles. Subsequently, the VW share price fell significantly and the scanal triggered a severe crisis in the entire automotive industry (Welt, 2015).

The above example is a classic principal-agent dilemma that is characterized by the following aspects:

(a). Conflict of interest. The manager ("agent") receives the assignment from the shareholder ("principal") to run the business with duly care. However, the manager also has an interest of his own that may differ from that of the "principal". For example, due to his personal performance award, the manager prefers short-term financial gains to strategically important investments in the company's future. For the pursuit of personal power, the manager is also prone to highly risky actions.

(b). Information asymmetry. The principal has only limited insight into the business process, the actions of the manager, the risks, etc. Thus, the manager can take advantage of the situation that the principal is not able to understand the company in its operative business due to lack of information.

The problems arising from such a principal-agent dilemma in complex stakeholder relationships can be improved through more effective stakeholder relationship management.

10.3 Stakeholder Relationship Management and CSR Strategies

With the constant advancement of stakeholder interests in the business world, the initial focus on customer relationship management is expanded to include holistic stakeholder relationship management (SRM) (Crane & Matten, 2016, S. 199 ff.).

In the past, stakeholder relationships were mostly conceived in a confrontational constellation. The adventurous protests by environmental and animal rights activists, the calls for boycotts against exploiters of child labour, the occupy movements, the withdrawal of funding by creditors, are only a few examples of negative impacts of stakeholder relationships. However, in recent times, stakeholder relationships have become increasingly cooperative. Companies have recognized the advantages of active approaching stakeholders, so as to develop harmonious strategies. The cooperation between companies and stakeholders has often been observed in the following fields (Seitanidi & Crane, 2014, S. 201):

- Cooperation with supervisory authorities or NGOs in favour of environment management and social projects.
- Marketing projects as cooperation with aid organizations.
- Partnership with governmental institutions to address social, educational, health and transport issues.
- Cooperation with NGOs, trade unions and government organizations to improve working conditions and to combat child labour and other human rights violations in developing countries.

Building a collaborative stakeholder relationship is a costly process. This necessary expense often imposes a barrier for medium-sized companies that is difficult to overcome (Crane & Matten, 2016, S. 203). In addition, the company needs to focus on the strategically important stakeholders, since it is little possible to satisfy all stakeholders at the same time (Jones & Hill, 2013). Depending on the business strategy, the selection of stakeholders could be made based on (Mitchell, 1990):

- the perceived potential power of the stakeholders to actively impact the business operations;
- the perceived legitimacy of the stakeholders to impact the business operations and if such influences are perceived as desirable and appropriate;
- to what extent the demands of the stakeholders must urgently be attended to.

References

Crane, A., & Matten, D. (2016). *Business ethics. Managing corporate citizenship and sustainability in the age of globalization* (4th ed.). Oxford University Press.

Friedman, M. (1970) *The social responsibility of business is to increase its profits*. New York Times Magazine, 13 September 1970, 122–126.

Freeman, R. E. (2010). *Strategic management: A stakeholder approach*. Cambridge University Press.

Freeman, R. E., Harrison, J. S., & Wicks., A. C. (2007). *Managing for stakeholders*. Yale University Press.

Ghosthal, S. (2005). Bad management theories are destroying good management practices. *Academy of Management Learning and Education, 4*(1), 75–92.

Helmold, M., Dathe, R., Dathe, T., Groß, D.-P., & Hummel, F. (2020). *Corporate social responsibility im internationalen Kontext: Wettbewerbsvorteile durch nachhaltige Wertschöpfung*. Springer Gabler.

Jones, G., & Hill, C. (2013). *Strategic management theory: An integrated approach* (11th ed.). Cengage Learning.

Mitchell, W. (1990). Interest groups: Economic perspectives and contribution. *Journal of Theoretical Politics, S., 2*, 85–108.

Parkinson, J. (1993). *Corporate power and responsibility*. Oxford University Press.

Rowley, T. (1997). Moving beyond dyadic ties: A network theory of stakeholder influence. *Academy of Management Review, 22*(4), 887–910.

Seitanidi, M., & Crane, A. (2014). *Responsible business and social partnership: A research handbook*. Routledge.

Welt. (2015, September 21). 16 Milliarden – die teuerste Dummheit der VW-Geschichte. Von https://www.welt.de/wirtschaft/article146646993/16-Milliarden-die-teuerste-Dummheit-der-VW-Geschichte.html, retrieved 01.12.2021.

The State and Civil Society 11

Nearly all men can stand adversity, but if you want to test a man's character, give him power.

Abraham Lincoln

11.1 The State and Regulations

The government is the highest political institution of a state. In the economic context, the objectives of governmental regulations for the market are mainly seen in the following fields (Benz et al., 2007, S. 74 ff.):

1. Natural monopoly. Due to the nature of business, the competition in some business sectors is very limited due to the market entry barriers, the enormous investment requirements and the strong economies of scale etc. The main reason for governmental supervision could be ensuring of a nationwide infrastructure and primary care with affordable prices and tariffs.
2. Negative externality. Externality means that the business activities of the company cause economic, ecological or social impacts on bystanders. The externality can be both positive (e. g. increase in job offers) and negative (e. g. environmental pollution). The main goal of state supervision is to internalize the costs of negative externality, e. g. promoting environment-friendly technical systems by taxation of emissions, in order to reduce pollution.
3. Information asymmetry. The state of information asymmetry is discussed in the classical principal-agent theory. The main focus of government regulation in this

T. Dathe et al., *Corporate Social Responsibility (CSR), Sustainability and Environmental Social Governance (ESG)*, Management for Professionals,
https://doi.org/10.1007/978-3-030-92357-0_11

regard is consumer protection. Especially in the financial sector, market entry is restricted by special regulations. In the service sector, the supervisory authorities may request the service providers to provide guarantee to their customers.

Some regulations are not initiated by the public sector, but by private companies, business associations or civil law organizations ("non-governmental organizations", NGOs), in order to harmonize ethical standards in business practices. Such regulations are typically enforced through market mechanisms. Regulations initiated by private organizations are called private regulations. In the financial industry in particular, the most regulatory provisions often come from private institutions, for example from the Financial Conduct Authority (FCA) or the Prudential Regulation Authority (PRA) in the United Kingdom, as well as the Securities and Exchange Commission (SEC) in the United States. Many NGOs make special economic, social and environmental contributions to the society through their political activities (Götz, 2008).

The business organisations are often interested in self-regulation on a voluntary basis. The self-regulation is often advocated in the literature with the following arguments (van Calster & Deketelaere, 2001):

- By acting proactively, companies can shape the rules in an economically compatible way, e. g. that the CSR activities are better rewarded or can be better linked to their own economic activities.
- The freedom of design (e. g. the free choice of technology for emissions certificates) can reduce administrative costs.
- The implementation of voluntary regulations is not bound to timely obligations, thus there is little time pressure.

Regulations play an important role in corporate CSR performance and can be shaped by the state, NGOs or companies. In practice, there are different constellations of co-operations of the above actors as designers of regulations (see Fig. 11.1):

i. Regulations by the government. In particular in the form of nation states, the state plays a central role in administering regulations. Despite their growing importance in regulation, the cross-border governmental institutions such as the UN or the OECD (Organization for Economic Co-operation and Development) have yet to address the enforcement rules with awards and sanctions due to lack of effective legal means.

ii. Self-regulation of private business. The codes of conduct is a well-used CSR instrument for self-regulation. There are also a number of professional and industry-related rules of conduct as a result of the cooperation of individual companies and professional associations.

iii., iv. and V. Regulation through co-operations between the government, NGOs and private companies. The contribution of the government and NGOs in such co-operations has an indicative function and is usually universally formulated.

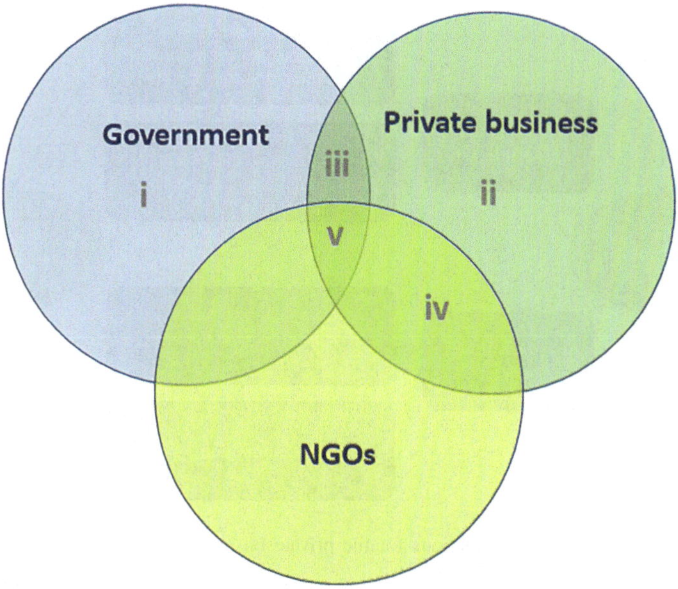

Fig. 11.1 Designers of regulations. (Based on Crane and Matten, 2016, S. 518 ff.)

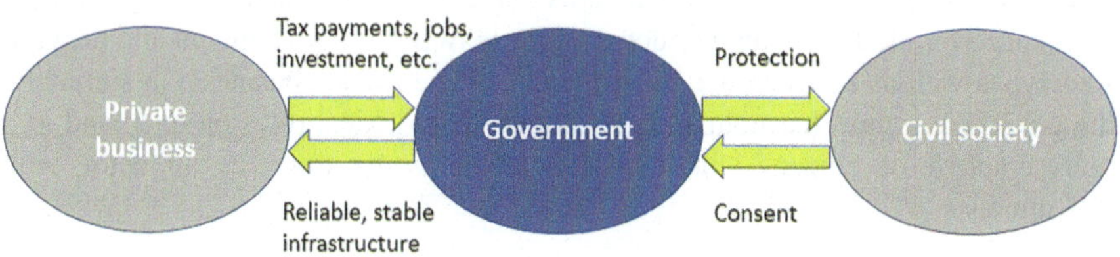

Fig. 11.2 The government's role between the private sector and the civil society. (Based on Mitchell, 1990)

11.2 The Role of Government

The government plays a complex role between private business and civil society (see Fig. 11.2 The government's role between the private sector and the civil society. (Based on Mitchell, 1990).

First, the government bears the responsibility to protect the interests of the general public with regulatory mechanisms and the civil society depends on the protective function of the government as a natural representative of the interests of the citizens. Secondly, the government also depends on the consent of society for self-preservation. Next, in order to meet the economic requirements of the civil society, such as high employment rate and stable improvement of income levels, the government also needs the contribution of private companies in terms of tax payments, job

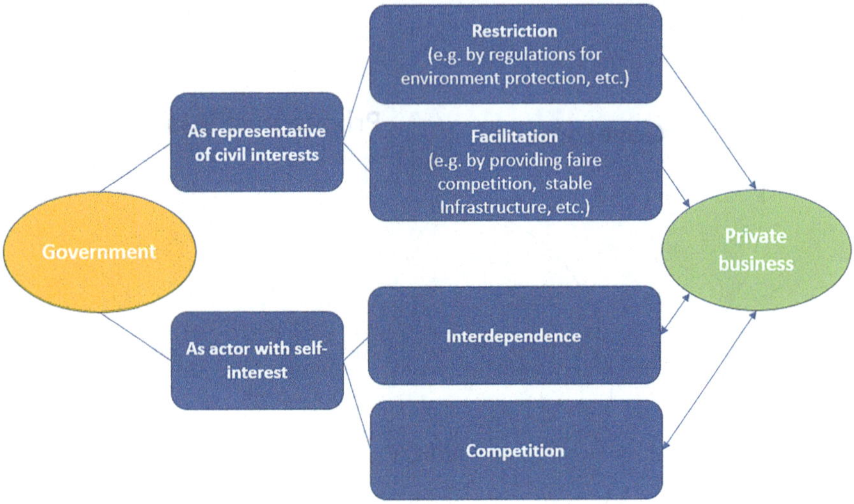

Fig. 11.3 The government's functions for the private business. (Based on Crane and Matten, 2016, S. 493)

offers, investments, etc. On the other hand, the economic achievements of the private sector also rely on the infrastructures that can only be guaranteed by the government. Overall, there is an interdependence between the government and the civil society, as well as between the government and the private business. In summary, the government must harmonize its apparently paradoxical roles on one hand as a representative of citizens' interests and at the same time, as an actor with self-interests.

11.3 Political Power of Private Business

In reality, the government is often criticized for representing the political interest of the private sector and suppressing citizens' interests. The influence of companies on the state can be described mainly in three dimensions (Getz, 1997):

- Access to the decision maker. Personal contact is a form of direct access. Examples of indirect access include advertising and media campaigns that support or question certain political decisions.
- Public access to information. The influence of the companies can be made public and thus visible to the general public, or private, i. e. the politicians are addressed behind closed doors without the knowledge of the general public.
- type of arguments. This dimension describes whether the companies try to convince the decision-maker through factual arguments or put pressure in the foreground.

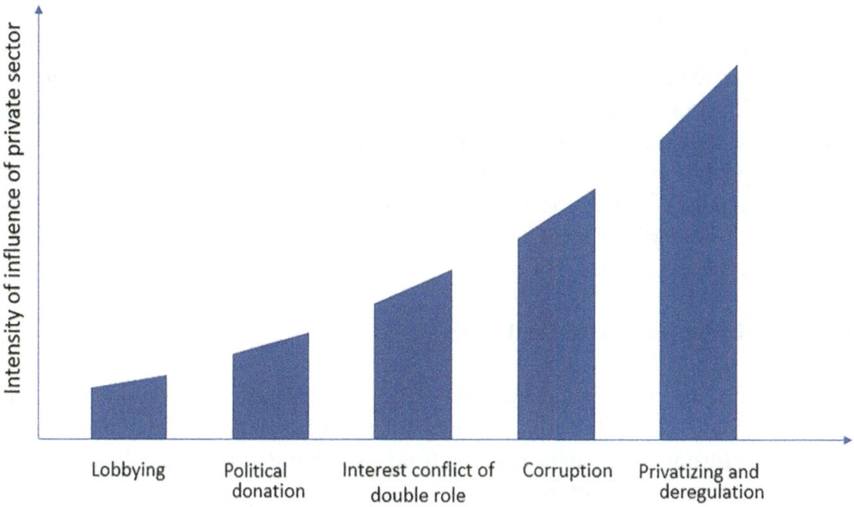

Fig. 11.4 Various forms of political influence of private sector

Ethical problem cases occur increasingly when companies exert private influence through direct access to politics. With increasing intensity, the political influence of the companies can be described in the following grades (see Fig. 11.4):

- lobbying.
- Party donations.
- Conflict of interest due to a dual role.
- corruption.
- privatization and deregulation.

Lobbying

Lobbying is an attempt of the business sector to access lawmakers by providing convincing arguments rather than exerting explicit pressure. Lobbying is the weakest form of direct influence of private sector on the government. However, it can be particularly problematic when politicians are put under pressure with one-sided information (McGrath, 2005).

Due to the enormous potential impact of such influence on the legislature, lobbying is nowadays often engaged with profession efforts. Lobbying is usually operated by:

- Professional lobbyists,
- Managers or internal departments for government relations or public affairs,
- Specialized consulting firms
- Industry and trade associations.

Political Donations

In a democratic system, the political parties are often dependent of party donations. On one hand, the parties have a legitimate need for donations ("legitimacy"). On the other hand, as a representative of the interests of civil society, they are obliged to disclose the information about the donations ("accountability").

In the public, donations to political parties by the private sector are generally viewed critically as a "fee" to enforce their political decisions. Some NGOs are also suspected of supporting the political parties financially to implement their own strategic goals (Harris & Lock, 2002).

Conflict of Interest Due to Dual Roles

- As the formal head of the most powerful national state, the President of the United States Donald Trump also embodies the business empire of the Trump family. His important advisors come from close family members who also have a strong economic background.
- The former Italian Prime Minister Silvio Blusconi dominated the media landscape in the country parallel to his political activities through his possession of 3 influential television stations and a large publishing house.
- The former Chancellor of Germany Gerhard Schröder took on important posts in the private sector, including as chairman of the supervisory board of Nord Stream AG (whose operating object is the pipeline operation for the transport of natural gas from Russia to Germany) of the Russian mineral oil company Rosneft, in addition to other lobbying activities.

The list can go on indefinitely. Overall, it almost seems to be a trend that important political offices become subsequently business representatives or that politicians are involved in private business. In addition, former politicians ("elder statesman") are also criticized for overtly paid consulting activities and lecture fees after they have given up their mandates. However, some people see the strong link between politicians and the economy as an advantage in that they are better able to make more optimal economic and political decisions in the interest of the general public. Others, however, view this connection with doubts and suspect if the politicians are likely to misuse their power to change the "rules of the game" in favour of the private business.

Corruption

Corruption is an abuse of power and can be understood as a violation of the public interest to specific individual advantages (Rogow & Lasswell, 1963, S. 132–133). While the previously mentioned forms of attempts by private firms to take political influences arouse ethical concerns, the act of corruption is a clear breach of legal and ethical standards. It is particularly problematic in cultures and regions where corruption is widespread and interpreted as a "service of friendship". It is often difficult for companies not participating in corruption even to gain a foothold at the regional market.

Privatization and Deregulation

Privatization is the formal transformation of public assets into private property. Deregulation is the dismantling of restrictive regulations by the government. In core replaces the private business the government in a partial function (Schubert & Klein, 2021).

For example, Deutsche Bahn was converted into an AG under private law in 1994. However, due to the financial crisis, the planned IPO was stopped and the company remains 100% in public hand to this day. In general, privatization and deregulation may increase cost efficiency. However, the lifting of institutional protections could result in disadvantages, especially for sparsely populated rural regions, since the focus for infrastructure planning is no longer on political but on economic considerations.

Despite various concerns about the increasing political power of private business, companies have proven in the past that they can also make a particularly positive contribution to the general public with their political power. For example, the MNEs use their global influence to improve the environmental, socio-political and human rights standards for individual citizens in different political and cultural environments.

11.4 NGO and Social Enterprise

NGO is the abbreviation for "Non-Governmental Organization". A non-governmental organization is not legitimized by a public mandate, nor does it aim at profit, but represents the interests of the civil society through its commitment, especially in the environmental and socio-political issues (cf. Bundeszentrale für

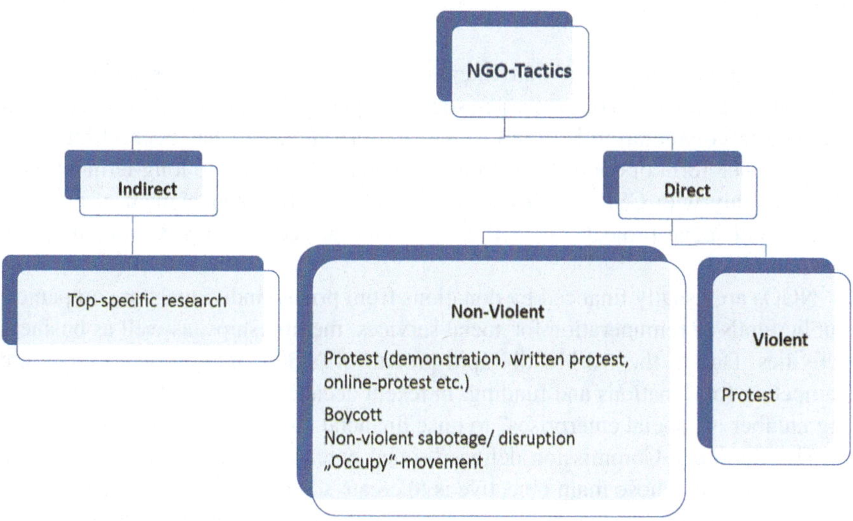

Fig. 11.5 Taktics of NGOs

politische Bildung, 2017). Greenpeace and World Wide Fund for Nature WWF are examples of the most influential NGOs.

NGOs tend to be strong at promoting their cause, mostly by attracting public attention, their chosen tactics are ethically not always undisputed (see Fig. 11.5 Taktics of NGOs.).

Indirect Action: Topic-Related Research in Advance

In the past, NGOs have often been criticized for spreading misleading information. Today, they make more efforts for objective research, although for some smaller anti-economic groups the subjective interpretation of the facts is still in the foreground. Overall, however, NGOs enjoy more trust in civil society than private companies (Whawell, 1998).

Direct Action with Use of Force

The use of force for a good cause is highly controversial in a civilized society. The past experience shows, however, that the NGOs effectively generate publicity with this approach. The use of force during protest actions is particularly popular with people who see no alternatives to attracting social attention (Crane & Matten, 2016, S. 451).

Direct Action: Without Use of Force

For the most part, however, the NGOs act non-violently, often choosing from the following measures:

- Protest (demonstration, written protest, online protest, etc.);
- Boycott;
- Non-violent sabotage or disruption;
- "Occupy" movement.

A variety of today's NGOs are internationally active, focusing on topics such as environment protection or combating social inequality. Despite conflicting goals, an increase in collaboration between NGOs and private sector has been observed in practice. The form of cooperation ranges from simple project to long-term partnerships, mainly with CSR objectives, in particular for the management of environmental and social projects, as well as economic projects (Crane & Matten, 2016, S. 451).

NGOs are usually financed by donations from private individuals or companies, public funds or remuneration for social services, memberships, as well as business activities. Due to the worldwide rapid growth of NGOs, many organizations are competing for donations and funding. In recent decades, there has been an increasing number of "social enterprises" to raise financial means for desired social goals.

The European Commission defines "social enterprise" as: "… an actor in the social economy whose main objective is to create social impact rather than make a profit for its owners or shareholders". It deals with an entrepreneurial and innovative provision of goods and services for the market and uses its profits primarily to achieve social goals. It is run openly and responsibly and particularly involves employees, consumers and stakeholders who are affected by its business activities (EUROPEAN COMMISSION, 2011).

Social enterprise can be understood as an intermediate form of NGO and a classic business organisation. Like NGOs, social enterprises pursue charitable CSR goals, while at the same time strive for reasonable profit. The social enterprises model offers a solution to the increasing difficulty for funding of non-profit activities as an alternative to dependence on charitable donations and government funding. With the economic success, social enterprises are able to secure their sustainable pursuit of the social goals.

The collaboration of non-profit organizations with the private sector often brings about bilateral benefits: while the NGO can improve the financial standing as a basis for the sustainable achievement of the social missions, the business benefits from the market-effective publicity. However, there are some critical opinions about this connection:

- The private business often has dominant influence in the joint activities. Ultimately, the business benefits far more than the intended recipients of the social benefits.
- Due to the close collaboration, the NGOs are "contaminated" ("co-opting") with economic thinking. In other words, they tend to adopt the point of view of the business.

A healthy distance from the private business is critical for the NGOs, since their credibility is mainly based on their independence.

(Vgl. (Crane & Matten, 2016, S. 471 ff.))

References

Benz, A., Lütz, S., Schimank, U., & Simonis, G. (2007). *Handbuch governance.* Hrsg.

Bundeszentrale für politische Bildung. (2017, October 1). *NGOs – Nicht-Regierungsorganisationen.* Von http://www.bpb.de/nachschlagen/zahlen-und-fakten/globalisierung/52808/ngos, retrieved 01.12.2021.

Crane, A., & Matten, D. (2016). *Business ethics. Managing corporate citizenship and sustainability in the age of globalization* (4th ed.). Oxford University Press.

European Commission. (2011, October 25). *Communication from the commission: Social business initiative: Creating a favourable climate for social enterprises, key stakeholders in the social economy and innovation.* Von Abgerufen 17.12.19: https://eur-lex.europa.eu/LexUriServ/LexUriServ.do?uri=COM:2011:0682:FIN:EN:PDF abgerufen.

Getz, K. (1997). Research in corporate political action: Integration and assessment. *Business & Society, 36*(1), 32–72.

Götz, N. (2008). Reframing NGOs: The identity of an international relations non-starter. *European Journal of International Relations, 14*(2), 231–258.

Harris, P., & Lock, A. (2002). Sleaze or clear blue water? The evolution of corporate and pressure group representation at the major UK party conferences. *Journal of Public Affairs, 2*(2), 136–151.

McGrath, C. (2005). Towards a lobbying profession: Developing the industry's reputation, education and representation. *Journal of Public Affairs, 5*, 124–135.

Mitchell, W. (1990). Interest groups: Economic perspectives and contribution. *Journal of Theoretical Politics, 2*, 85–108.

Rogow, A. A., & Lasswell, H. D. (1963). *Power corruption and rectitude*. Prentice-Hall Englewood Cliffs.

Schubert, K., & Klein, M. (2021). *Das Politiklexikon: Begriffe. Fakten. Zusammenhänge*. J.H.W. Nachf: Dietz Verlag.

van Calster, G., & Deketelaere, K. (2001). The use of voluntary agreements in teh European Community's environental policy. In E. Orts & K. Deketelaere (Eds.), *Environmental contracts* (pp. 199–246). Kluwer.

Whawell, P. (1998). The ethics of pressure groups. *Business Ethics: A European Review, 7*(3), 178–181.

Shareholders 12

Let your joy be in your journey, not in some distant goal.

Tim Cook

12.1 Shareholders and Stakeholders in Corporate Governance

Stakeholders are the challengers and drivers of a corporate organisations from inside (Executives, Managers but also labour representatives in workers councils) and outside (Governments, Non-profit organisation NGOs, Regulators, Competitors, and others). For public-traded companies, shareholders are as the same time stakeholder from an outside point of view.

Company shares can be distributed in many pieces known as stock shares by public listed companies on stock exchanges e.g., New York's Dow Jones, Nasdaq, or London's FTSE. On another hand, large investment companies mainly from the Wall Street can hold higher numbers of share. e.g., Blackrock or Vanguard with its Exchange-traded funds also known as ETFs. Further, individuals are also being shareholders and can express its influence through their voting rights at the annual shareholder meeting to support and not support the Executive team. The shareholder earnings are dividend payment and share price increasing which is the basis of the success of the Corporate America model in which executive and shareholders working together to enhance the financial output of a company (Zingales, 1994; Lazonick & O'Sullivan, 2000).

The corporate management needs to cover those stakeholders and is carried out by professional executives who shall commit to the following behaviour (Parkinson, 1993, S. 76–100):

T. Dathe et al., *Corporate Social Responsibility (CSR), Sustainability and Environmental Social Governance (ESG)*, Management for Professionals,
https://doi.org/10.1007/978-3-030-92357-0_12

- Duty to trade for the benefit of the company.
- Duty of professionalism – to run the company organisation in the most professional and effective way.
- Due diligence – dealing with company affairs with the expected level of commitment.

According to Friedman's classic shareholder value approach, the only responsibility of managers is their responsibility to shareholders (Friedman, 1970). In the stakeholder theories, too, shareholders are among the most important stakeholders in any company (Freeman, 2010).

As a rule, the individual shareholders own too small numbers of shares with voting rights to have a significant influence on business transactions. However, they are entitled to ask questions on the summarizing annual reports, to exercise their voting rights at the Annual General Meeting or to resell the shares at their own discretion (Zingales, 1994; Lazonick & O'Sullivan, 2000).

The manager generally has in-depth specialist knowledge and has a direct influence on ongoing business. This gives them the de facto opportunity to manipulate the information to be made available to the shareholders. As a rule, his personal interest does not match the interests of the shareholders. For example, the takeover of a company (Merger & Acquisition) would have a negative economic impact on the company value and be disadvantageous for the shareholders, because the manager could still find this opportunity attractive because it expands his personal power. Further, the rule for forward looking statements is described in the International Safe Harbor Privacy Principles (Corwell law school, 2021). Moreover, companies need to apply data privacy rule according Safe Harbor act (Court of Justice of the European Union, 2015).

This type of corporate constellation (see Table 12.1 Constellation of shareholder and manager in the principal-agent relationship) of different objectives and simultaneous information asymmetry is referred to in the literature as the principal-agent dilemma. The problem is that goal achievement by the principal depends on the agent's action. However, the agent has its own goals that do not coincide with those of the principal. Solutions are sought for the principal, with which he can change the agent's mind to act in his own interest.

The entirety of rules, processes and structures with which the shareholders exert influence on the company via the managers, for example by helping to shape the strategic goals, exercising supervision and awarding or punishing management, are referred to in the literature with the term "corporate governance" summarized (Parkinson, 1993, S. 157).

An important body of the corporations is the supervisory board, which is mandated by the shareholders to advise, monitor and control the management (the board of directors). Due to the necessary independence, the following principles, among others, should apply when appointing the non-executive members of the supervisory board (Boyd, 1996):

Table 12.1 Constellation of shareholder and manager in the principal-agent relationship

	Manager (agent/contractor)	Shareholder (principal/client)
Task	Carry out the order in the interests of the shareholder	Assess or reward the manager's performance
Goal setting	Maximizing personal income, the power base in the company or in the industry as well as future career	Maximizing the share price and the dividend yield (shareholder earnings) Profit maximization of the company
Direct impact on business operations	Strong	Small amount
Knowledge of business	Usually incoming	Usually superficial
Information content about current business	Detailed (operational responsibility)	Compact
Source of information	Internal operating units and divisions	Executive manager

Parkinson (1993, S. 157)

- The appointment should be made independently of the management, i. e. either at the general meeting by the shareholders directly or by the supervisory board (term is limited and a usually an age limited is incorporated in the appointment)
- The personalities to be appointed should be able to obtain information about the company or to assess the company's business situation objectively. Nowadays, Diversity and Inclusion is part of the process for the board members and is an important factor for the society and environment.
- The personalities to be appointed should not have any personal financial interest in the company that is different from the interests of the shareholders. This means, among other things, that the remuneration for your work may not significantly exceed a reasonable framework for your time or other expenses.
- The personalities to be appointed should, if possible, come from outside the company. However, there are independent and depended Board members. Independent ones are e. g. scientists, business peers and business influencer. Dependent one's member of financial institutions and worker council representatives.
- The order should only be valid for a limited period of time in order to prevent the development of dependency on the company.

However, the implementation of the above principle of independence often proves to be difficult in practice. Due to the high demands on the competence of the members, they often come from the same circle as the managers (as former managers or managers of other companies), so that their neutrality is questioned by critics (Gorden, 2002). In particular, there is criticism when the chairman of the board of directors' changes to the chair of the supervisory board after leaving the board of directors. It is criticized that this creates a great risk that previous wrong decisions can lead to new wrong developments. In Germany, there is a cooling off period of two years (Bundesministerium der Justiz und für Verbraucherschutz, 2021). But after this period, the independency of former colleagues and peer is questioned.

It is not uncommon for members of the supervisory board to hold several supervisory board mandates at the same time. The question that arises here is whether the quality of the control work will suffer if there are several mandates. Further ethical questions arise when the same person holds mandates at competing companies. Also, quite common especially in US companies is that the CEO is also permanent member of the Board of Directors and not just a guest member. To sum up, independency is important but not always give be in public listed Companies.

In Germany, at least one employee representative must be elected to the supervisory board in order to exercise the co-determination rights for employees as stakeholders in the company. The involvement of the union-related employee representative also increases the complexity of corporate governance. (Bundesministerium der Justiz und für Verbraucherschutz, 2021).

In order to induce the managers in the above-mentioned principal-agent relationship into a mode of action preferred by the shareholders, it is now common practice to agree a performance-related bonus with the managers. The main problem in this practice is that the effect of such bonus payments is hardly measurable, since the performance of the manager cannot be viewed in isolation from the performance of the organization as well as from other external influencing factors. This effect has the signal, that the share price is driver of the business and not the CSR baseline. To improve this situation Environmental Social Governance ESG guidelines was created based on the Corporate Social Responsibility CSR principles (Gupta, 2021).

In the past, the high manager bonus payments have repeatedly caused high-profile discussions about justice. Society questions whether managers really do so much more than the average employee (Luttmer, 2021). Such headlines do not cast a positive light on companies with regard to the CSR issue.

12.2 Shareholders and Stakeholders in the Financial Market

Shareholders are confronted with other stakeholders in the financial market which have different goal settings and inspirations.

Rating Agencies

The risk for the shareholders already exists when they decide to enter the stock market as a market participant. If the market value is far above the real value of the shares, one speaks of a bubble ("price bubble", "economic bubble" or "baloon") e. g. the Dotcom bubble in 2000s. One of the first recorded bubbles was the tuple mania in Amsterdam which is referend in literature and movies like Wallstreet: Money Never Sleeps (Stone, 2010). Since after the stock bubble has popped, the expected future payments of new shareholders will be significantly below the market value of the shares or the shares held will most likely only be obtained at a much lower price when resold, so buying the overvalued shares means a losing deal for the shareholder. The creditworthiness analysis of the rating agencies provides a decision-making aid (Topol, 1991).

The rating agencies (Eng. “Credit Rating Agency CRA”) are private companies that try to evaluate the creditworthiness (= creditworthiness) of states, companies and other corporations or financial products, etc. The rating agencies are obliged, among other things, to determine a true and fair view of the financial situation of a company or to assess the trustworthiness of an investment opportunity.

The most influential rating agencies worldwide include the following service providers that dominate the United States (“Big Three”) (McLean & Joe, 2010):

- Standard & Poor’s Financial Services
- Moody’s Investors Service and
- Fitch Ratings.

The result of your analysis is expressed in predefined credit ratings, ranging from “AAA” for “best quality” to “C” or “D” for “insolvent”. The rating interprets a probability of the extent to which the companies will exist in the long term or can repay their debts due (e. g. due dividend payments).

Lenders such as banks also use the rating information for their decision on lending. Depending on the risk level, you determine whether you accept a loan application or with what risk premium (McLean & Joe, 2010). The rating information is intended to reduce the information asymmetry between shareholders and the company.

There are also some repeated criticisms against the practice of the rating agencies:

- The rating agencies can only work with existing data. This implies that possible misleading “balance sheet cosmetics” from the individual companies will be reflected in the rating result.
- Particularly negative results arouse concern and can even trigger financial emergencies in the companies assessed (self-fulfilling prophecies).
- The rating agencies carry out the evaluation for relatively high fees. As a company from the private sector, you yourself are interested in receiving orders in the future. The intention to retain customers could flow into the rating process and thus falsify the result, especially for their clients.

The issue of rating financial instruments against fees was one of the sources of the Financial Crisis in 2008, where subprime markets for real estate obligations and instruments like CDOs collapse and the world economy was fallen in one of its biggest economic crises like the Covid 19 downturn in 2020 (McLean & Joe, 2010).

Accounting Firms

Confirmation by independent auditors increases the credibility of the annual reports. This is intended to reduce the information asymmetry for corporate governance. Most often it concerns the examination of the regular final reports.

Upon receipt of the audit assignment, the examiners are prompted to determine the focus of the examination and the examination schedule, to carry out the examination work properly and then to document the result. If the test is passed, the company receives an auditor's report.

The final examination essentially includes the following content (ICAS, 2019):

- The control tests;
- The examination of the overall business situation;
- The process investigation, especially in the area of accounting, as well as other core areas e. g. sales, purchasing, etc.;
- The system check, in particular regarding the ERP system (Enterprise Resource Planning = Business Resource Planning) or MIS (Management Information System);
- On the authorization plan or implementation;
- On the error-free implementation of the transactions;
- The substantive audit procedures;
- Examination of individual cases: further examinations of specific business transactions based on the preceding risk-oriented random sample examination;
- Checking the accuracy of the data contained in economic reports by random sampling, including checking the source documents;
- Random check of business transactions in payroll accounting;
- Several samples are necessary for each type of transaction;

The aim of the audit is to reduce the information asymmetry between the shareholders and the company. Due to their knowledge and their international network, the large companies usually only commission the largest auditing or accounting firms ("Big Four"):

- Deloitte
- Ernst & Young EY
- KPMG
- PricewaterhouseCoopers PwC.

In addition to auditing, the above companies also offer other services, in particular tax advice, transaction advice and their own corporate or management consultancy. Because the audit firms themselves are economically dependent on the engagements, their dependence on the general public is often called into question as seen in the Wirecard and Enron scandal (Fröndhoff, 2021).

Furthermore, they are in particular criticized because of the creation of tax optimization plans for large multinational customers. It is felt to be injustice that the large corporations are relieved of tax with the help of specialists, while normal employees, smaller individual and medium-sized companies, have to bear the higher taxes (Süddeutsche Zeitung, 2015). In particular, big tech companies like Amazon and Microsoft are in the news about this issue (Sackmann, 2021).

After the Wirecard scandal in 2020 and the bankruptcy of DAX listed company, the German regulation are under review especially the rotation of the accounting firms every 10 years e. g. Deutsche Post is rotating from PricewaterhouseCoopers PwC to Deloitte in 2023 (Fröndhoff, 2021). The regulators would like to reduce it further in the future. Other results of the accounting scandal of Wirecard and Ernst & Young EY, was the enhancement of the German Blue chips index DAX from 30 to 40 companies in 2021 (Fröndhoff, 2021; Cünnen, 2021).

Insider Trading

Although every investor tries to get as much information as possible about the company, for example through the annual reports or the evaluations of the rating agencies. In insider trading, however, the limit of ethical behaviour is exceeded.

Insider trading means the use of non-public information (inside information) for stock market transactions (Moore, 1990). In doing so, an attempt is made to achieve an unfair profit maximization with financial instruments with the information advantage over the rest of the investors.

Insider trading is clearly an unfair act that violates ethical norms. The reprehensibility of this action can be justified with the following arguments (Moore, 1990):

- **Fairness.** The information asymmetry gives the person with the information advantage an unfair advantage over other stock market participants.
- **Misappropriation of property.** Using valuable information that Insider Traders are not authorized to access. This is tantamount to misappropriating the property of the company concerned.
- **Damage to investors and the market.** Insider traders could benefit at the expense of ordinary investors, making the market riskier and threatening market confidence.
- **Undermining the trust relationship.** The insider trader uses the information advantage in the principal-agent relationship for his personal advantages. In doing so, he destroys trust as the basis for a solution to the dilemma.

Insider trading is also one of the Discussion point for ESG behaviours which is seen as not acceptable for the UN initiative (Gupta, 2021; PRI Association, 2021).

In most cases, insider trading is not only a violation of ethical norms, but also a criminal act that can destroy investors' confidence in the market and thus impair the functionality of the capital market (Carroll & Buchholz, 2012). The US SEC (U.S. Securities and Exchange Commission SEC) has launched the Regulation FD (Fair Disclosure) 17 CFR 240, 243, and 249 to define a fair disclosure of data. Many financial supervisory authorities such as the American SEC (U.S. Securities and Exchange Commission; eng. = US stock exchange supervisory authority) constantly check the stock market for noticeable price movements. One of the most recent known cases of exposed insider trading involves Raj Rajaratnam, founder of the Galleon hedge fund group. He was accused of having illegally obtained around US $ 64 million in profits through 2009 through illegally obtained in-house information. He was found guilty of insider dealing in 2011 by the US District Court in

Manhattan, New York, and his sentence was set to 11 years in prison. Before him, 13 compiles were also convicted (Spiegel Online, 2011).

12.3 Responsible Shareholding

As important stakeholders, the shareholders can use their influence on the CSR performance of the company.

One speaks of shareholder democracy when it comes to the fact that individual shareholder (groups) come together to vote together democratically on individual matters for the current business or, if necessary, to oppose the implementation of corresponding CSR goals Decision of managers to enforce. This approach can be implemented particularly well in practice if a few shareholders with significant company share pacts share similar ethical ideas (Parkinson, 1993, S. 160–166). Otherwise, a fundamental distinction is made between the approaches of "shareholder activism" and "socially responsible investment SRI".

In the situation of "shareholder activism", activist individuals or groups (e. g. NGOs) invest in order to put themselves in the shoes of shareholders or, by exercising their rights as shareholders in the company, to make ethical decisions for the operational business influence. The influence can take place as follows:

- Obtaining internal information (right to information).
- By defining rewards or penalties that direct managers towards desirable behaviour.
- At the general meeting, the shareholders and management should expressly draw their attention to CSR issues.
- Increase the pressure on managers through media-effective appearances.

However, the communication effort with shareholding or activism is often relatively high, so that practicable compromises have to be made.

Next to CSR, also ESG is supporting the approach of sustainable investing and shareholding (Gupta, 2021; PRI Association, 2021). With "Socially Responsible Investments SRI", the socially-oriented shareholders invest exclusively in companies that not only promise economic success, but also meet a number of ethical criteria.

The three-pillar model should be used as the basis for establishing SRI criteria. Accordingly, the ethical goals can be defined in the following three dimensions also known as ESG:

- **Environmentally oriented goals**. e. g. emissions control, use of environmentally friendly new technologies.
- **Socially oriented goals**. e. g. donations for education and art, charitable sports activities.
- **Economic goals**. e. g. new job offers, fair salary level.

Table 12.2 Examples of SRI criteria

Negative criteria	Positive criteria
Abortion	Equal opportunities for women and men
Alcohol consumption	Equal opportunities about ethnic origin
Animal testing	Funding for education
Birth control	Organic farming
Child labor	Promotion for art
Genetic engineering	Reduction of greenhouse gas emissions
Occupational safety	Support for socially disadvantaged households
Political influence of religion	
Pornography	
Tobacco use	
Use of atomic energy	
Use of fossil energy	
Weapons production	

Based on (Crane & Matten, 2016, S. 264

Other objectives are also conceivable.

According to the empirical studies, some activist hedge funds have achieved well above average returns. This implies that activist shareholding can be not only more socially acceptable, but also more economically profitable for investors (Wood & Dysart, 2015). In other words, investors' interest in directly influencing corporate CSR strategies can be both idealistic and economically motivated. Consequently, the SRI criteria can be determined according to the ideology of the shareholder, but can also be based on the results of a previous market research (Mackenzie, 1998). The Selection rules can be both positive and negative and do not have to correspond to general ethical norms (see Table 12.2 Examples of SRI criteria. Based on. (Crane & Matten, 2016, S. 264).

To sum up, CSR and ESG are the driver of ethical and responsible shareholding and influencing the stock market and the public-listed companies in the future.

References

Boyd, C. (1996). Ethics and corporate governance: The issues raised by the Cadbury report in the United Kingdom. *Journal of Business Ethics, 15*, 167–182.

Bundesministerium der Justiz und für Verbraucherschutz. (2021). *Aktiengesetz*. Von https://www.gesetze-im-internet.de/aktg/ abgerufen 11.09.2021.

Carroll, A., & Buchholz, A. (2012). *Business and society: Ethics, sustainability and stakeholder management* (8th ed.). South-Western Cengage Learning.

Corwell law school. (2021). *15 U.S. Code § 78u-5 – Application of safe harbor for forward-looking statements*. Von https://www.law.cornell.edu/uscode/text/15/78u-5 abgerufen.

Court of Justice of the European Union. (2015). *Judgment in case C-362/14 maximillian schrems v data protection commissioner: The court of justice declares that the commission's US safe harbour decision is invalid. Court of Justice of the European Union*. Von https://curia.europa.eu/jcms/upload/docs/application/pdf/2015-10/cp150117en.pdf abgerufen.

Crane, A., & Matten, D. (2016). *Business ethics. Managing corporate citizenship and sustainability in the age of globalization* (4th ed.). Oxford University Press.
Cünnen, A. (2021). *Handelsblatt*. Von Die zehn Aufsteiger stehen fest – wie die Vergrößerung den Dax verändern wird.: https://www.handelsblatt.com/finanzen/anlagestrategie/trends/dax-40-die-zehn-aufsteiger-stehen-fest-wie-die-vergroesserung-den-dax-veraendern-w abgerufen.
Freeman, R. E. (2010). *Strategic management: A stakeholder approach*. Cambridge University Press.
Friedman, M. (1970, September 13). The social responsibilty of business is to increase its profits. *New York Times Magazin*.
Fröndhoff, B. (2021). *Deloitte wird neuer Abschlussprüfer der Deutschen Post. Handelsblatt*. Von https://www.handelsblatt.com/unternehmen/dienstleister/wirtschaftspruefer-deloitte-wird-neuer-abschlusspruefer-der-deutschen-post/27154094.html?ticket=ST-3791857-C abgerufen.
Gorden, J. (2002). What Enron means for the management and control of the modern business corporation: Some initial reflections. *University of Chicago Law Review, 69*, 1233–1250.
Gupta, P. (2021). *Understanding and adopting ESG – An overview part I: The evolution of ESG from CSR:*. Von https://www.rhtlawasia.com/wp-content/uploads/2021/03/ESG-Part-I-The-Evolution-of-ESG-from-CSR.pdf abgerufen 11.09.2021.
ICAS. (2019, December 18). *Tests of control and substantive testing*. Von https://www.icas.com/education-and-qualifications/tests-of-control-and-substantive-testing-student-blog abgerufen 11.09.2021.
Lazonick, W., & O'Sullivan, M. (2000). Maximizing shareholder value: A new ideology for corporate governance. *Economy and Society, 29*(1), 13–35.
Luttmer, N. (2021). *Boni für Manager: „Das System krankt als Ganzes" Frankfurter Rundschau*. Von https://www.fr.de/wirtschaft/boni-fuer-manager-das-system-krankt-als-ganzes-90661458.html abgerufen 11.09.2021.
Mackenzie, C. (1998). The choice of criteria in the ethical investment. *Business Ethics: A European Review, 7*(2), 81–86.
McLean, B., & Joe, N. (2010). *All the devils are here: The hidden history of the financial crisis, portfolio*. Penguin.
Moore, J. (1990). What is really unethical about insider trading? *Journal of Business Ethics, 9*, 171–182.
Parkinson, J. (1993). *Corporate power and responsibility*. Oxford University Press.
PRI Association. (2021). *Principles for responsible investment. PRI association*. Von https://www.unpri.org/pri/about-the-pri abgerufen 03.09.2021.
Sackmann, C. (2021). *Focus Online*. Von 123 Milliarden Euro Steuern gespart: Wie US-Tech-Riesen auch in Europa den Fiskus austricksen: https://www.focus.de/finanzen/boerse/konjunktur/debatte-um-globale-mindeststeuer-80-milliarden-euro-steuern-gespart-wie-us-tech-riesen-auch-in-europa-den-fiskus-austricksen_id_13363679.html abgerufen 11.09.2021.
Spiegel Online. (2011, Oktober 13). *Richter straft die Wall Street ab*. Von https://www.spiegel.de/wirtschaft/unternehmen/historisches-insider-urteil-richter-straft-die-wall-street-ab-a-791747.html abgerufen 11.09.2021.
Stone, O. (2010). *Wall Street: Money never sleeps. Movie. 20th Century Fox*. Von https://en.wikipedia.org/wiki/Wall_Street:_Money_Never_Sleeps abgerufen.
Süddeutsche Zeitung. (2015, Januar 31). *Luxemburg-Leaks – Warum ein Professor PwC für eine Gefahr für die Gesellschaft hält*. Von https://www.sueddeutsche.de/wirtschaft/luxemburg-leaks-steuertrickser-vom-dienst-1.2208497-2 abgerufen 11.09.2021.
Topol, R. (1991). Bubbles and volatility of stock prices: Effect of mimetic contagion. *The Economic Journal, 101*(407), 786–800.
Wood, J., & Dysart, T. (2015, July 23). *Assessing the merits of an activist investor's point of view*. Von Transaction Advisors: https://www.transactionadvisors.com/user?destination=node/3466 abgerufen 11.09.2021.
Zingales, L. (1994). The value of the voting right: A study of the Milan stock exchange experience. *Review of Financial Studies, 7*, 125–148.

13 Consumers

Change will not come if we wait for some other person or some other time. We are the ones we've been waiting for. We are the change that we seek.

Barack Obama

13.1 Consumer Protection

Customers are the starting point of company's success. On the other hand, customer protection is part of the CSR and ESG approaches (Gupta, 2021; PRI Association, 2021).

The basis of the private sector's social obligations lies in its economic success. This includes, above all, that the companies offer long-term useful products or services as required by the public at reasonable conditions and price according to the launched marketing and price strategy (Schindler, 2012).

In terms of economic activities, consumers are generally disadvantaged, among other things by the stronger financial position or the knowledge advantage of the companies and thus their enormous contractual advantages. Nevertheless, society demands that the most important consumer rights are guaranteed, which include above all the right of access to non-dangerous products, the right to just and sustainable economic and social development, and environmental protection (UNCTAD, 2016).

In the EU and in particular in Germany there are Customer protection NGO's like Stiftung Warentest institution which are an independent organisation under civil law. The base line of the customer protections to perform comparison tests, inform customers and give public advises (Warentest, 2021).

T. Dathe et al., *Corporate Social Responsibility (CSR), Sustainability and Environmental Social Governance (ESG)*, Management for Professionals,
https://doi.org/10.1007/978-3-030-92357-0_13

In the UK, there is customer protection rights under law in regards of (Gov UK, 2021):

- Builders;
- Contracts;
- Counterfeit goods;
- Credit and store cards;
- Faulty goods;
- Poor service;
- Rogue traders.

Next to Customer protection is also in the objective of the society to reduce customer and price discrimination (Png, 1991)as well as investigate quality aspects of customer products as an essential comparable point in the online and offline market especial in the retail market (Xu et al., 2021) (see Fig. 13.1 Retail shopping card (photo: Dr. René Dathe).)

The United Nations Conference on Trade and Development (UNCTAD) has set up a set of principles called United Nations Guidelines to support legislators, law enforcement agencies and the arbitration boards of the member states in promoting consumer protection Nations for consumer protection ("United Nations Guidelines for Consumer Protection") published (UNCTAD, 2016) (see Table 13.1 Objective of the United Nations guidelines for consumer protection).

Fig. 13.1 Retail shopping card. (Photo: Dr. René Dathe)

Table 13.1 Objective of the United Nations guidelines for consumer protection (UNCTAD, 2016)

C	Assisting countries in achieving or maintaining adequate protection for their populations as consumers
O	Assisting countries in curbing abusive business practices by all companies, nationally and internationally, that adversely affect consumers
N	Encourage the development of market conditions that allow consumers more choice at lower prices
S	Facilitating production and distribution in response to consumer needs and desires
U	Facilitating the development of independent consumer groups
M	Promote a high level of ethical behavior among those in the production or distribution of goods and services to consumers
E	Promotion of international cooperation in the field of consumer protection
R	Promotion of sustainable consumption

Table 13.2 Scope of legitimate consumer needs (UNCTAD, 2016)

P	Access to sufficient information for consumers to make informed decisions based on individual wants and needs
R	Availability of effective arbitration or settlement of consumer disputes
O	Consumer access to essential goods and services
T	Consumer education, including education about the economic, social and environmental consequences of consumer choices
E	Freedom to set up consumer and other relevant groups or organizations, including the opportunity for such organizations to express their views in the decision-making processes that affect them
C	Promotion and protection of the economic interests of consumers
T	Promotion of sustainable consumer behavior
I	Protecting consumers from threats to their health and safety
O	Protection of consumer privacy and the free flow of information around the world
N	Protection of vulnerable or disadvantaged consumers
S	The level of security for consumers using e-commerce that is no less than for other forms of business

The United Nations guidelines for consumer protection also specify the scope of the legitimate needs of consumers as follows and thus increase the operationality of the above-mentioned principles (see Table 13.2 Scope of legitimate consumer needs). The guidelines also aim to promote international cooperation between the member states and the exchange of experience on consumer protection (UNCTAD, 2016).

In accordance with the United Nations guidelines for consumer protection, the European Commission has issued a series of EU consumer protection regulations under the designation Consumer Contract Law, to deal with contractual issues relating to business transactions between companies and consumers, e.g. Right of withdrawal, legal guarantee and unfair contractual conditions to regulate. These concerns the following binding legal provisions (see Table 13.3 Consumer contract law (Europäische Kommission, 2019).

Table 13.3 Consumer contract law (Europäische Kommission, 2019)

Legislation	Detailed content
Consumer rights directive	Regulations for consumer information and other contractual questions, e.g. distance selling or contracts conclude outside of business premises, consumer sales rights for public auctions, transfer of existing contracts between consumers, pre-contractual information, the right of withdrawal, delivery, transfer of risk, fees for the use of payment methods
Consumer sales and warranty policy	Consumer sales and warranty policy with aim to harmonize consumer contract laws about legal and commercial guarantees The consumer goods seller must guarantee that the goods are in conformity with the contract for a period of at least two years from delivery of the goods If the goods are not in accordance with the contract, the consumer can request that the goods be repaired, replaced, and reduced in price or that the contract be terminated
Pricing policy	The sales price or the price per unit of measure (unit price) for all products that retailers offer to consumers must be indicated to make it easier for consumers to compare prices The selling price must be unambiguous, easily identifiable and clearly legible
Unfair contract terms directive	Protecting consumers from unfair standard contractual clauses imposed by traders The policy applies to all types of contracts for the purchase of goods and services, such as online or offline purchases of consumer goods, gym subscriptions, or contracts for financial services such as loans

As a result of the above-mentioned legal regulations, the relevant norms of behaviour have become legal norms and thus form the lower limit of ethical norms.

For the UK after the Brexit in 2020, updated guidelines with a certain transition period might be expected (Competition and Consumer Protection Commission, 2021). Customer protection is also linked to customer satisfaction that products are good and clean as well as service and goods in a satisfied condition (see Fig. 13.2 Customer satisfaction as basis for services and products.)

13.2 Pricing Strategies

It is part of the economic responsibility of the private sector that the products and services are offered at fair prices (Schindler, 2012).

Opinions about where the fair prices are can vary greatly among providers and consumers. Usually, producers want to get the highest possible price in order to maximize their profit. On the other hand, private households want to buy at the lowest possible prices in order to optimally satisfy individual needs with their disposable income or to build up their own wealth (Schindler, 2012; Xu et al., 2021; Png, 1991).

According to neoclassical theory, fair prices are the result of a functional or perfect market where a balance between supply and demand is achieved (Ferguson, 2008). This means that the information is transparent and generally accessible, and

Fig. 13.2 Customer satisfaction as basis for services and products. (Photo: Dr. René Dathe)

that all economic players can enter or leave the market at any time. If the price rises, the sale will be more lucrative and there will be more vendors entering the business. As a result, the total supply on the market increases, so that the providers tend to have to lower the selling price in order to win over consumers. On the buyer's side, demand will decline when the price rises, which further exacerbates the competition and its consequences. If the market price falls, the business will yield less returns and some providers will leave the market. This reduces the supply and if the demand remains the same, the providers can achieve a higher price. When the price falls, demand also rises, which drives the market price up further (Ferguson, 2008). However, the customers react differently to the market price variations. This phenomenon is described as price elasticity (Browning, 1992; Parkin et al., 2003).

$$E = \frac{\Delta Q / Q}{\Delta P / P}$$

E price elasticity of demand for a good
ΔQ quantity change
Q quantity of the good demanded

ΔP price change

P price of the good demanded

Unethical behaviours of commercial providers of products and services can disrupt fair market price mechanism. *Typical examples of such unethical behaviours are:*

Exorbitant Price

The providers take advantage of the emergency or the weakness of the customer and offer the products or services at excessive prices e. g. Mask shortage during Covid-19 pandemic worldwide in Spring 2020. The reason can be, for example, an information asymmetry, i. e. the providers have a knowledge advantage over the consumers about the market; or they are existential products such as food, living space, etc., so that consumers cannot leave the market despite the inflated price. According to German jurisprudence, usurious transactions or immoral transactions are void (BGB, 2019)]. In individual cases, however, the submission of the exorbitant price must be proven. Similar rules are also applicable in Anglo-saxony markets and companies need to be more ethical according the UN ESG set up.

Price Agreement

In some business cases there are few providers versus many consumers. The competing companies coordinate with each other in order to enforce a sales price that differs from the fair price. The profits generated in this way through excessive prices are a burden for the general public. This type of competition agreement is also known as a price cartel and is prohibited in Germany by the Act against Restraints of Competition. A good example was the Standard Oil Monopoly in the US. However even today Oil cartels are continuing e. g. OPEC Organization of the Petroleum Exporting Countries cartel (OPEC, 2021).

Ruinous Competition

Large companies can take advantage of their strong financial position and offer their products and services at disproportionately low prices. With the aggressive pricing strategy, they win the market and eliminate the competitors. Subsequently, the prices are again increased disproportionately to the burden of the consumer. The ruinous competition mainly destroys smaller companies and start-ups and damages society. In Germany, such behaviour is combated by the Act against Unfair Competition (UWG) and the Act against Restraints of Competition (GWB).

Deceptive Pricing

It is deliberately misleading pricing that misleads customers into the false assumption that they are paying a lower price that is below the actual market price. Often encountered are, for example, hidden or concealed fees/additional taxes, discount sales based on increased prices or with hidden additional costs.

13.3 Marketing Strategies

Marketing strategies are long-term planned approaches with which companies attempt to gain competitive advantages to achieve their marketing objectives. The important items in marketing strategies include the choice of product ranges, customer target groups and marketing communication (Schindler, 2012).

A typical misconduct in the choice of customer target groups is the exploitation of vulnerable customer groups ("consumer vulnerability") who can be easily manipulated for example due to the following conditions (Smith & Cooper-Martin, 1997):

- Unable to assess the consequences of their actions due to a lack of education or product information;
- Old age or senility;
- Physically or emotionally in a state of emergency due to illness, grief or other unfortunate circumstances;
- Too young to make rational decisions;
- Under pressure due to poverty.

In their own economic interests, the companies tend to eliminate the unattractive customer groups ("consumer exclusion"), for example by refusing the admission of medical care for elderly members, or dismantling service centres or branches (e. g. post, transport or banks) in sparsely populated regions (Kempson & Whyley, 1999).

Marketing communication is the communication of the marketing mix with the help of various channels or instruments such as advertising, sales promotion, sales (direct sales), branding and online advertising (Krizan et al., 2007, S. 15). The main objectives of marketing communication are (Crane & Matten, 2016, S. 345):

- To inform consumers about the product mix, and
- to convince consumers to buy.

There are two main variations of marketing mix includes (Kusumawati et al., 2014):

- Marketing strategy for the classical consumption goods: **4P's (Price – Promotion – Place – Product)** (see Fig. 13.3 Marketing strategy for the classical consumption goods).
- Service marketing strategy: **7P's** (Price – Promotion – Place – Product – People – Physical evidence – Process) (Fig. 13.4).

A typical problem field in marketing communication is consumer deception, whereby consumers are led into false assumptions about the characteristics of the products or services, or their rational purchase decisions are impaired in some other way (Boatright, 2012).

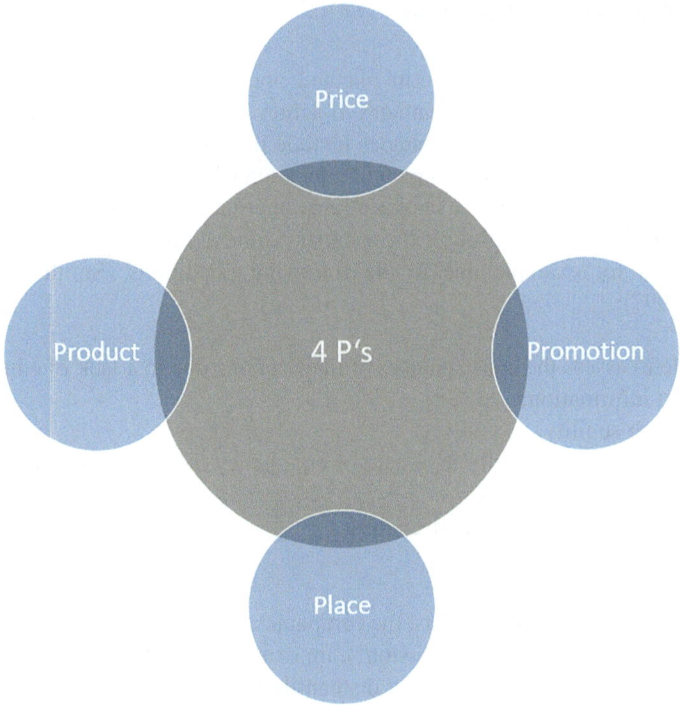

Fig. 13.3 Marketing strategy for classic consumption goods. Based on (Kusumawati et al., 2014)

Data protection for consumers also deserves attention in market-related ethical discussions. With the General Data Protection Regulation (GDPR) which came into effect in May 2018, the European Union ensures a uniform set of rules for all member states in order to protect consumers from unauthorized or unwanted collection of personal data. Firms relying on collection of personal data (e. g. Facebook Inc. selling personalized advertisements on its platforms) need to rethink the business models when the costumers become increasingly conscious of the personal data protection.

13.4 Sustainable Consumption

As a result of the growing consumer awareness, the CSR concept and the ESG initiative have become an important guideline for the strategy development in the politics and the private business sector (Gupta, 2021; PRI Association, 2021).

To avoid market sanctions due to negative impact on the ecological, social, or economic development of society, private firms voluntarily distance themselves from the business partners (especially suppliers and customers) who are threatened by ethical scandals. For example, the world's second largest fashion retailer H&M

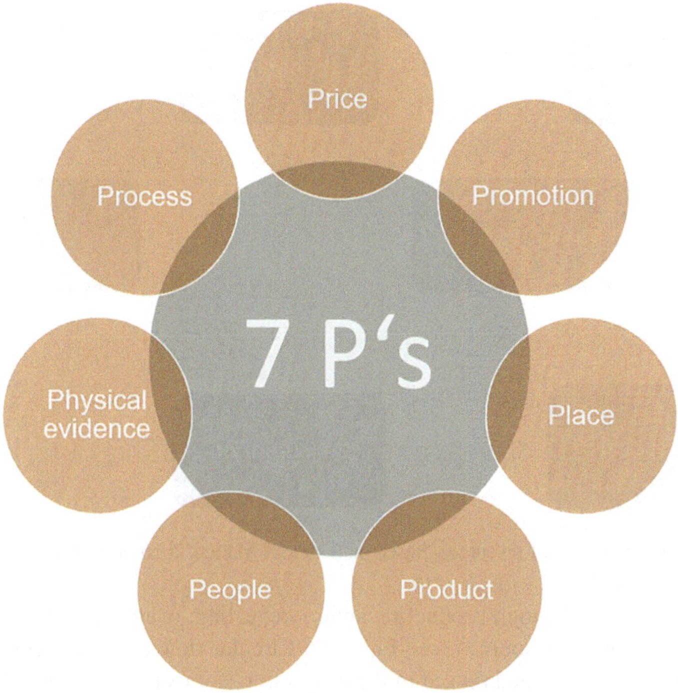

Fig. 13.4 Service marketing strategy. Based on (Kusumawati et al., 2014)

Fig. 13.5 Linear flow of resources. Based on (Crane & Matten, 2016, S. 369 ff)

stopped purchasing leather from Brazil, after the country's cattle ranching was suspected of being responsible for the deforestation of the Amazon rainforest.

There is evidence that globally, a significant proportion of all purchase decisions came about through a positive judgment about the producer, including positive ethical behaviours. In other words, the ethical behaviour of private business is rewarded by the market (Devinney et al., 2010). The conscious engagement of consumer influence is often referred to as "sustainable consumption". As a result, there is an increasing demand for product using environment-friendly technology, e. g. electric vehicles (e-mobility). However, there is also critics for "green washing", that the technology is sometimes not as sustainable as it is advertised (for example, although electric vehicles reduce toxic exhaust gas, the production of eCars uses Carbon-based materials and causes environment pollution.

Another trend of sustainable consumption is "refurbishing", i. e. in contradiction to the classic flow of resources (see Fig. 13.5 Linear flow of resources), the waste

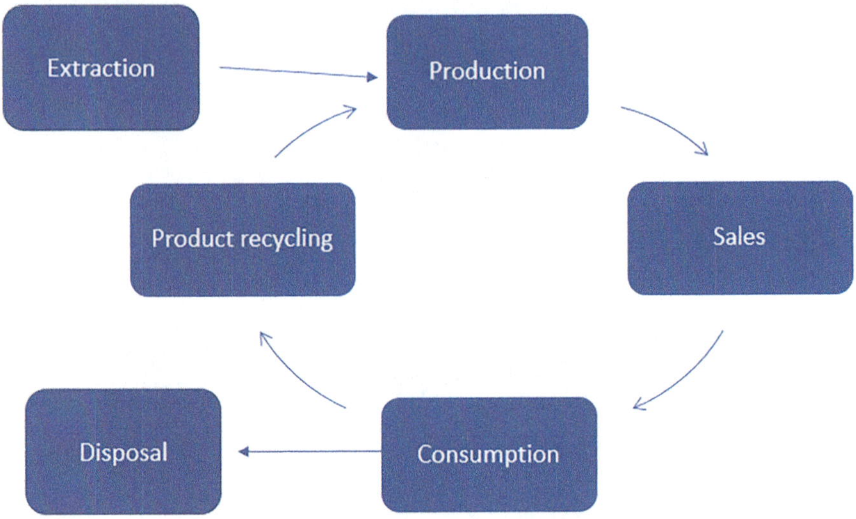

Fig. 13.6 Circular flow of resources. Based on (Crane & Matten, 2016, S. 369 ff)

material is reused through product recapture, recycling, overhaul and others. With the circular flow of resources (see Fig. 13.6 Circular flow of resources), valuable materials may be obtained reused in the production (for example Apple iPhone dismantling robot Daisy).

Consumers also make a direct contribution to sustainability by reducing their own consumption and foregoing convenience. For example, with the car-sharing concept, the providers (e. g. We Share from Berlin, Germany; Didi from China, Grab from Singapore or Uber as a global provider) offer consumers the possibility to travel with the shared cars at their convenience, so that they can give up the ownership of a private vehicle and reduce the overall carbon footprint (Crane & Matten, 2016, S. 369 ff.).

References

BGB. (2019). *Bürgerliches Gesetzbuch § 138 Sittenwidriges Rechtsgeschäft; Wucher*. Von Bundesministerium für Verbraucherschutz: https://www.gesetze-im-internet.de/bgb/__138.html. Abgerufen 03.09.2021.

Boatright, J. (2012). *Ethics and the conduct of business* (7th ed.). Pearson.

Browning, E. (1992). *Microeconomic theory and applications*. HarperCollins.

Crane, A., & Matten, D. (2016). *Business ethics. Managing corporate citizenship and sustainability in the age of globalization* (4th ed.). Oxford University Press.

Devinney, T., Auger, P., & Eckhardt, G. (2010). *The myth of the ethical consumer*. Cambridge University Press.

Europäische Kommission. (2019). *Consumer contract law*. Von https://ec.europa.eu/info/law/law-topic/consumers/consumer-contract-law_de. Abgerufen.

Ferguson, C. (2008). *The neoclassical theory of production and distribution*. Cambridge University Press.

Gov UK. (2021). *Consumer rights.* Von https://www.gov.uk/consumer-protection-rights. Abgerufen.

Gupta, P. (2021). *Understanding and adopting ESG – An overview part I: The evolution of ESG from CSR.* Von https://www.rhtlawasia.com/wp-content/uploads/2021/03/ESG-Part-I-The-Evolution-of-ESG-from-CSR.pdf. Abgerufen 11.09.2021.

Kempson, E., & Whyley, C. (1999). *Kept out or opted out? Understanding and combating financial exclusion*. Policy Press.

Krizan, A., Merrier, P., Logan, J., & Williams, K. (2007). *Business communication* (7th ed.). South-Western College Publication.

Kusumawati, R. D., Oswari, T., Utomo, R. B., & Kumar, V. (2014). The influence of 7P's of marketing mix on buying intention of music product in Indonesia. *Procedia Engineering, 97*, 1765–1771.

OPEC. (2021). *Our mission.* Von https://www.opec.org/opec_web/en/about_us/23.htm. Abgerufen.

Parkin, M., Powell, M., & Matthews, K. (2003). *Economics European edition* (5th ed.). Addison-Wesley.

Png, I. (1991). Most-favored-customer protection versus price discrimination over time. *Journal of Political Economy, 99*(5), 1010–1028.

PRI Association. (2021). *Principles for responsible investment. PRI Association.* Von https://www.unpri.org/pri/about-the-pri. Abgerufen 11.09.2021.

Schindler, R. (2012). *Pricing strategies: A marketing approach.* SAGE.

Smith, N., & Cooper-Martin, E. (1997). Ethics and target marketing: The role of product harm and consumer vulnerability. *Journal of Marketing, 61*, 1–20.

UNCTAD. (2016). *United Nations conference on trade and development.* Von Guidelines for consumer protection: https://unctad.org/en/PublicationsLibrary/ditccplpmisc2016d1_en.pdf. Abgerufen 03.09.2021.

Warentest. (2021). *Stiftung Warentest.* Von So ist die Stiftung organisiert.: https://www.test.de/unternehmen/stiftungsgremien-5017311-5017322/. Abgerufen 11.09.2021.

Xu, J., Huang, Y., Avgerinos, E., Feng, G., & Chu, F. (2021). Dual-channel competition: The role of quality improvement and price-matching. *International Journal of Production Research Suppliers and Competitors*. https://doi.org/10.1080/00207543.2021.1931725

Suppliers and Competitors

14

All your dreams can come true if you have the courage to pursue them.

Walt Disney

14.1 B2B Relationships in the Supply Chain Network

The business relationships could be business-to-business (referred to as "B2B") or business-to-consumer (referred to as "B2C"). The global B2B relationships make up a complex supply chain network (see Fig. 14.1 supply chain network). The companies are suppliers to their own customers, and customers to their suppliers. In addition to existing business partnerships, the companies often maintain relationships with a plethora of potential customers and suppliers. These contacts are sources for business growth and solution for delivery bottlenecks.

Unlike suppliers and customers, competitors only have indirect business relationships with companies. Classically, the interactions among the competitors are presented as zero-sum games, i. e. the competitors try to win the largest possible market share for themselves with a fixed total business volume. The suppliers and potential suppliers also see each other as competitors.

The business partners in the B2B relationships as suppliers or customers are mutually dependent.

The buyers need the products and services from the suppliers, in order to be able to make their own products or services available for the market. Their ability to make high-quality purchases at low prices is an important factor for their economic success.

The profit of the seller depends in turn on what prices the customers are willing to pay and how much money is left after deducting their own costs at the end of the

T. Dathe et al., *Corporate Social Responsibility (CSR), Sustainability and Environmental Social Governance (ESG)*, Management for Professionals,
https://doi.org/10.1007/978-3-030-92357-0_14

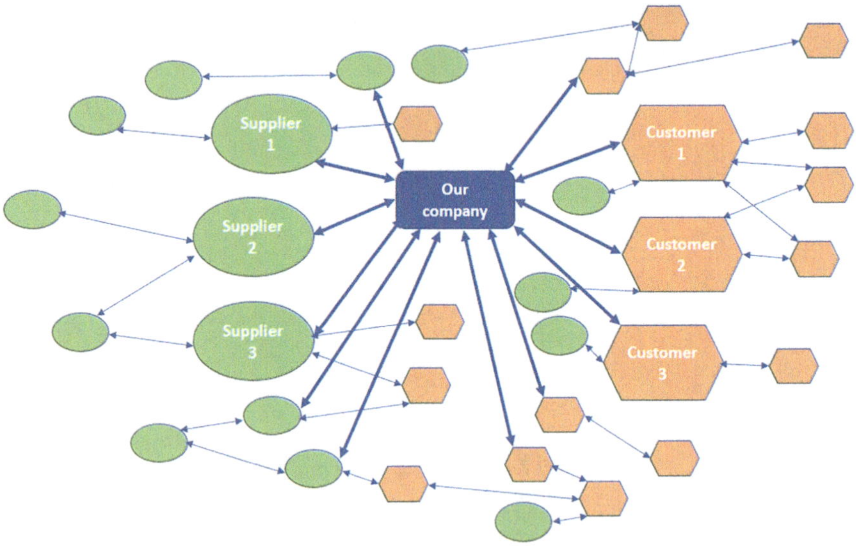

Fig. 14.1 Supply chain network

value creation process. Despite the mutual dependency, the economic interests of the B2B business partners diverge: the buyers want to pay the lowest possible purchase price, while the sellers try to achieve the highest possible sales price.

Furthermore, the companies need to react to the competitors, in order to remain successful in the market. In the general sense of justice, the competitors are entitled to fair treatment.

14.2 Dealing with Suppliers

Supplier management is a major component of global supply chain management. The quality assurance of suppliers from various locations and stable supplier relationships are often the main objectives (Shah & Lim, 2021). To maintain long-term collaborative relationship with the business partners, corporates are increasingly foregoing the confrontational approach with the suppliers to achieve short-term cost savings. Rather, attempts are made to create a win-win situation, in order to benefit from a long-term partnership with the supplier (Daugherty, 2011). However, the empirical research highlights a number of practical ethical dilemmas that arise in such sourcing partnerships. Supplier management is also an important element for the economic sustainability.

14.2.1 Fair Trade and Ethical Trade

The power position of the business partners essentially determines the distribution of profits, as well as the type of ethical dilemmas in the interactions (Porter, 2008). The company has a strong position of power when there are several alternative suppliers or when the purchased goods and services can be substituted for the value creation process in their own company. On the other hand, there is a weak position of power if the alternatives are very limited or if the goods and services purchased are rather indispensable for one's own business.

Companies can take advantage of their strong position of power and dictate delivery terms. Large corporations such as supermarket chains (e. g. Carrefour in France and Walmart in the US) typically have such power advantages over their suppliers.

In Germany, the Top Four grocers Edeka (incl. Netto), Schwarz Group (Lidl and Kaufland), REWE (incl. Penny) and Aldi (Nord and Süd) use around 60% of the total market volume ((Lebensmittel Zeitung, 2018). The supermarkets can determine favourable purchase prices based on their market position. Furthermore, you can dictate the terms of delivery to shift your business risks onto the suppliers, such as:

- *Listing fee* (a fee for the suppliers to be allowed to deliver to the supermarket)
- *Bans or restrictions* on deliveries to other supermarket chains
- *Retroactive price reductions* (e. g. subsequent rebate requests)
- *Returning unsold products* (including fresh products that can no longer be sold)
- *Short-term changes* to orders and delivery quantities.
- *High contractual penalty* for inadequate delivery quantities.
- *Additional claims for subsidies* for advertising costs, sales promotions, new openings, etc.

REWE banned several US brands due to a different understanding of price development in 2020 and remove the products from Kellogg's, Mars-Wrigley's und Eckes-Granini from their supermarkets. This is an example of showing the market power of grocery stores in an oligopoly market to their suppliers (Berliner Zeitung, 2021).

The constant price pressure on suppliers' forces suppliers to save on production and development costs and often puts smaller companies in danger of their existence. As a result, the product quality or choice for the consumer is reduced, so that the private labels of the supermarket chains move into the focus of the consumers, which in the end can no longer be substituted as a brand with the competitors.

The Bakery competition battle has shown when supermarkets offer fresh baked products and industrial driven bakery chains entering the market. Being in direct competition with traditional Bakeries, the amount of bakery has been dropped to half to 11.000 handcrafted marketplaces (Dierig, 2019).

Due to consumer movements and more and more awareness of the ESG aspects, companies are sensitized to improve their image through CSR activities with regard to B2B partnerships (Gupta, 2021; PRI Association, 2021).

The typical approaches are:

- Fair trade
- Ethical trade

Fair Trade

With the participation of the fair-trade organizations, the companies ensure that, especially in the case of imported goods from developing countries (e. g. banana and coffee plantations), the producers receive a fair price for their products. With the long-term supply relationships, the economic and social situation, as well as the environment in the regions of the producers, should be sustainably improved (fairtrade.de, 2020)].

Fair trade needs to be scalable to be accessible to more people. However, there is difference in fair and free trade in the economies of scale models (Maseland & de Vaal, 2002).

Ethical Trading

When selecting suppliers, companies pay attention not only to economic aspects, but also to how their potential business partners fulfil their social responsibility. Often in combination with an auditing process, the companies implement their Code of Ethics with their business partners, which typically includes the well-being of employees (e. g. decent working conditions and renouncement of child labour), environment preservation and other social aspects (Freidberg, 2003). In the quality assurance agreement, ethical standards and ESG KPIs are often implemented to support the Code of Ethics in a global context. Nowadays the ethical performance is usually incorporated in sustainability report and annual reports to overlook the investment (Perego & Kolk, 2012).

14.2.2 Conflict of Interest & Integrity

The personal interests of purchasers may collide with the interests of the company. Many "salespeople" try to lure the potential customer's purchaser with attractive gifts, entertainment and other benefits. Such behaviours are not to be tolerated in ESG terms (Gupta, 2021; PRI Association, 2021).

Personal integrity is required so that the interests of the company can be guaranteed. The term "personal integrity" describes the quality of a person who stands firm by his values and is therefore incorruptible (Kesselring, 2007). Sometimes, the conflict of interest does not arise on a personal level, but on an organizational level. For example, the rating agencies e.g. S&P, Moddy's and Fitch have the professional task of assessing the creditworthiness of companies independently and objectively like during the 2008 Financial Crisis (McLean & Nocera, 2011). Since the agencies have their own economic interests and are interested in follow-up appointments, the institutional integrity can come under pressure, especially if their clients perform poorly. Similar situations can also arise with auditing firms e. g. EY and the Wirecard scandal (Handelsblatt, 2021).

In order to counteract the unethical temptations, large companies have often set the framework for action for buyers or suppliers by means of a code of conduct. The following Code of Conduct of the Chartered Institute of Procurement & Supply (CIPS), an international professional association for buyers, shows the typical content of such a document (CIPS, 2020):

"As a member of CIPS I will:

Enhance and protect the standing of the profession, by:

- never engaging in conduct, either professional or personal, which would bring the profession or the Chartered Institute of Purchasing & Supply into disrepute
- not accepting inducements or gifts (other than any declared gifts of nominal value which have been sanctioned by my employer)
- not allowing offers of hospitality or those with vested interests to influence, or be perceived to influence, my business decisions
- being aware that my behaviour outside my professional life may have an effect on how I am perceived as a professional.

Maintain the highest standard of integrity in all business relationships, by:

- rejecting any business practice which might reasonably be deemed improper
- never using my authority or position for my own financial gain
- declaring to my line manager any personal interest that might affect, or be seen by others to affect, my impartiality in decision making
- ensuring that the information I give in the course of my work is accurate and not misleading
- never breaching the confidentiality of information I receive in a professional capacity
- striving for genuine, fair and transparent competition
- being truthful about my skills, experience and qualifications

Promote the eradication of unethical business practices, by:

- fostering awareness of human rights, fraud and corruption issues in all my business relationships
- responsibly managing any business relationships where unethical practices may come to light, and taking appropriate action to report and remedy them
- undertaking due diligence on appropriate supplier relationships in relation to forced labour (modern slavery) and other human rights abuses, fraud and corruption

- continually developing my knowledge of forced labour (modern slavery), human rights, fraud and corruption issues, and applying this in my professional life

Enhance the proficiency and stature of the profession, by:

- continually developing and applying knowledge to increase my personal skills and those of the organisation I work for
- fostering the highest standards of professional competence amongst those for whom I am responsible
- optimising the responsible use of resources which I have influence over for the benefit of my organisation.

Ensure full compliance with laws and regulations, by:

- adhering to the laws of the countries in which I practise, and in countries where there is no relevant law in place I will apply the standards inherent in this Code
- fulfilling agreed contractual obligations
- following CIPS guidance on professional practice."

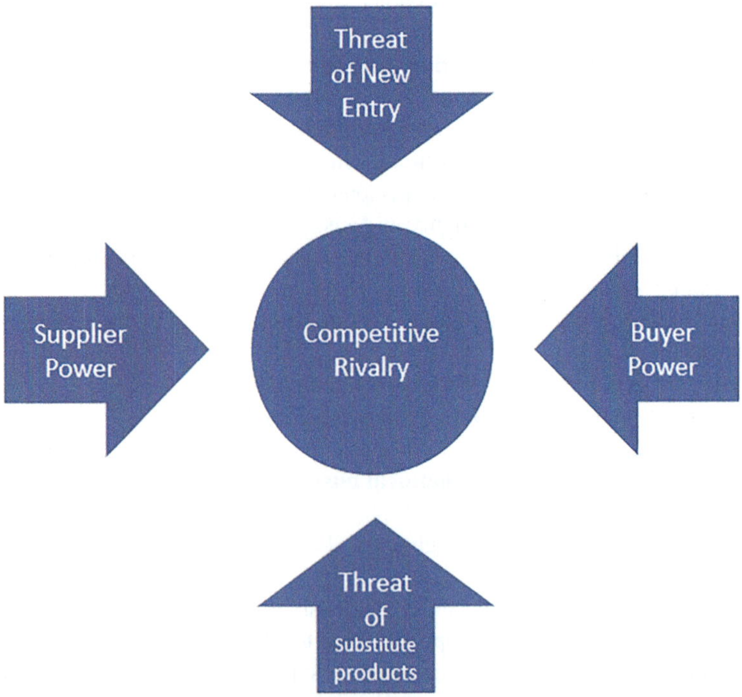

Fig. 14.2 Porter's five forces. Based on (Porter, 1980)

14.2.3 Fair Competition

14.2.3.1 Social Interest in a Functioning Market

The society has a strong interest for a functioning market, in which the market price is determined by the interplay of supply and demand. If the price rises, the supply increases because of the profit potential and the demand decreases, because fewer customers are willing to pay the higher price. Due to the competition with a higher total supply and decreasing demand, the price begins to decrease again. Otherwise, when the price falls, the market supply decreases and demand increases at the same time. As a result, the price recovers, till a stable market price level is reached. In theory, the maximum benefit for the public with the available resources could be reached with the market mechanism.

The market success can be influenced by the following factors in the 5-force model according to Porter (see Fig. 14.2 Porter's Five Forces) (Porter, 1980):

- Rivalry among existing competitors (central influencing factor);
- Threat of new competitors entering the market;
- Threat from substitute products;
- Suppliers' negotiating power; and
- Bargaining power of customers.

Fair treatment of competitors is an important social responsibility of the private sector. By acting immorally, companies can override market functions and increase the short-term profits, but run the rist to damage the long-term corporate image. Examples of such conceivable misconduct by companies include:

Unfair Competition

The competitors are eliminated with unfair methods so that the companies from a quasi-monopoly position can disproportionately increase the price at the expense of the consumer e.g., Standard oil or Microsoft case 253 F.3d 34 (D.C. Cir. 2001 as anti-trust law case (Justia US law, 2021)).

Shopping Cartel

The few competing companies secretly agree on higher sales prices to take advantage of the customers.

In the following section, the problems of unfair competition are discussed in more details.

14.2.3.2 Barriers to Competition and Protectionism

Companies sometimes breach moral norms, in order to gain economic advantages at the expense of the society. Under certain conditions, such unfair behaviour can also be a violation of the law ("unfair competition"),

According to the federal laws of Germany, the following acts are considered unfair competition(Bundesamt für Justiz, 2019, S. §§ 4–7):

- Negative advertising towards the competition (disparagement);
- Bribery;
- Industrial espionage;
- Sabotage of competitor property ownership;
- Brand theft, unauthorized imitation or forgery;
- Decoy offers;
- Misleading designation and description of your own products or services;
- Disguise the corporate identity;
- Misleading cost structure for billing.

Ruinous competition is a typical act of unfair competition. Large companies exploit their financial strength and undercut their competitors at disproportionately low prices. After the competitors have left the market, the remaining providers raise the prices abruptly by market dictation.

Protectionism is the attempt by the government to create trade barriers, in order to protect domestic companies from international competition. The French government attempts to build up "National Champions" through a protectionist approach. The merger of the pharma-firms Sanofi-Synthelabo and Aventis, as well as the merger of Gaz de France with Suez to form GDF SUEZ (now known as Engie) are examples of a protectionist industrial policy against a total sell-out of advanced technologies (Tariq Anwar, 2008).

The Franco-German Airbus was supported by the European governments to counteract US supremacy in the aviation industry. At present, the European Union is debating over institutional promotions of European digitization industry to counteract on the US FAAG companies Facebook, Amazon, Apple and Google (Nonnast, 2006).

The opposite of protectionism is free trade. According to the theory of international trade, the macroeconomic optimum can only be achieved through free trade. However, the theory does not take into account the interests of the individual economic sectors at the national level, that due to the market entry of more cost-efficient foreign competitors, certain national employee groups can no longer be competitive and have to fear corresponding economic cuts. With the protectionist policy, the local politicians primarily want to stimulate the votes in these industrial sectors and avoid protest voters.

Protectionism's instruments include (Eibner, 2006, S. 107–110):

- Import duties: Taxing imported goods increases the costs for suppliers. To offset the additional costs, the sales prices must also be increased. The aim is that the goods become less attractive and that the domestic products, which are expensive due to higher labour costs, remain on the market and can be sold.
- Subsidies: The state subsidizes certain economic sectors (e. g. agriculture, lignite and hard coal mining or new technologies such as solar technology or e-mobility) that are otherwise not competitive on the market with the existing structure. The subsidies can take various forms, e. g. as tax relief, granting of preferential loans or direct financial aid. Export subsidies are a special type of subsidy, with the aim

of ensuring that domestic products can assert themselves on the world market through state subsidies.

- Import quotas: by setting an upper limit for certain types of import goods, the volume of import transactions is limited.
- Conformity requirements: The national standards for certain product groups can represent an additional barrier for foreign suppliers when entering the market, which can also be shown in an analysis of the Five forces according to Porter (Porter, 1980).

The primary goal of protectionism is to protect one's own economy in the hope of sustainable employment and international competitiveness.

Considerations relating to national security or global political strategies can also provide further motivation for protectionism. The ongoing trade dispute between China and the USA, as well as the current various debates about the use of the communication systems of the Chinese radio network equipment supplier Huawei in various countries can be cited as an example (Bowler, 2020).

Protectionism represents a state intervention in the market economy and is therefore often criticized by supporters of market liberalization for disrupting the market mechanisms and consequently for reducing overall prosperity.

The British business journalist Joe Studwell reproaches the critics of protectionism with the fact that in the Asian region it is precisely the countries such as the Philippines, Thailand and Indonesia that are facing economic difficulties today, following the recommendations of the International Monetary Fund (IMF) and receiving subsidies for the national one Producers have waived. Other countries such as China and South Korea, on the other hand, have supported domestic industries through protectionist measures in the cost-intensive initial phases and helped them achieve lasting success on the international market (Studwel, 2014).

References

Berliner Zeitung. (2021). *Rewe verbannt mehrere Produkte aus den Regalen*. Von https://www.berliner-zeitung.de/news/rewe-verbannt-mehrere-produkte-aus-den-regalen-li.145577. Abgerufen 11.09.2021.

Bowler, T. (2020). *BBC*. Von Huawei: Why is it being banned from the UK's 5G network?: BBC. https://www.bbc.com/news/newsbeat-47041341. Abgerufen 11.09.2021.

Bundesamt für Justiz. (2019). *Gesetz gegen den unlauteren Wettbewerb (UWG)*. Von § 4 Mitbewerberschutz: https://www.gesetze-im-internet.de/uwg_2004/__4.html. Abgerufen.

CIPS. (2020). *CIPS code of conduct*. Von Chartered Institute of Procurement & Supply: https://www.cips.org/Documents/About%20CIPS/2/CIPS_Code_of_conductv2_10_9_2013.pdf. Abgerufen 11.09.2021.

Daugherty, P. (2011). Review of logistics and supply cain relationship literature and suggested research agenda. *International Journal of Physical Distribution & Logistics Management, 41*(1), 16–31.

Dierig, S. (2019). *Bäckereisterben – „Zahl der Betriebe bereits fast halbiert"*. Von https://www.welt.de/wirtschaft/article191460415/Fachkraeftemangel-Sterben-der-traditionellen-Baeckereien-geht-weiter.html. Abgerufen 11.09.2021.

Eibner, W. (2006). *Anwendungsorientierte Außenwirtschaft: Theorie und Politik*. Oldenbourg Wissenschaftsverlag.

fairtrade.de. (02. Januar 2020). *Was ist fairer Handel?* Von https://www.fairtrade.de/index.php/mID/1.1/lan/de#Mehr_als_nur_ein_fairer_Preis. Abgerufen 11.09.2021.

Freidberg, S. (2003). *The contradictions of clean: Supermarket ethical trade and african horticulture*. Von International Institute for Environment and Development, Sustainable Agriculture and Rural Livelihoods Programme. https://pubs.iied.org/pdfs/6361IIED.pdf. Abgerufen 11.09.2021.

Gupta, P. (2021). *Understanding and adopting ESG – An overview part I: The evolution of ESG from CSR*. Von https://www.rhtlawasia.com/wp-content/uploads/2021/03/ESG-Part-I-The-Evolution-of-ESG-from-CSR.pdf. Abgerufen 11.09.2021.

Handelsblatt. (2021). *Nach der Veröffentlichung des Geheimreports: Nun kann sich keiner mehr rausreden"*. Von Der vom Handelsblatt zugänglich gemachte Report über das Versagen von EY im Fall Wirecard schlägt hohe Wellen. Anwälte, Anlegerschützer und Politiker begrüßen die Veröffentlichung. https://www.handelsblatt.com/finanzen/banken-versicherungen/banken/wambach-bericht-zu-ey-nach-der-veroeffentlichung-des-geheimreports-nun-kann-sich-keiner-mehr-rausreden/27795562.html?ticket=ST-2113825-mo6hSsvoqFjclnX9vKzb-ap1 retrieved 16.01.2022.

Justia US law. (2021). *United States of America, Appellee v. Microsoft Corporation, Appellant, 253 F.3d 34 (D.C. Cir. 2001)*. Von https://law.justia.com/cases/federal/appellate-courts/F3/253/34/576095/. Abgerufen 11.09.2021.

Kesselring, T. (04. Mai 2007). *Mens sana in corpore sano. Integrität aus ethischer Sicht*. Von Beitrag zur Tagung von „Berner Gesundheit": Wieviel Körper darf es sein?: http://www.bernergesundheit.ch/download/Referat_Kesselring.pdf. Abgerufen 11.09.2021.

Lebensmittel Zeitung. (März 2018). *Top 30 Lebensmittelhandel Deutschland 2018*. Von Lebensmittel Zeitung: https://www.lebensmittelzeitung.net/handel/Ranking-Top-30-Lebensmittelhandel-Deutschland-2018-134606. Abgerufen 11.09.2021.

Maseland, R., & de Vaal, A. (2002). How fair is fair trade? *De Economist, 150*, 251–272.

McLean, B., & Nocera, J. (2011). *All the Devils Are Here: The Hidden History of the Financial Crisis*. New York: Portfolio Penguin.

Nonnast, T. (2006). *Software AG sieht Airbus als Vorbild*. Von Handelsblatt: https://www.handelsblatt.com/unternehmen/it-medien/kooperation-europaeischer-software-firmen-software-ag-sieht-airbus-als-vorbild/2676864.html, retrieved 16.01.2022.

Perego, P., & Kolk, A. (2012). Multinationals' accountability on sustainability: The evolution of third-party assurance of sustainability reports. *Journal of Business Ethics, 110*, 173–190.

Porter, M. (1980). *Competitive strategy: Techniques for analyzing industries and competitors: With a new introduction*. Free Press.

Porter, M. (2008). The five competitive forces that shape strategy. *Harvard Business Review, 86*(January), 79–93.

PRI Association. (2021). *Principles for Responsible Investment. PRI Association*. Von https://www.unpri.org/pri/about-the-pri. Abgerufen 11.09.2021.

Shah, M., & Lim, C. (2021). Quality assurance in the domestic third-party arrangement in Australia. *International Journal of Educational Management, 35*(4), 866–878.

Studwel, J. (2014). *How Asia works: Success and failure in the world's most dynamic region*. Profile Books.

Tariq Anwar, S. (2008). Creating a national champion or a global pharmaceutical company: a tale of French connection. *Journal of Business & Industrial Marketing, 23*(8), 586–596. https://doi.org/10.1108/08858620810913399

15 Employees

Don't discount yourself, no matter what you're doing. Everyone has a unique perspective that they can bring to the world.

Mark Zuckerberg

15.1 Employees' Contribution

Employees are the driving force behind corporate innovations and the value creation process. In times of globalization, the business organizations rely largely on the employees' commitment to obtain competitive advantages for sustainable business growth.

To optimize the internal process, employers make great efforts for example in recruitment of qualified staff, professional trainings and knowledge-transfer etc. The ethical behaviour of employers not only fulfils corporate social responsibility, but motivates the employees to better performance, so that the business in turn benefits from higher productivity and efficiency.

15.2 Employer's Duty of Care

Corporates have important duties of care towards their employees (see Table 15.1 Some of employer's duty of care).

T. Dathe et al., *Corporate Social Responsibility (CSR), Sustainability and Environmental Social Governance (ESG)*, Management for Professionals,
https://doi.org/10.1007/978-3-030-92357-0_15

Table 15.1 Some of employer's duty of care

Employer's duty of care	Content
Working conditions	Accident prevention and work safety; Protection from health hazards; Overtime limit; Work-life-balance, including flexible working time, etc.
Inclusion	Elimination of discrimination; Equal opportunity; Prevention of sexual harassment etc.
Privacy	Physical privacy; Social privacy; Data protection; Psychological privacy.

15.2.1 Working Conditions

In some regions, profit-oriented companies are still taking advantage of their position of power to exploit their workforce by paying starvation wages. Women and children are particular easy prays who are forced into inhumane working and living conditions.

In most industrialized countries, however, employers have a wide range of welfare obligations that are laid down in a series of statutory regulations, which aim to protect employees from health hazards and the risks of accidents in the workplace. The employee overtime is limited by the labour law and the agreement with the trade union to avoid disproportionate interference of private and social life of the employee, which, under certain circumstances may cause physical or psychological illnesses ("burn-out").

The term "work-life balance" can be understood as an employee-friendly state of life, with the professional activities organized in a manner that is compatible with the family life of the employees. Especially during the Covid-19 pandemic, many employers offer the employees flexible working time and place (e. g. home office) to facilitate less stressful daily routines. With the current demographical development and tendential increasing retirement age, such flexibility becomes even more necessary in the future.

However, the flexible working time also causes a blur between the professional and the private life. As a result, the working time can no longer be limited and the employees often have to remain available in their private time, especially by using the smartphone. This topic is gaining increasingly attention in public discussions.

Since the quality of life of employees is significantly influenced by their occupation, they have a legitimate interest in helping to shape their work environment. The employees are usually represented by the workers' council when participating in the decision-making process of the business operations. The participation of employees may take place in various manners (Crane & Matten, 2016, S. 306):

- Task expansion. Employees are empowered to make more autonomous decisions in the workplace, for example, to control the results of their own work.
- Information. The employer provides the employees with additional background information, such as corporate strategies, the general business performance of the company, to facilitate a better understanding of the overall business operations and to motivate the employees with the feelings of trust.
- Hearing. The management-employee communication is no longer a one-way street. Instead, the employees are given the opportunity to express their own opinions on the operational matters that would significantly change their working environment.
- Participation. Employees have a codified right to participate in decision-making, for example when hiring new employees or in the event of individual dismissals. This is the highest possible form of participation by the employees in a company.

15.2.2 Inclusion

Inclusion in workplace means equal treatment and equal opportunities for all employees.

Many countries have anti-discrimination laws and regulations to protect the interests of minorities. Employers are expected by the public to behave according to higher ethical standards, so as to ensure the elimination of discrimination against individuals or individual groups among the employees. That is, no one should be disadvantaged based on his/her skin colour, ethnicity, social origin, age, gender, sexual orientation, religion, political convictions, physical or mental disabilities, etc.

"Equal opportunity" means, the job positions and rewards of the employees should be determined according to their performance and capabilities, without taking into account irrelevant personal traits. Equal opportunities should already begin with the recruitment process. The business practising equal opportunity benefit from a wider range of talents from various cultures and regions, which may be an essential competitive advantage in future global and local development.

Sexual harassment is a serious offence. In severe cases, the victims are put under pressure with possible job opportunities or wages and abused physically, verbally or emotionally, etc. In practice, there is a blur line between harassment and mere teasing is blurred. More and more companies are taking this issue seriously and have designed measures to better protect potential victims.

15.2.3 Employee Privacy

Important aspects of privacy include mainly (Simms, 1994):

- **Physical privacy**: "own" space that should remain physically inaccessible to others.
- **Social privacy**: free decision-making about one's own behaviour in private life.

- **Data protection**: autonomous decision on how, when and which private, personal data should be released for third parties.
- **Psychological privacy**: the control over one's own emotional or cognitive inputs and outputs without being forced to reveal one's private thoughts and feelings.

The protection of privacy for employees is often controversially discussed. The employee promises to undertake certain tasks in interests of the employer. However, the employee may misuse the employment relationship and act against the employer's interest. The protection of employees' privacy makes it easier for the employee to cover up of his wrongdoings. In public opinions, the employee's privacy is weighted again the employer's right for employee's service. For example, in a warehouse for hazardous chemicals, it is widely accepted that the employer could order regular drug tests for the employees, since the potential danger the general public is exposed to in case of drug misuse outweighs the employee's need to protect his personal privacy.

15.3 Fair Wage and Sustainable Employment

15.3.1 Fair Wage

The amount of wage the employee receives from the employer should match the job performance. The legislators in many countries have created a legal framework to protect employees from exploitation, e. g. through the introduction of minimum wages or regulations on equal pay for men and women for the same job.

In some professions (e. g. sales), it is common for the employer to agree to a performance-based remuneration which is often referred to as bonus payments. In practice, it is often not trivial to define fair individual performance objectives.

The top manager bonuses are often the subject of diverse media debates. It is questionable whether the performance of the executives justifies exorbitant amount of the bonus, which is exponentially higher than the income of the employees. The high payments are often justified with the high level of responsibility and market value and are intended to motivate managers to perform better. The company and all stakeholders should benefit from the positive business result. It is particularly problematic if the managers receive a large bonus despite poor performance.

15.3.2 Dismissal Protection

Job security is a major demand of the employees. Statutory regulations that restrict termination of the employment relationship are summarized as " dismissal protection". The dismissal protection usually requires a minimum notice period and justification of termination by employer.

15.3.3 Sustainable Employment

In the classic industrial production, a higher efficiency is achieved by specializing of the production process. As a result, the workers are burdens with monotonous or dulling assignments. With the concept of "re-humanized workplaces", an attempt is now being made to enable more variety in individual workplaces by changing the distribution of tasks, in order to increase job satisfaction. This can be achieved, for example, by empowering employees with the following variants:

- Job enlargement: The employee gets additional tasks;
- Job enrichment: The employee is given more freedom to make decisions about the work process or design of their own tasks.

The progressive automation of production processes and the progressive digitization has lead to increasing unemployment in old occupational fields. This trend potentially separates the working population into two groups:

- Highly qualified workers with sustainable, well-paid jobs who can adapt due to the level of education and qualification;
- Low-skilled workers cannot maintain previous wage levels over time and have to fear social decline.

The governments make different attempts to mitigate the above increasing social inequality. A radical reduction of standard working time, in order to create more jobs, and an unconditional basic income are among the most popular proposed solutions.

Another trend of sustainable employment is the promotion of "green jobs", which are the jobs related to environment-friendly technologies or contribute to environmental protection, e. g. the use of renewable energies or e-mobility. (Crane & Matten, 2016, S. 327 ff.)

References

Crane, A., & Matten, D. (2016). *Business ethics. Managing corporate citizenship and sustainability in the age of globalization* (4th ed.). Oxford University Press.

Simms, M. (1994). Defining privacy in employee health screening cases: Ethical ramification concerning the employee/employer relationship. *Journal of Business Ethics, 13*, 315–325.

Index

T. Dathe et al., *Corporate Social Responsibility (CSR), Sustainability and Environmental Social Governance (ESG)*, Management for Professionals,
https://doi.org/10.1007/978-3-030-92357-0

The manufacturer's authorised representative in the EU is Springer Nature Customer Service Centre GmbH, Europaplatz 3, 69115 Heidelberg, Germany. If you have any concerns regarding our products, please contact ProductSafety@springernature.com

Printed and bound by CPI Group (UK) Ltd, Croydon, CR0 4YY
28/09/2026
02224090-0004